Subverting
the Family Romance

Subverting the Family Romance

Women Writers, Kinship Structures, and the Early French Novel

Charlotte Daniels

Lewisburg
Bucknell University Press
London: Associated University Presses

© 2000 by Associated University Presses, Inc.

All rights reserved. Authorization to photocopy items for internal or personal use, or the internal or personal use of specific clients, is granted by the copyright owner, provided that a base fee of $10.00, plus eight cents per page, per copy is paid directly to the Copyright Clearance Center, 222 Rosewood Drive, Danvers, Massachusetts 01923. [0-8387-5410-4/00 $10.00 + 8¢ pp, pc.]

Associated University Presses
440 Forsgate Drive
Cranbury, NJ 08512

Associated University Presses
16 Barter Street
London WC1A 2AH, England

Associated University Presses
P.O. Box 338, Port Credit
Mississauga, Ontario
Canada L5G 4L8

The paper used in this publication meets the requirements of the American National Standard for Permanence of Paper for Printed Library Materials Z39.48-1984.

Library of Congress Cataloging-in-Publication Data

Daniels, Charlotte, 1959–
    Subverting the family romance : women writers, kinship structures, and the early French novel / Charlotte Daniels.
    p. cm.
    Includes bibliographical references and index.
    ISBN 0-8387-5410-4 (alk. paper)
    1. French fiction—18th century—History and criticism. 2. French fiction—19th century—History and criticism. 3. French fiction—Women authors—History and criticism. 4. Kinship in literature. I. Title.
2000
843'.509355—dc21   99-33520
                                                                                  CIP

PRINTED IN THE UNITED STATES OF AMERICA

Contents

Introduction 7

1. Françoise de Graffigny's *Lettres d'une Péruvienne* and the Privatization of the Family
   - Receptions 19
   - The Eighteenth-Century Family Romance: Marriage, the Family, and the Origins of the Novel 22
   - The Novel and the New Family Unit 25
   - How Utopian Is Peru?: Graffigny's Exploitation of the Exotic Novel Form 29
   - Marriage Plots 34
   - Graffigny's "Indispensable Pivot": Incest and the Structure of *Lettres* 41
   - Recovering a Tradition of *Tendre Amitié*: Graffigny and Her *Précieuses* Predecessors 51

2. The Mother–Daughter Plot in Isabelle de Charrière's *Lettres écrites de Lausanne*
   - After Rousseau 57
   - The Woman Writer in the Age of Rousseau: A Case Study 66
   - The Mechanics of the Marriage Plot 70
   - The Chastity Lessons 78
   - Marrying Motherhood 83
   - Public and Private Transgressions 87
   - Resisting (En)closure: Charrière's Open Ending 92
   - Reading Beyond the Ending: Part Two 96

3. After the Revolution(s): George Sand's *Indiana*
   - Transitions 103
   - Cross-Voicing in *Indiana* 108
   - Old Plots 115
   - New Plots 120
   - All in the (Saint-Simonian) Family 128
   - After the Fall (at Bernica): Indiana and Sir Ralph's "Natural Marriage" 132

Conclusion	143
Notes	146
Works Cited	172
Acknowledgments	180
Index	181

Introduction

> L'histoire de l'homme doit être représentée dans les romans; ...
> les fictions doivent nous expliquer, par nos vertus et nos sentiments, les mystères de notre sort.
> —Germaine de Staël, preface to *Delphine*, 1802

IN ANSWER TO HIS OWN QUESTION, "LES LIVRES FONT-ILS LES RÉVOLUtions?," Roger Chartier describes "un processus d'intériorisation par des lecteurs de plus en plus nombreux ... des manières de penser proposées par les textes philosophiques." Chartier underlines the transformative power of words on readers, attributing to them the ability to "make" the individuals who will eventually carry out the French Revolution: "Si les Français de la fin du dix-huitième siècle ont fait la Révolution, c'est parce que préalablement, ils avaient été transformés, 'faits,' par les livres."[1] Chartier's reference to "textes philosophiques" includes a great number of different types of works. Certainly philosophical texts of all sorts—pamphlets, educational treatises, essays—were passing through readers' hands during the prerevolutionary period, and all undoubtedly played their role in planting the seeds of change in the minds of readers. But revolutionaries and citizens are not "made" through engaging the intellect alone. The enormously complex task of constructing "les Français [qui] ont fait la Révolution" demanded significant changes on the level of feelings as well. Indeed, Chartier's words about "textes philosophiques" and their role in constructing revolutionary subjects are perhaps *most* suggestive when applied to the plethora of less overtly philosophical memoir and epistolary novels that flooded Paris and the provinces in the decades preceding the French Revolution. For clearly something about the supposedly frivolous novel, scorned yet feared by the reigning conservative literary establishment, through a series of complex and subtle sexual and emotional mechanics, seduced readers into radically new conceptions of who they were and who they might be.[2] Just what were these mechanics?

What was it about this somewhat bastard[3] genre that rendered it such an agent (and fine calibrator) of social change, an agent that arguably played a role in undermining the power structure of absolute monarchy?

Novels, written in modern French prose, did not require a traditional Latin-based education or erudition to be understood and experienced. For the first time, readers were invited to interpret and feel without the mediation of clergymen or teachers. Moreover, novels addressed themselves to the emotions as much as to the intellect of their readers. The only golden rule in the novel form—and on this both foes and supporters of the genre agreed—was that passionate love, in some relation to marriage, constitute its primary subject matter. The attention given to the passions, combined with a focus on confessional explorations of the "I" in the memoir novel, and of the "I–you" in epistolary novels, invited readers to empathize with characters on the most visceral level and thereby conceive of themselves in (literally) novel ways.

The novel's focus on the intimate details of an intensely experienced inner life was paralleled by the increased privacy of the reading experience itself. Unlike the novels of the seventeenth century, which were often read in a public space—in fact, historians of the family teach us that it is only late in the seventeenth century that the notion of private space comes into existence—eighteenth-century novels, more plentiful and therefore more readily available, could be read away from the watchful eyes of others. The form and content of the novels coupled with the privacy of the reading experience itself fostered the conditions necessary for the development of a theretofore unknown terrain of inner life.

Paradoxically, this inner life was, at one and the same time, intensely private and intensely public: "En même temps que le siècle affirme l'individu comme différence et territoire autonome, [il] ne cesse d'en référer à la communauté sociale, au devoir de communication avec autrui et d'ouverture à l'autre." For writers as well as readers, "exhiber l'intime serait donc l'inscrire dans un échange social, dont il semble *a priori* la négation."[4] From the beginning the modern concept of private life existed always in relation to the private lives of others. While readers experienced their own emotional responses to novels on an individual basis, they were reading the same stories as other French readers who were having their own seemingly private reactions. Novels thereby facilitated the creation of a shared set of intensely private emotional patterns that, while seeming deeply personal and, as such, intrinsically one's own, actually existed in dialectic relation to the new public systems of production and exchange that brought them into readers' hands. For this very reason, novels constitute a privileged locus for the study of the emergence of modern models of identity in their relation to larger social and economic realities.

Just how this new collective private life worked in the production and reproduction of a particular set of gender relations has been a matter of debate, much of which emerges from differing interpretations of Jürgen Habermas's *Structural Transformation of the Public Sphere* (1962). Published for the first time in the early 1960s, at the height of the structuralist mania to exclude all extratextual material, the work was paid scant attention by scholars of French literature and was not translated into French until 1978 and into English until 1989.[5] While Habermas is a social scientist, and not a literary historian, his work nevertheless has provided a helpful framework for literary critics exploring literature in relation to social and economic change. Indeed, despite some recent criticism,[6] *The Structural Transformation of the Private Sphere* has provided arguably the most useful theoretical context for the collaborative exchange between literary critics and historians exploring the ever-elusive relationship between literary and historical change.

Habermas's thesis is well known. With the implementation of mass publishing, both licit and illicit, the written word could for the first time be used to rally public resistance to the unitary truths presented in the literature sanctioned by the monarchy. While the press had its origins within the public authority of the state and was intended to uphold this authority, the increase in the number of writers and readers in France eventually created the possibility for organized opposition to it. As "the publisher replaced the patron as the author's commissioner and organized the commercial distribution of literary works,"[7] a sphere of readers emerged beyond the direct control of the state. This sphere, consisting of private individuals capable of reasoning and therefore of questioning the state's absolute and unitary nature, is referred to by Habermas as the "bourgeois public sphere":

> The bourgeois public sphere may be conceived above all as the sphere of private people come together as a public; they soon claimed the public sphere regulated from above against the public authorities themselves. . . .[8]

The bourgeois public sphere is not to be confused with the "representative publicness" of the state. Rather the bourgeois public sphere is one face of a bipartite private sphere (because composed of private individuals) that defined itself *against* the representative publicness of the state. This bipartite private sphere consisted then in what Habermas refers to as an "authentic" or "bourgeois" public sphere on the one hand and, on the other, the "intimate sphere"—which eventually, and only eventually, becomes the nuclear family as we have inherited it.[9] Habermas describes the emergence of a new bourgeois subject in terms of the relationship between these two domains, and it is here, for all the reasons discussed above, that the novel plays such a key role.[10] The new "je" emerged through a double role for the bourgeois in a market-based society, part public and private (or, if you will, part private and part intimate): "As a privatized individual, the bourgeois was two things in one: . . . *bourgeois* and *homme*."[11] The process of constructing this economically necessary individual subject involved a marriage of inclination, and a family united by bonds of affection. To perceive of himself as a private agent in the new world of the market, emancipated to some degree from governmental directives and controls, the subject needed a sense of being a private entity, and this sense came through reading and identifying with new subjectivities within the symbolic or literal depiction of new family patterns. In a sense, Habermas suggests that early capitalism depended on the novel to "create" a certain kind of subject for its own needs.

While this description suggests a rather passive subject, Habermas emphasized that this "je" had a strong sense of its (his) own individualism and a capacity to think critically about the world. He felt that the oppositional public sphere was a *positive* development because it liberated individuals by giving them a voice critical of institutional authority. Indeed, it was in part to restore the Enlightenment's emancipatory impetus in the wake of critique by his Frankfurt School predecessors, especially Theodor Adorno and Max Horkheimer, that Habermas wrote *The Structural Transformation of the Public Sphere*.

The model provided by Habermas in the *The Structural Transformation of the Public Sphere* would seem, at first, an odd choice for scholars interested in issues of female subjectivity before and during the revolutionary period. Unsurprisingly perhaps, given the time during which he was writing, Habermas never directs his full attention to issues of gender. His use of the masculine "homme"—"the bourgeois was two things in one: *bourgeois* and *homme"*—points toward a tendency, prevalent among the French revolutionaries whose subjectivity he is studying, to present the masculine as the universal in such a way that the feminine is for the most part rendered invisible. And yet, by the simple fact that Habermas's model ties together family, economy, and state, it has facilitated an analysis of gender in the revolutionary project. Once having overcome what Nancy Fraser calls "the gender blindness" of Habermas's model of public and private spheres, scholars (including Habermas himself[12]) have been asking new questions. While men were being transformed into the "je" who would carry out the French Revolution, what was happening to women? Was the development of the public sphere good for women? Did it increase their sense of being autonomous individuals?

Fraser and other feminist scholars have convincingly shown that the public sphere with its focus on individual freedom was, as Joan Landes has put it, "essentially, and not just contingently, masculinist."[13] The creation of a public sphere where men could participate in a new economy and critically hold forth depended on the simultaneous creation of a feminized private sphere. As France moved from old regime to republic, men, in Madelyn Gutwirth's words, were gradually "being driven toward all the forms of self-realization, including the sexual, yet all the while needing to contain, or recontain, these same drives in women."[14] Even a brief study of the political doctrines and iconography of the revolutionary period certainly supports the contention that as men evolved into citizens, women increasingly came to be defined as tender mothers and loving wives, the guarantors of a new domestic unit from which men could sally forth into a larger world but from which women themselves should rarely stray. Especially in the post-revolutionary National Assembly, republican discourse made it abundantly clear that women who ventured across the public/private divide to participate in the masculinized world of politics or business were treading on dangerous territory indeed.

Fraser has argued that Habermas's celebration in *The Structural Transformation of the Public Sphere* of the development of a new oppositional social order based on a division between public and private spheres implicitly legitimizes "the division which is the lynchpin of women's oppression."[15] Certainly (as Fraser herself recognizes) the situation is more complicated. A return to the novel genre—in a very real sense the mediator between the public and private spheres—and more specifically to female-authored novels, provides us a means of thinking anew about gender in its intricate interactions and intersections with the public/private divide constructed by literary discourse.

I use the term "family romance" in this project to invoke a relationship between the modern affectionate "family" and the eighteenth-century "romance," that is, the modern psychological novel. But, of course, the term "family romance" evokes more than a simple corollary between the development of the nuclear family and that of the novel genre. My argument is that the patterns of gender identity and family formation that Freud will describe over two hundred years later are already, in some sense, under construction in the novels of the eighteenth and early nineteenth centuries.[16] Freud's theory of psychoanalysis is founded on the assumed eternal existence of the nuclear family from which the subject emerges. The work of Habermas, especially considered in conjunction with recent work of cultural historians, suggests that this family structure is not eternal at all but rather rooted in a particular, and fairly recent, historical moment. Such a conclusion "casts doubt upon the assumptions that the particular kinds of infantile traumas upon which Freud laid so much stress have been suffered by the whole of the human race at all times and in all places."[17] In *The Structural Transformation of the Public Sphere*, Habermas mentions Freud only once and then briefly: "Freud discovered the mechanism of the internalization of paternal authority."[18] Others, however, have looked to the eighteenth-century novel as the crucible in which was forged the peculiar set of gendered emotional intensities and matching taboos that guarantee the production and reproduction of subjectivity within the modern nuclear family.

Jean-Claude Bonnet, for example, in a project he calls "[l]'archéologie de la recherche de Freud," and Paul Pelckmans, in a project he calls the search for "une préhistoire du discours freudien," both trace the origins of the Freudian Oedipus complex to eighteenth-century literature.[19] Calling our attention to what they see as the emergence of the "family romance" in eighteenth-century literature, they focus on the development of the father figure, at once threatening and exalted, as a marker of the Oedipus complex, and both agree that this figure became an important presence in the second half of the eighteenth century. While the work of scholars like Bonnet and Pelckmans is valuable in that it historicizes the unconscious "rules and regulations"[20] described by Freud, and thereby opens the way for an exploration of the role literature plays as both reflector and definer of kinship rules, their work follows Freud in being concerned primarily with fathers and sons in what have become canonized works, that is, works written by men.[21]

In this study, I follow Pelckmans's and Bonnet's return to the early French novel as a space in which the "family romance" was imagined but, instead of focusing on fathers and sons in works written by men, I consider the development of mothers, daughters, and sisters in works written by women. Bonnet explains the emergence of the ambivalent father figure in literature in terms of the lived experience of Enlightenment writers: "Fils qui ont craint d'être maudits et rejetés dans l'anti-nature pour avoir contesté les valeurs de la tradition, les écrivains du dix-huitième siècle ont produit une image du père surtout conciliatrice en se l'appropriant dans leur projet positif."[22] The "projet positif" to which Bonnet refers is the replacement of "la société d'ordres avec ses rites séparés, par une société plus homogène et plus égalitaire." A study of women-authored fiction makes it almost impossible to ignore the ways in which the replacement of "la société d'ordres avec ses rites séparés, par une société plus homogène et plus égalitaire" involved radical changes in the conception of gender as well. Moreover, as the century progressed, "writer-daughters" had at least as much reason to fear being "maudites" and "rejetées dans l'anti-nature" as did their male counterparts. Indeed, the professionalization of the career of writer entailed a corresponding defeminization of the novel genre that, throughout the seventeenth and into the early eighteenth century, had been viewed as a domain in which women excelled. By the late eighteenth century and, especially, the early nineteenth century, women writers, frequently portrayed as unnatural, lonely, or sexless creatures, were forced to choose between working within a family-romance framework defined by male authors or being excluded altogether. Susan Jackson's comment that "the female novelist's work [was] made to consist, not so much in doing, as undoing, stitch by careful stitch, the ever-so-tightly woven tapestry of novelistic convention," in other words, becomes more and more pertinent as one moves through the eighteenth century and into the nineteenth.

Françoise de Graffigny's *Lettres d'une Péruvienne* (1747, 1752), written well before the French Revolution and before Rousseau had published his major works, reminds us that the official gendering of the public as a male domain and the private as a female one during the revolutionary period was the result of a long struggle between a variety of gender, as well as social and political, alternatives. In her feminist reading of *The Structural Transformation of the Public Sphere,* Marie Fleming rightfully points out that Habermas's model of public and private spheres is based on both continuity and rupture with the past.[23] On the one hand, Habermas emphasizes that rational critical debate emerges from courtly salon activity; on the other, that it is dependent on a new family structure that constitutes a definite rupture with courtly openness. In my reading of Graffigny's *Lettres d'une Péruvienne* in chapter 1, I explore the juncture between these two aspects of the emergence of the public sphere, especially in relationship to the incest taboo.

After Rousseau published his major works, a generalized tendency emerged, in all sorts of discourse, to posit a "natural" order defined in opposition to the supposed artificialities of the "public women" associated with the court. And this feminization of the court in republican discourse did indeed eventually place enormous limits on the possibilities for women to participate in the new oppositional public sphere. But the "public women" of the court, as novelists and as *salonnières,* were in fact at the crossroads between two systems: on the one hand, representative publicness and, on the other, an oppositional public sphere. Just as the printing system, which had its origins within the sphere of representative publicness, was eventually turned against the representative publicness from which it emerged, so those women novelists and *salonnières* who played a role in upholding court society were in multifarious ways the predecessors of men and women whose writing activities later resisted the social order of the old regime.[24] The early forms of the public, far from excluding women from any access to a public voice, provided women novelists an astonishing and unprecedented means to shape the mental terrain of France. In fact, during this time of "new definitions in which nothing was firmly defined," the public sphere provided women writers with a forum for participating in negotiations on just what the new collective private life could be and on what it would mean in terms of who would hold what position in the structures opening up in society.[25]

Just over thirty years later, when Isabelle de Charrière published her *Lettres écrites de Lausanne* (1782), this was far less true. Charrière wrote her work in Switzerland, a country, like France, marked by the textual/emotional imprint of Rousseauian "family values." And yet, even as the public/private divide became more well defined along gender lines, and even as novels played an increasing role in this process, there continued to be something about the genre itself that maintained a necessarily *ambiguous* relationship to gender. The novel was the place in which the intimate familial sphere was imagined, yet its presentation of this sphere was always to a public and distributed through public channels of exchange. This position, on the very brink between public and private, the recorder/creator of an interior to be presented to a public in the exterior world, made it neither obviously feminine, nor obviously masculine. Rousseau himself claimed that writing feminized men (by contagion with womanly concerns) and masculinized women (by contagion with a world extending beyond the confines of the domestic interior). In chapter 2, I explore how Charrière's *Lettres écrites de Lausanne* exploits this inherent genre/gender instability to present a "mother–daughter plot," subverting the rules of post-Rousseauian Oedipal romance even as it seems to follow them.

By the time George Sand wrote her *Indiana* in 1832, the privatized family had become one agreed-upon constant in the midst of great social and political turmoil. Once an integral part of a bipartite *oppositional* sphere, the family had become part of the official story. At the same time, novels of the period, mostly written by men, tended toward romantic tales of strong individualistic heroes and the most angelic of heroines. With her novel *Indiana*, Sand sends forth an ambiguously gendered narrator to make "his" way through this highly conventionalized literary landscape. In chapter 3, I consider the ways in which Sand's use of a "cross-voiced" and, eventually, cross-dressed narrator, allows her to play with the gender assumptions of the nineteenth-century family romance.

Like their male counterparts, Graffigny, Charrière, and Sand certainly participated in the move toward representing, and thereby creating, the private sphere. But at the same time, in varying ways corresponding to different historical moments, each also used the novel genre to question the impermeability of the border between public and private. I will argue that women writers in the period I consider used the novel first to imagine different social rules that might define alternative kinship systems (Graffigny), and later to find—and create—loopholes within a firmly entrenched system of official and unofficial familial law (Charrière and Sand).

Subverting
the Family Romance

❋ 1 ❋
Françoise de Graffigny's *Lettres d'une Péruvienne* and the Privatization of the Family

> Il y a chez tout écrivain qui cherche à se réaliser dans l'expression d'une pensée une part de passivité, où cet esprit n'est qu'un reflet, un miroir inerte de son temps, mais aussi une part d'activité où l'écrivain s'efforce d'influer lui-même sur ceux qui l'entourent et qui le lisent.
> —Georges Noël, *Une Primitive oubliée de l'école des coeurs sensibles: Madame de Graffigny*, 1913

RECEPTIONS

Graffigny's novel *Lettres d'une Péruvienne* (1747, 1752), the first epistolary novel written and published by a woman in France, met with enormous success. The definitive version (1752) went through twenty-eight editions in the author's lifetime and more than one hundred by 1835, including translations of the novel into English (1748), Italian (1754), Russian, (1791), German (1792), Spanish (1792), Portuguese (1802), and Swedish (1832).[1] Despite the efforts of a few scholars who returned to original editions and who made mention of the novel thereafter, the work fell into obscurity by the mid-nineteenth century and remained there until just a few decades ago.[2] In 1967, Gianni Nicoletti published an annotated edition of the novel. Following the work of English Showalter and Jürgen von Stackelberg in the 1970s, Clifton Cherpack in 1983 included a substantive reading of the novel in *Mythos and Logos: Ideas and Early French Narratives*. The same year Garnier-Flammarion published a paperback edition of *Lettres*, making Graffigny's novel accessible to a wide reading audience for the first time since the eighteenth century. With the publication of the Garnier-Flammarion edition (which includes the novel among a series of novels in the form of love letters) and, especially the recent bilingual edition of *Lettres*, Graffigny's novel has become a mainstay on literature syllabi across the country and a bestseller among academics.[3] Beginning over a decade ago, such scholars as Janet Altman, Julia Douthwaite, Katharine Jensen, Nancy Miller, Elizabeth MacArthur, and Jack Undank began creating a body of scholarship that continues to enrich our understanding and appreciation of what Showalter calls Graffigny's "eighteenth-century best-seller," ensuring it an enduring place in the French literary canon. Indeed, perhaps no single author has both gained more from and contributed more to the wave of recent studies devoted to the eighteenth-century novel and the foundational role played by women in the genre than has Graffigny.

Graffigny's exotic tale of a young Inca princess forcibly removed from the Temple of the Sun in Peru by Spanish colonialists on the very day of her marriage appealed to eighteenth-century readers' penchant for exotic literature. It met with the approval of most critics as well.[4] Even the Abbé Jacquin, perhaps the most vehement contemporary foe of the novel genre, bestowed praise upon the work, citing it moreover as the *only* decent example of the genre that he had recently read.[5] Nevertheless, in a century in which, as Nancy Miller has pointed out in *The Heroine's Text*, the majority of heroines ended up married, confined to a convent, or dead, Graffigny's heroine, who ends up rich, educated, and accountable to no one, was bound to raise a few eyebrows (and pens) among critics. The most notable example is provided by a journalist by the rather unfitting name of Pierre Clément who had warm praise for the novel as a whole but suggested that, once the Peruvian heroine is betrayed by her Peruvian lover, Aza, "il faut ici tuer quelqu'un."[6] And Clément left little doubt as to whom that somebody might be.

Most critics spared Zilia her life in their recommended changes, though few were willing to grant her financial and emotional independence. Turgot, the future minister and a frequent guest at Graffigny's salon on the rue Sainte-Hyacinthe in Paris, in his recommendations for "quelques changements qui n'y feraient point de mal," included the marriage of Zilia and Aza at the novel's conclusion. He went on to justify this proposed alteration of Graffigny's text with a manifesto concerning what he viewed as a primary function of the novel: "Il y a longtemps que je pense que notre société a besoin qu'on lui prêche le mariage et le bon mariage."[7] In his *Lettres sur quelques écrits* (1749), Fréron, too, complained of the intolerable state of "insatisfaction" in which Graffigny leaves her reader, and suggested that Zilia's fate might perhaps be altered, but this time by a union with Déterville: "Comme on ne dit pas ce que devient Déterville, j'aime à me persuader que ses vertus, ses bienfaits et sa constance auront enfin triomphé de la délicatesse outrée de Zilia. . . ."[8] Given their proclivity for the marriage plot, these critics must have been relieved when, in 1749, Hugary de Lamarche-Courmont published *Les Lettres d'Aza*, a collection of letters telling Zilia's story from Aza's point of view and, predictably enough, ending with the wedding of the Peruvian lovers.

Despite the published words of Turgot, Fréron, and (indirectly) Lamarche-Courmont, we should be careful not to assume that their view on the role of marriage in the novel was the only, or even the prevalent, one. Indeed, it would be a mistake to conclude from the reactions of these critics that Graffigny's ending was simply an aberration within a well-defined novelistic tradition. In 1747, seven additional letters were published anonymously that seem to anticipate the "marriage endings" so favored by Turgot, Fréron, and Lamarche-Courmont, and to refute them in advance. This short collection includes a letter from Céline to her brother, Déterville, in which she encourages him to be more persistent in his efforts to win over Zilia. Zilia, however, intercepts the letter and, in no uncertain terms, affirms in a letter of her own that Céline is not the only model for women, that she, Zilia, has the right to be different (and not to marry):

> Hé quoi! peut-on sans justice juger les Vierges dévouées au Soleil et élevées dans son Temple, parce que [Céline] définit le caractère général des Femmes? N'est-il qu'un modèle, qu'une règle pour juger? Le Créateur, qui diversifie ses ouvrages en mille manières . . . a-t-il voulu que les caractères seuls fussent semblables partout, et que tous les êtres raisonnables pensassent de même? Pour moi, j'ai de la peine à me le persuader.[9]

The author of these additional letters clearly understood the stake of commentary among critics with regard to Graffigny's ending and points to the fact that there was room for alternative models. Zilia's words underline the way Graffigny exploited the still-inchoate form of the novel as a forum to preach not for the modern marriage of inclination but rather for alternative models of "le caractère général des femmes."

When, in 1752, Graffigny republished her novel, she chose not to heed the advice of Turgot or Fréron, nor did she make changes to accomodate *Les Lettres d'Aza*. In fact, far from making concessions to her critics, Graffigny actually reinforced her marriageless ending by adding several letters critical of the institution of marriage in France. The fact that Graffigny's novel in its 1752 version continued to sell extremely well—Graffigny in fact earned ten times as much for this edition written after the critiques of her ending as she did for the first edition—suggests that Graffigny's ending was compelling to many readers. In his 1910 study of personal library collections between 1750 and 1780, Daniel Mornet found that Graffigny's *Lettres* was one of the books that most commonly adorned the shelves of eighteenth-century readers.[10] One must conclude that the views of these readers did not coincide with those of Turgot or Fréron. At the very least, the continuing sales suggest the presence of a great deal of public ambivalence concerning the role of women in the new "sex/gender system" emerging in the early eighteenth century.

My reading focuses on these explicit and implicit reactions to Graffigny's *Lettres*, that is, on changing conceptions of marriage and the family and on their relation to the novel genre. To better understand the context in which Graffigny wrote her novel and ways in which critics reacted to her work, I begin by briefly considering the work of family historians who have begun to explore in some detail the eighteenth-century family. After exploring the familial and marital changes underway in France during the period in which Graffigny was writing her *Lettres*, I consider the following: the relationship between familial changes and the novel genre in view of the theories of Jürgen Habermas and Paul Pelckmans, scholars with very different approaches; the ways in which Graffigny exploits the popular "spy novel" form to address issues of gender; the patterns of marriage in this novel; and finally the function of incest in *Lettres*.

The Eighteenth-Century Family Romance: Marriage, the Family, and the Origins of the Novel

Cultural historians have provided us with convincing evidence that notions about marriage and the family were undergoing vast change beginning in the last half of the seventeenth century and continuing at an accelerated pace in the first half of the eighteenth century.[11] Changes in architecture, shifts in the tone of confessional manuals and etiquette books, inscriptions on gravestones, new and plentiful endearments in the correspondence between husband and wife—all suggest that the traditional family of the sixteenth and early seventeenth century was being replaced in the imagination, and at least to some degree in reality as well, by a smaller, more nuclear unit.

Throughout the seventeenth century and to a lesser extent into the eighteenth, the traditional family relied on strong ties with larger kinship and community groups for its support. Houses and communities were built with much communal space and little private space. In a sense, *everything* was public. Within this extremely hierarchical Great-Chain-of-Being model of the universe, it was natural to look on the monarch as a superpatriarch, and the father as a mini-sovereign:

> Under the ancien régime, there was a continuity between public power and familial power, or in any case, an implicit homology. The dependence in which family members found themselves with respect to their head was not substantially different from that of the family with respect to the men or agencies above it. Moreover, the head of the family received aid and protection for maintaining his power over his own—witness the *lettres de cachet de famille*—precisely insofar as this power was in keeping with the requirements of the public order.[12]

Intrafamilial affection was not a systematically necessary part of such a structure, and often it was not present at all.[13] Men and women spent a good part of their lives with a mate whom their parents had chosen, the choice most often having been dictated less by considerations of compatibility than by concerns of lineage, that is, by rules emerging from a well-defined system of social alliances. Relationships between children and their parents were also characterized by adherence to clearly set out rules. Early confessional manuals encouraged obedience to one's parents in the same way they did obedience to any social superiors. When a baby died—and this occurred frequently[14]—it was often buried beneath a tombstone that carried neither its name nor any other inscription. Philippe Ariès uses this (among other phenomena) as evidence for his claim that the whole notion of innocent childhood with its own set of rites, toys, and games was alien to this world, which considered young children to be more animal than human. Finally, the iron law of primogeniture, which encouraged parents to favor the eldest son to the detriment of sisters and younger brothers, did little to encourage the development of loving feelings between siblings.

In his seminal essay, "Ideology and Ideological State Apparatuses," Louis Althusser makes a useful distinction between between Repressive State Apparatuses (RSAs) and Ideological State Apparatuses (ISAs).[15] Both ensure the reproduction of a given system of power relations but they do so in different ways. While both state apparatuses function through an overt display of force by the state, the latter function in the realm of more private relations. Antonio Gramsci presents a similar distinction in historical terms. The traditional authoritarian state used more concretely coercive forces of police and judicial authority to ensure social control, while in the modern state more private institutions such as the family, in less overtly violent ways, have taken over some of this work.[16]

As Jean Flandrin has shown, the modern meaning of the French word *famille*, used to designate the unit formed by parents and their children, was used for the first time by le Chevalier de Jaucourt in an article published in *L'Encyclopédie*.[17] Until late in the seventeenth century, the term had two meanings: 1) a broad group of individuals related by blood, often including grandparents, cousins, and others in addition to parents and children; and 2) all those individuals who lived under one roof, including servants, and frequently immediate and less immediate family members.[18] This linguistic shift reflects a general move toward that Ideological State Apparatus that we continue to think of today as simply the "family." Architectural records suggest that it was during the eighteenth century that families began to retreat from broader community and kinship groups and to cloister themselves off in their houses, or in special parts of their houses, which were closed to the public. With the beginnings of contraception, fewer babies were born, and those who were lived longer. When a baby did die, the tombstone more frequently showed the child's name and often included an inscription expressing sadness at the family's loss. There is evidence that even before laws made it official, parents began to treat their children more as equals, and that the laws of primogeniture relaxed. In confession manuals, we find for the first time the assumption that parents are responsible to some degree for the happiness of their children. As early as 1713, Antoine Blanchard asks of fathers: "N'avez-vous point forcé [votre fils] à contracter un mariage avec une fille pour laquelle il avait de l'aversion, quoique vous eussiez prévu ou dû prévoir qu'ils feraient mauvais ménage ensemble?"

It must be emphasized here that, while it is a simple matter to describe these sociological changes in a few paragraphs, such a pat presentation is misleading. It is important for my reading of *Lettres d'une Péruvienne* to recognize that the shifts described by cultural historians, and theorized by Marxist historians, were by no means unidirectional or inevitable. In fact, the nuclear family experienced a long period of shaky beginnings and was not the dominant family model in France until close to the end of the eighteenth century. It is fair to say that when Graffigny wrote, marriage and the family, if not in a state of crisis, were certainly in a state of uneasy confusion.[19]

The debate about whether the above-mentioned changes were beneficial or detrimental to women began the moment historians turned their attention to the family. Edward Shorter, for example, emphasizes the ways in which the domestic family liberated women and suggests that, in the eighteenth century, "romantic love" became a code word for female autonomy. Women were beginning to be freed from parental dictates and might live with a husband they loved; moreover, the new focus on motherhood gave them a legitimate "profession," which allotted them a visibility they had not previously enjoyed. But Laurence Stone, a few years later, points out that the changes had disadvantages as well:

> The decline of ties with the kin deprived the wife of much external help which had previously been available to her in the difficult tasks of adjusting to life under a husband, and of child-rearing and child-care. She lacked support in case of marital conflict, and advice in case of serious incompatibility; her life became more isolated and more tedious while the children were young for lack of relatives to share the burden of baby-sitting and education; and her existence was more empty and lacking in social or economic function when the children had left home.[20]

While the question of whether the new womanhood represented progress or regression, an increase or decrease in the power allotted women in society by comparison to that allotted them under the ancien régime is intriguing, my focus is more specifically on the role played by early French novels in this process.

The Novel and the New Family Unit

The novel in France soared in popularity in the early decades of the eighteenth century. New publishing conditions and the market economy made its distribution possible on a scale never before conceivable. As we have seen, Habermas in *The Structural Transformation of the Public Sphere* has suggested that changing marriage and family patterns were inextricably tied up with the concomitant emergence of the market economy and of the novel. He describes the development of a newly self-conscious individual subject in terms of what he calls public and private spheres, a "je" that needed a sense of being a private entity to perceive himself as a private agent in the new world of the market, emancipated to some degree from governmental directives and controls, and governed by standards of profitability. According to Habermas, an essential sense of self as a private entity came about through the creation of the "intimate sphere" of the nuclear family. He argues that it is in the novel, the genre that emerged more or less in tandem with the market economy, that we find a concurrently imagined space for this newly formulated "je."

Habermas's work is certainly suggestive in terms of the link he describes among the changing economic sphere, the novel, and the development of a new subjectivity. While Habermas's "je" is never explicitly *not* female, it is implicitly male. Given both the time during which he wrote and the fact that he is not by profession a literary scholar, it is not surprising that Habermas's model neither considers the female "je" nor considers the "je" of eighteenth-century women authors nor looks more broadly at issues of gender. The recent publication of many eighteenth-century novels by women, however, invites us to consider anew the relationship between the new genre and new sex/gender systems. Graffigny's very successful *Lettres d'une Péruvienne* indicates that, at the midpoint of the eighteenth century, the novel genre continued to be a space of intense negotiation and dialogue on just what the new sexual/social order might be.

In her study of early seventeenth-century *salonnières*, Erica Harth writes:

> It is tempting to think of [these women] as speaking what Richard Rorty has called "abnormal discourse" in contradistinction to "normal" masculine discourse. Such a formulation would ignore, however, the historical conditions of paradigm formation. In the first half of the seventeenth century... there was no "normal discourse" with agreed-upon terms of discussion. Educated women and men alike faced the uncertainties of discursive change.[21]

Harth's comment regarding the "uncertainties of discursive change" faced by men and women in early salon activity was equally true for France a full century later. Especially before Rousseau's works were published, the country, and indeed most of Europe, experienced a long period during which numerous value systems articulated in various discourses coexisted in complicated relation to each other, sometimes conciliatory, sometimes overtly antagonistic. There was no one well-developed power structure that controlled what Althusser calls Institutional State Apparatuses.[22]

Along these lines, Joan Landes has suggested we understand the (oppositional) public sphere as being far more multifaceted than Habermas (in 1962) supposed:

> The oppositional public sphere was not one (universal sphere of discourse, as Habermas implies), but many. Critical distinctions are to be drawn—not just between society and its critics—but among the oppositional publics themselves. . . .[23]

Beginning within the salon context explored by Harth, and continuing into the eighteenth century, especially as mass publishing developed, novels especially afforded women a privileged means of entry into a larger literary and intellectual world and access to social and political events from which they would have been otherwise largely excluded. It is hardly surprising then that early eighteenth-century female-authored novels, including Graffigny's *Lettres,* do not fit into the Habermassian model, a model whose definition of subjectivity is that of "universal" masculine, free to float between private and public spheres, and which, by implication, would confine women to the domestic sphere.[24]

Graffigny's novel provides a case in point of the multifaceted nature of the oppositional public sphere at the midpoint of the eighteenth century. Zilia, who writes that novels in France are "la critique générale des moeurs," is a critic herself. But whereas Habermas links the nuclear family with the emergence of the critical "je" of the public sphere, Zilia's female "je" extends her criticism to aspects of discourses beginning to make a tender maternal figure the (literal) centerpiece of a new family model. To cite but one example, in the third of her letters, Zilia makes reference to "l'humiliant avantage" of mothering Aza's children:

> Si tu étais un homme ordinaire, je serais restée dans l'ignorance à laquelle mon sexe est condamné; mais ton âme, supérieure aux coutumes, ne les a regardées que comme des abus; tu en as franchi les barrières

pour m'élever jusqu'à toi. Tu n'as pu souffrir qu'un être semblable au tien fût borné à l'humiliant avantage de donner vie à ta postérité.[25]

Given what we have learned from the work of cultural historians, Zilia's rebellious stance against the Inca patriarchal traditions must have resonated among the real French readers of her letters. Zilia, in a "Peruvian" framework, refuses to acquiesce to social pressure and accept a subordinate role within an increasingly privatized family. The words "humiliant avantage" suggest that while woman's ability to bear children may be revered within Zilia's culture, it is also linked to her low status and her exclusion from participation as a full subject in the social structure: "je serais restée dans l'ignorance à laquelle mon sexe est condamné." We might see in Zilia's critique of childbearing an indirect response to the incipient pressures of the cult of true motherhood emerging at just this time in France.[26]

Habermas's theory is convincing when we consider the work of Rousseau (as we will do in chapter 2), but less so when we consider the work of Graffigny. While, as we will see, Graffigny's novel provides clear evidence that the family and marriage were undergoing massive transformations—as is suggested by the Habermassian model and much other historical work—in the case of *Lettres,* the outcome clearly suggests a resistance to the nuclear family "solution" rather than its affirmation. The novel, particularly in its pre-Rousseauian—or I should say rather in its pre-*La Nouvelle Héloïse*—rendition, constituted a space of intense negotiation concerning the role of gender in the emerging socioeconomic structure. Graffigny's *Lettres,* written in precisely the period Habermas treats in his work, constitutes a vehicle for expressing the possibility of independence for women and participation in an evolving social structure *outside* the newly imagined role of loving wife and mother within a privatized family.

In *Le Sacre du père,* Paul Pelckmans, like Habermas, focuses on the relationship between the novel and the emergence of the nuclear family in the development of a model of modern subjectivity. And his primarily psychoanalytic perspective offers a useful complement to Habermas's model. Pelckmans proposes that the modern notion of the Oedipus complex as defined by Freud has its roots not in the universal psyche, always already there, but rather in the particular collective imagination of the mid- to late-eighteenth century. While Pelckmans does include a few female-authored novels, even then he focuses exclusively on the male subject. In the few pages he devotes to Graffigny's novel, for example, he places Aza, Zilia's lover-brother, in the maternal position, and reads the novel as charting Zilia's breaking away from this mother figure. He uses Graffigny's novel, with its clear focus on incest, to illustrate, if not a full-fledged reflection of the Oedipal structure, at least the beginnings of the pattern that will come to dominate family life in the nineteenth and twentieth centuries. By placing Zilia in a male position to make his point about the development of the Oedipus complex, and by reading *Lettres* as just one step along the way to the better-developed Oedipal structures we find in later novels, Pelckmans betrays how indebted he is to Freud's categories even as he calls the Oedipus complex "un mensonge romantique."

Pelckmans's reading, however, is valuable for this study in that it points to incest as an active force in the eighteenth-century imagination inseparable from the issues of marriage and the family we have considered. He goes beyond simply noting the obsession with incest in literary texts of the day—which many scholars have done—to wrestle with an explanation for why this might be the case. But, whereas Pelckmans traces the development of an Oedipal structure that will make possible the domestic family, I argue that in Graffigny's novel, incest serves a different purpose. Graffigny's *Lettres* is indeed composed around the pivotal issue of incest, but it is intersibling incest that is at issue rather than parent–child incest. Moreover, it is presented in such a way that a principled and self-aware woman is forced by society to reject, rather than accept, the kind of marriage and family situation that was becoming an imagined and to some degree historical reality in France at precisely the time Graffigny was writing. The very structure of Graffigny's novel opens up a space "in between" the two patriarchal cultures she presents in her novel, sixteenth-century Peru and eighteenth-century France, allowing Graffigny to subvert the notion that, within the new socioeconomic order, exchange (of property, money, words) need be the exclusive domain of men.

How Utopian Is Peru?: Graffigny's Exploitation of the Exotic Novel Form

We learn in the historical preface to Graffigny's novel that the Peruvian Temple of the Sun, contrary to what its name might lead one to expect, is a fully enclosed, dark space, entirely cut off from any actual warmth or light from the sun. This space is occupied almost exclusively by girls and young women and their governesses, known as "mamas," who look after their needs. The title of the women, "Vierges du Soleil," suggests that they are virgins, untouched by men, just as the temple itself is a dark invisible space not to be penetrated by men. But we soon discover that what seems at first like a feminocentric sanctuary is actually a space entirely circumscribed by a masculine tradition. The Temple of the Sun is controlled by a man who wields immense cultural power: the Capa-Inca, an exotic version of the absolute monarch. The Capa-Inca's wife (who is also his sister or next of kin) is conspicuously absent from the affairs we hear about in the novel. This is already clear in Graffigny's presentation in the historical introduction of the Capa-Inca and Mama Oello:[27]

> Le soleil . . . que [les Péruviens] appelaient leur père, et qu'ils regardaient comme leur Dieu, touché de la barbarie dans laquelle ils vivaient depuis longtemps, leur envoya du Ciel deux de ses enfants, un fils et une fille, pour leur donner des lois, et les engager, en formant des villes et en cultivant la terre, à devenir des hommes raisonnables. C'est donc à Mancocapac et à sa femme Coya-Mama-Oello-Huaco que les Péruviens doivent les principes, les moeurs et les arts qui en avaient fait un peuple heureux. . . . (251)

Though one is immediately struck by the fact that the myth of Inca origins presented in the historical preface includes mention of a daughter as well as a son and, moreover, that it suggests both participate in production and continuation of principles, customs, and arts, a closer look reveals that this brother–sister dyad is hardly an indication of egalitarian relations between the sexes in Peruvian culture.[28] It is the father-Sun who sends forth these male and female children, and there is no mention of the mother-Moon's role in this foundational act of Inca culture. There is, in fact, nothing in the historical introduction or in the novel as a whole suggesting that the daughter figure was actually associated with legislation in any systematic way.

Within the Inca culture as Graffigny presents it in the novel, Mama Oello is defined primarily by her role as spouse of the Sun and producer of his children: "[Les Péruviens] avaient aussi beaucoup de vénération pour la Lune, qu'ils traitaient de femme et de soeur du Soleil. Ils la regardaient comme la mère de toutes choses" (253–254). Similarly, all the women contained in the temple are defined entirely in terms of their relationships to men. Even those women destined to join the eternal male Sun remain under the control of the reigning human male Inca, who alone has access to the temple.

One passage in particular underscores the fact that control of this sacred place is the prerogative of the reigning Capa-Inca:

> Il y avait cent portes dans le temple superbe du Soleil. L'Inca régnant, qu'on appelait le Capa-Inca, avait seul le droit de les faire ouvrir; c'était à lui seul aussi qu'appartenait le droit de pénétrer dans l'intérieur de ce temple. (254)

This striking image, not to be found in Garcilaso, suggests the Capa-Inca's control, not only over the body of the mother but over that of all the women confined within the temple, over "les cent portes," which he alone has the right to open or leave shut: "C'était à lui seul ... qu'appartenait le droit de pénétrer dans l'intérieur de ce temple." This presentation of Peruvian culture as strongly patriarchal does not end with the historical preface, but continues throughout Graffigny's *Lettres*. Zilia writes in her second letter:

> C'est toi, mon cher Aza, c'est toi qui dans la suite comblas mon âme de délices en m'apprenant que l'auguste rang de ton épouse m'associerait à ton coeur, à ton trône, à ta gloire, à tes vertus. . . . (264)

Graffigny's Peru is hardly a feminist utopia presented in contrast to patriarchal France. Indeed Zilia, like her female ancestors the Moon and Mama Oello, would not have shared the throne with the man who was to be her husband, even if the Spanish had not colonized the country and prevented her marriage. Rather, to use her own words, Zilia would have been "associated" with what would clearly remain Aza's throne (*ton* trône). She has become educated to some degree in Peruvian culture only because Aza is different from other husbands. As we will see in the course of this chapter, if Zilia eventually does occupy the symbolic space of the throne, it is despite, rather than because of, the Inca tradition from which she emerges.

To better understand Graffigny's vision of Peru, it is useful to return to the original text of Garcilaso's *Histoire des Incas: Rois du Pérou*, her primary source for "facts" about the Inca culture. The work, inspired by highly personal motives, was an impassioned plea to sixteenth-century (ruling-class) Spanish readers for acceptance and respect. Garcilaso, born of an Inca mother and conquistador father, was particularly concerned with protecting the rights of mestizos like himself in the face of Spanish colonization. Written against a flood of contemporary Spanish colonial accounts that most often depicted the Incas as a race of barbaric tyrants, it emphasized those aspects of Inca culture most likely to ingratiate Renaissance Spain. James Higgins writes that "Garcilaso depicts a near-perfect society which links his work to the utopian literature of the period."[29] Publishing history indicates that this "near-perfect society" appealed to early eighteenth-century readers in search of alternative social models. Over the course of the century, three editions of *Histoire des Incas* appeared in French, one of them in 1744—three years before Graffigny published her *Lettres d'une Péruvienne*.[30]

Graffigny's novel consists in a transformation of Garcilaso's sixteenth-century vision of Peru for decidedly eighteenth-century ends. The most significant change that Graffigny makes in her transposition of Garcilaso's Peru involves replacing the point of view of a man with that of a woman. When subjected to the female gaze, Garcilaso's supposedly utopian view of the Golden Age of Peru is undermined. Passages such as the one in which Zilia critiques the "humiliant avantage" of Peruvian women to provide their husbands with children suggest that, from her protagonist's perspective, Garcilaso's Peru was far from idyllic.

This is not to say that Zilia does not present the Peruvian culture in glowing terms. We need go no further than the introduction to see that the Peru from which Graffigny's protagonist emerges is, in Enlightenment terms, almost Edenic: "La nation était encore dans l'enfance [à l'égard des sciences], mais elle était dans la force de son bonheur" (255). But when the protagonist begins to describe her experiences in other cultures, her critical vision is sharpened. As she does so, the dichotomy set up in the introduction and opening pages between an "us"—vanquished Peru, Aza, and Zilia—and a "them"—the bloodthirsty Spanish conquistadors—breaks down.

Quite early in the novel, the "us" and "them" dichotomy begins to give way to a new division based on gender rather than nationality. We learn in the second of Zilia's letters that Aza's fate among the Spaniards is quite different from Zilia's among the French. Zilia compares "les honneurs qu'ils rendent [à Aza]" with "la captivité où ils [la] retiennent" (262). The fact that he is honored whereas she is not is based on the fact that he is a man and she a woman rather than on any difference between the Spanish and the French.

Already in this letter we find foreshadowed Aza's decision to assimilate fully into the Spanish cultural and marriage system, and Zilia's to remain outside of and distrustful of the French (European) system, and here already her vision is linked to her marginal status as a woman. Aza, who had more power in the Inca tradition, is blind to the workings of power among the Spanish. Zilia protests to him:

> Tu crois sincères les promesses que ces barbares te font faire par leur interprète, parce que tes paroles sont inviolables; mais moi qui n'entends pas leur langage, moi qu'ils ne trouvent pas digne d'être trompée, je vois leurs actions. (262)

We see here one of the ways in which Graffigny genders the very popular ethnographic novel form. Zilia gains a gendered vision of power relationships among her captors that she did not have among the Peruvians and that is unavailable to Aza in either culture. We find another more pointed example of this phenomenon in Zilia's fifth letter, written aboard the boat that carries her toward France. Zilia, sick and close to dying—as she is more often than not through at least the first half of her letters—lies confined to her bed by her French captor-saviors. Once these men have allowed her access to her precious *quipos* again, she "writes" the following words:

> Sans compter un nombre infini de petites contradictions, ils me refusent, mon cher Aza, jusqu'aux aliments nécessaires au soutien de la vie, jusqu'à la liberté de choisir la place où je veux être: ils me retiennent par une espèce de violence dans ce lit, qui m'est devenu insupportable: je dois donc croire qu'ils me regardent comme leur esclave, et que leur pouvoir est tyrannique. D'un autre côté, si je réfléchis sur l'envie extrême qu'ils témoignent de conserver mes jours, sur le respect dont ils accompagnent les services qu'ils me rendent, je suis tentée de penser qu'ils me prennent pour un être d'une espèce supérieure à l'humanité. (271–272)

Zilia presents her captivity and Aza's relative freedom as a new phenomenon under Spanish colonialism. But this remarkably modern analysis of the dichotomous role that women play in patriarchal culture could as well describe Zilia's position in Peruvian culture where she was revered as a princess, but enslaved in a temple. Her vision is sharpened in the new culture to see and critique that which she frankly admired in Peruvian culture.

Marriage Plots

Zilia's introduction into the world beyond the temple is violent and bloody, strikingly reminiscent of a rape. Clinging to the altar of the Inca temple, she is grabbed by Spanish colonialists who forcibly bring her forth from the shadowy matrix of the temple into a world pervaded by bright clear light from the sun. Blood and women's cries imbue the scene: "Les pavés du temple ensanglantés, l'image du Soleil foulée aux pieds, des soldats furieux poursuivant nos Vierges éperdues et massacrant tout ce qui s'opposait à leur passage; nos mamas expirantes sous leurs coups . . ." (259). The dramatically described invasion of Cuzco, which ruptures the lawful sexual order of the Incas, also serves a more banal but no less important purpose.

The Spanish invasion and its aftermath place physical distance between Zilia and her fiancé, Aza, and thereby justify the letters that follow. At the same time, the confrontation between East and West breaks off Zilia's wedding plans and places Graffigny's heroine in an unusual position for a woman in the epistolary tradition. Zilia becomes a traveling letter-writer (rather than an abandoned one)[31] and begins to explore her "je" at the precise moment she is wrenched away from an initial marriage plot. We find in the novel's first letter the beginnings of an exploration of female subjectivity outside of marriage and within writing, which finds its full expression in the final pages of the novel when Zilia retires to the country house she owns to spend her days absorbed in literature and friendship.

Before we consider further the treatment of marriage in *Lettres*, it is useful to consider once again Graffigny's use of Garcilaso's text, this time as it regards the institution of marriage. We have seen that Graffigny replaces the male point of view presented by Garcilaso with a female point of view. The second major way in which Graffigny transforms Garcilaso's *Histoire* is to present romantic love as an integral part of the Peruvian conjugal union. In other words, she adds the crucial element of a love story. Nowhere in Garcilaso's account is any evidence that love functioned as an essential ingredient in the formula that united royal spouses. On the contrary, we read in Garcilaso that the Capa-Inca had access to numerous concubines in addition to the wife allotted him by the rigid Inca marriage system; the virgins in various convents around the capital city of Cuzco were always available as mistresses to the king, "à qui on les livrait à la première demande" (342). Graffigny does borrow from Garcilaso the extremely rigid and incestuous model of marriage for her Peruvian characters, which places an emphasis on the Aristotelian link between the authority of God and that of his son, Aza, the reigning Inca: "[Les Incas], devaient toujours s'unir à leurs soeurs, ou à leur défaut à la première princesse du sang qui était Vierge du Soleil" (254), but the Inca love story is her own invention. In the case of the intended marriage between Zilia and Aza, Graffigny superimposes an eighteenth-century modern marriage on the traditional system presented in Garcilaso wherein relationships are rigidly hierarchical and based on obedience to one's superiors.

The result of a love match conceived within the traditional framework provided by Garcilaso is a sort of Marivaudesque model in which the new concept of marriage based on love does not disrupt the old. Zilia's experience of love at first sight, for instance, does not interfere with the Peruvian patriarchal system of lineage:

> Je me rappelle ce jour fortuné où ton père, mon souverain seigneur, te fit partager, pour la première fois, le pouvoir réservé à lui seul d'entrer dans l'intérieur du temple. . . . Je ne sais quelles étaient les pensées de mes compagnes; mais de quels sentiments mon coeur ne fut-il point assailli! Pour la première fois j'éprouvai du trouble, de l'inquiétude, et cependant du plaisir. (263)

We find in this match the introduction of a romantic love that, far from upsetting old rules, is still imagined within their boundaries.

While this is the case for the proposed "Peruvian" marriage between Aza and Zilia, it is not true for the two "French" marriages we find in the novel: that of Déterville's unnamed elder brother, and that of his dear sister, Céline. When Zilia finally arrives in Paris, she is introduced to a stern woman who she soon learns is Déterville's mother:

> Elle embrassa [Déterville], mais avec une bonté si froide, une joie si contrainte, que si je n'eusse été avertie, je n'aurais pas reconnu les sentiments de la nature dans les caresses de cette mère. (288)

The terms that Zilia uses to describe Déterville's mother suggest something unnatural (". . . je n'aurais pas reconnu les sentiments de la nature . . .") about this mother's behavior because she is cold and reserved in her relations with her son. "Nature" is the equivalent then of the kind of tender maternal love beginning to be imagined in the period during which Graffigny writes. Déterville's mother, in other words, is associated with a notion of family being displaced by the new conception of a nuclear family. The role Madame Déterville plays in arranging and supporting the marriage of Déterville's elder brother and his future bride (both of whom remain unnamed) provides another example of her link to the ancien régime model of family. She desires to leave all her money to her firstborn son, an action that touches the lives of the more central characters, Zilia, Déterville, and Déterville's younger sister, Céline. This marriage of the elder Déterville son seems to be much in the tradition of the ancien régime model. Indeed, her own wishes as the parental figure and worries about the patrimony are the sole concerns of Madame Déterville, and they take precedence over anyone's interest in love and happiness.

Against this traditional marriage arrangement is posited a very different relationship: the one between Céline and an anonymous and handsome suitor. Zilia becomes aware of this relationship for the first time when the young man, taking advantage of the after-theater rush, approaches her and Céline and slips Céline a *billet doux*. While we saw that, in the case of Aza and Zilia, the love match was remarkably compatible with the more traditional model provided by Garcilaso, here there is definitely antagonism between Céline's desired new-style marriage and the traditional marriage preferred by her mother. All communications between the young lovers (in the eighteenth-century French sense of the word—presumably no sexual interactions have actually occurred) are forbidden. When Madame Déterville discovers Céline has a love interest that might lead to a marriage that would disrupt her own plans for the family, she promptly arranges for her daughter to be locked up in a convent:

> Madame Déterville, qui ne veut pas les unir, lui défend de le voir, et pour l'en empêcher plus sûrement, elle ne veut pas même qu'elle parle à qui que ce soit. Ce n'est pas que son choix soit indigne d'elle, c'est que cette mère glorieuse et dénaturée profite d'un usage barbare, établi parmi les grands seigneurs du pays, pour obliger Céline à prendre l'habit de Vierge, afin de rendre son fils aîné plus riche.[32] (302)

Madame Déterville is likewise afraid her son will woo the beautiful, but at this point poverty-stricken, Peruvian narrator and that the resulting marriage would hurt family interests:

Par le même motif, elle a déjà obligé Déterville à choisir un certain ordre, dont il ne pourra plus sortir, dès qu'il aura prononcé des paroles que l'on appelle voeux. (302)

In another of Zilia's letters, after some time has passed, we learn that Madame Déterville has died and made good her threat to leave all her worldly possessions to her eldest son:

La mère de Déterville est morte. Cette mère dénaturée n'a point démenti son caractère, elle a donné tout son bien à son fils aîné. On espère que les gens de loi empêcheront l'effet de cette injustice. Déterville, désintéressé par lui-même, se donne des peines infinies pour tirer Céline de l'oppression. Il semble que son malheur redouble son amitié pour elle; outre qu'il vient la voir tous les jours, il lui écrit soir et matin. (315)

There is much of interest in this peripheral story that weaves itself through a good part of the novel, particularly in the above passage. The adjectives describing Madame Déterville as "glorieuse et dénaturée" and of her actions as taking advantage of "un usage barbare établi parmi les grands seigneurs du pays" associate her with an outdated notion of motherhood, or rather I should say parenthood, because her position represents the interests of the father in the traditional model of marriage.[33] It is against this representative of the ancien régime family order that the brother–sister couple define themselves and their rights. The parental "oppression" reinforces a sense of injustice and shared rebellion among the French siblings, and suggests a new horizontal power replacing the more traditional vertical power structure of French society.

Increasingly, French citizens began to place themselves in society on the basis of their position vis-à-vis their peers in a developing public sphere, rather than in terms of their position within the strictly defined social hierarchy of the old regime. What is remarkable here is that this shift in power relations from vertical traditional lineage supported by traditional church values—Madame Déterville's chief activity, besides meddling in the amorous pursuits of her children, is, we are told "d'entourer gravement ses doigts d'un cordon qui pendait à un petit morceau d'or" (288)—to more horizontal relations, has the explicit support of changing laws: "On espère que les gens de loi empêcheront les effets de cette injustice" (315). Here in a fictional text we see the state explicitly portrayed as it is involved in the restructuring of family relations, a role previously fulfilled by the church. Thus we see both privatization and secularization of the family concept.

This Déterville family marriage drama also foregrounds the link between the shifting power structure and the problematics of incest inherent in such a shift. Déterville writes his sister, Céline, because he cannot write directly to Zilia, yet his devotion to his sister does intimate incestuous desire: "Il semble que son malheur redouble son amitié pour elle; outre qu'il vient la voir tous les jours, il lui écrit soir et matin" (315). In marked contrast to the cool reunion between Madame Déterville and her son, that of Céline and Déterville is characterized by great tenderness.

> La joie éclatait sur le visage [de Céline], sans en bannir un fonds de tristesse intéressant. Déterville l'embrassa la dernière, mais avec une tendresse si naturelle que mon coeur s'en émut. (289)

The "fonds de tristesse intéressant" that Céline experiences upon seeing her brother is not explained. Might it be jealousy in the face of her brother's return home with Zilia by his side? Regardless of whether we assume this to be the case, the parallel between the Déterville–Céline relationship and the clearly incestuous and love-invested Aza–Zilia relationship is made clear in the next line of Zilia's letter: "Hélas! mon cher Aza, quels seraient nos transports si après tant de malheurs le sort nous réunissait!" (289). Zilia's exclamation sets up a parallel between the Déterville–Céline relationship and the Zilia–Aza relationship, which emphasizes their comparability. This results in the eroticization of the sister–brother bond in the case of Déterville and Céline, and a corresponding "siblification," if I may use the word, of the erotic bond between Zilia and Aza.[34]

In this French drama of marriages, it is Céline's love marriage, supported by her devoted brother Déterville *and* the law, that is victorious[35]:

> Les juges ont rendu à Céline les biens dont sa mère l'avait privée. Elle voit son amant tous les jours, son mariage n'est retardé que par les apprêts qui y sont nécessaires. (321)

We find in this subplot threading its way through almost half of Zilia's letters to Aza the kind of plot that Habermas notes were typical of novels of this period. The nuclear family is imagined as a space at once freely chosen and affectionate, and it defines itself *against* rather than *within* traditional institutions, those Zilia refers to as the barbarous customs established by "les grands seigneurs du pays." In Céline's marriage, we see the triumph of a new set of social relations posited in terms of a marriage for love, and, by negative example in the case of Madame Déterville, the valorization of a more loving and less authoritarian relationship between parents and children. We also see new bonds of affection between the children themselves and perhaps even a flirtation with displaced incestuous desire (in the increasingly intense relationship that develops between Déterville and his sister Céline after he is forbidden contact with Zilia).

But in Graffigny's novel, Céline's story of the triumph of love within marriage is a subplot and only a subplot. It is *against* this plot that the main plot is presented, that is, the plot of Zilia's life that culminates in a career of writing and friendship outside the bounds of marriage. Against the backdrop of the Déterville marriages, Zilia's position points to Graffigny's rejection of *both* the traditional model of marriage, emblematized by that of Madame Déterville's elder son, *and* the bourgeois marriage of inclination represented by that of Céline. Graffigny does incorporate models of "modern marriage" in her novel, which would support Habermas's claim that this was generally (and generically) the case, but in Zilia's case these models are used to highlight a new female subjectivity *outside* of marriage.

Consider Zilia's overt critique of the limitations for women inherent in the new marriage of inclination, represented in *Lettres* by Céline's situation. Indeed, we see that Zilia's eventual decision not to marry Déterville is reinforced by her reactions to the marriage plans and ceremony of Céline. At one point during Zilia and Céline's stay in the convent, it seems that Zilia has come extremely close to recreating her previous situation in the Temple of the Sun:

> La chaise d'or que l'on conservait dans le temple pour le jour des visites du Capa-Inca ton auguste père, placée d'un côté de ma chambre en forme de trône, me représente ta grandeur et la majesté de ton rang. La grande figure du Soleil, que je vis moi-même arracher du temple par les perfides Espagnols, suspendue au-dessus, excite ma vénération, je me prosterne devant elle, mon esprit l'adore, et mon coeur est tout à toi. Les deux palmiers que tu donnas au Soleil pour offrande et pour gage de la foi que tu m'avais jurée, placés aux deux côtés du trône, me rappellent sans cesse tes tendres serments. (325)

She transforms her present situation of confinement in French culture into a situation of confinement similar to the one she knew in

Peru. In France, surrounded by the symbols of Inca culture, she continues to wait for Aza to arrive and sweep her away into domestic bliss. In this, her situation parallels that of Céline. Céline too is confined in a convent as she awaits the day of her marriage. Her subsequent marriage would seem to be similar to the destiny for which Zilia yearns. But Zilia, far from supporting the relationship in so many ways analogous to her own with Aza, is irritated by Céline and what she views as her friend's excessive concerns with love. This reaction does not seem to be the result of simple jealousy. Zilia could after all share Céline's fate by emerging from the convent to marry Déterville, a choice sanctioned by both the church and the social group represented by her French world, i.e., Céline and Déterville. She would thereby share with Déterville the social privileges bestowed on him by "sa haute naissance et par son mérite personnel" (307) and make up for most of what she lost in Inca culture.

In fact, the subjects of interest to Céline are, by this point in the novel, no longer compelling for Zilia. In her twentieth letter, Zilia writes of Céline:

> Je remarque dans les réponses qu'elle fait à mes questions, un certain embarras qui ne peut partir que d'une dissimulation maladroite ou d'une ignorance honteuse. Quoi qu'il en soit, son entretien est toujours borné aux intérêts de son coeur et à ceux de sa famille. (302)

Zilia, obligée to participate in the wedding festivities, shows little enthusiasm. Following the wedding ceremony, her irritation with Céline's preoccupation with her new husband at the expense of her friendship with Zilia becomes rather acrimonious:

> Toute occupée de son nouvel époux, à peine puis-je trouver quelques moments pour lui rendre des devoirs d'amitié.... Le monde et le bruit me devinrent plus importuns qu'à l'ordinaire; jusqu'à la tendre satisfaction de Céline et de son époux, tout ce que je [vois] m'[inspire] une indignation approchant du mépris. (333)

When the Spanish colonialists forced their way into the Temple of the Sun, Zilia herself had been "writing," actually knotting into her *quipos*, the story of her love and happiness in the context of her intended conjugal relationship with Aza:

> A peine [le jour] commençait-il à paraître, qu'impatiente d'exécuter un projet que ma tendresse m'avait inspiré pendant la nuit, je courus à mes

quipos, et profitant du silence qui régnait encore dans le temple, je me hâtai de les nouer, dans l'espérance qu'avec leur secours je rendrais immortelle l'histoire de notre amour et de notre bonheur. (258)

In Céline's marriage-period conversation, "borné aux intérêts de son coeur et de sa famille," we hear an echo of Zilia's own love story with Aza, "l'histoire de [leur] amour et de [leur] bonheur," at the moment of their own marriage. For Zilia, this was a tale begun but never to be completed.[36] Like the tragic heroine of *Lettres portugaises*, Zilia claims in her early letters to write to Aza only to express the depths of her anguish, both in love and at the hands of her brutal captors. In her subsequent development not only does she give up this conventional justification for women's writing (sorrow), she actually critiques it in a tragedy she attends in Paris where:

De belles femmes qu'apparemment ils persécutent, pleurent sans cesse, et font des gestes de désespoir, qui n'ont pas besoin des paroles dont ils sont accompagnés pour faire connaître l'excès de leur douleur. (297)

Zilia's reactions to Céline serve as marker of the heroine's evolution with regard to the marriage plot, her own aborted marriage plot as well as Céline's. Whereas Zilia was initially "impatiente d'exécuter [ce] projet," by the time Céline's marriage comes to pass, she has grown "impatiente" with the marriage plot itself, and longs to participate in stories that are not limited by what she terms, in the case of Céline, "une dissimulation malhonnête ou une ignorance honteuse."

Graffigny's "Indispensable Pivot": Incest and the Structure of *Lettres*

Flirtation with incest has been noted in many eighteenth-century novels. Lynn Hunt writes: "The possibility of incest, whether real or metaphorical . . . runs like a red thread through the eighteenth century novel."[37] Pierre Fauchery goes so far as to claim that "dans le roman—monde où le scandale est la loi—l'inceste se donne presque comme la relation familiale 'naturelle.' "[38] In light of the eighteenth-century changes in family structure thus far considered, it is hardly surprising that the issue of incest is such a familiar topos in the eighteenth-century novel. Indeed, within a family unit increasingly sexualized through both the eroticization of the conjugal couple and through the new affectionate bonds being developed between parents and their children, one would expect to find a great deal of anxiety concerning the proper border between the new "appropriate" affection among family members, and what must have continued to be considered "inappropriate" affection, that is, actual sexual relations between family members (other than husband and wife), relations that would undermine the continuing role the family played in a social system of alliance.

Habermas points to the dual role that the modern family has played since its origins in the eighteenth century:

> The ambivalence of the family as an agent of society yet simultaneously as the anticipated emancipation from society manifested itself in the situation of the family members: on the one hand, they were held together by patriarchal authority; on the other, they were bound to one another by human closeness.[39]

It is in fictions of the period, I believe, that the tensions between the family-as-emancipation-from-society and family-as-social-agent are confronted and resolved. We have seen that Pelckmans traces the development of the Oedipus complex in the novel during the pre-revolutionary period. He argues that, as one set of familial and social relations was imposed on another, the "glue" of the Oedipus complex, based on the ambivalent relation to incest, came into place to ensure the double role of the modern nuclear family. It is in the overlap of sexualized relations within the family and a continued concern for issues of alliance that the eighteenth-century obsession with incest emerges.

Michel Foucault writes eloquently on this precarious coexistence of concerns of alliance and intrafamilial love:

> Since the 18th century the family has become an obligatory locus of affects, feelings, love . . . sexuality has its privileged point of development in the family . . . for this reason sexuality is "incestuous" from the start. . . . In a society such as ours, where the family is the most active site of sexuality, and where it is doubtless the exigencies of the latter which maintain and prolong its existence, incest . . . occupies a central place; it is constantly being solicited and refused; it is an object of obsession and attraction, a dreadful secret and an indispensable pivot. It is manifested as a thing that is strictly forbidden in the family insofar as the latter functions as a deployment of alliance; but it is also a thing that is

continuously demanded in order for the family to be a hotbed of constant sexual incitement.[40]

We will see that Graffigny presents "the indispensable pivot" of incest in a way that upsets the delicate balance described by Foucault between incitement and taboo. Her decision to have the primary passionate love in her novel play itself out in the context of a brother–sister relationship serves a double purpose.[41] On the one hand, it provides the type of titillating touch of local color and historical authenticity so prized by Graffigny's contemporaries. On the other hand, and more importantly, it provides Graffigny's foreign heroine with an alternative social system to which her allegiance eventually allows her to *avoid* the marriage system in France. That is, in this period of changing familial relationships within a context of increasing privatization of the domestic space, Graffigny, consciously or unconsciously, takes advantage of the anxiety associated with the issue of incest. She does so *not* to imagine a situation in which these anxieties are resolved in an uneasy balance that makes the modern family possible, but rather to undermine the kind of familial relationships that Foucault describes above and to valorize other possible subjectivities, especially for women.

Zilia is faithful to Aza, her absent love, for the duration of her letters. The fact that the love Zilia shares with Aza is incestuous does not become important until the relationship comes to have power as a symbol of transgression—that is, once Zilia has been transplanted into a culture with a clearly defined incest taboo. The incestuous relationship and the symbolic role it continues to play in Zilia's life in France enable her to live in a way that would hardly be possible in either her own culture or in French culture. Indeed, it is the interplay between the two cultures, and the way that Graffigny plays them against one another, "rotating" them on what Foucault calls the "indispensable pivot" of incest, that make conceivable Zilia's eventual decision to live autonomously. When pressure is put on Zilia to conform to the "natural" marriage and family patterns demanded of her in France—patterns for which we find a model in Céline's relationship—Zilia is able to resist because of her love for Aza. When it becomes clear to Zilia that Déterville has fallen in love with her, she repeatedly takes refuge in undying feelings of tenderness for Aza:

> A présent je ne puis penser sans une sorte de mépris pour moi-même que je rends malheureuses deux personnes auxquelles je dois la vie; que

je trouble le repos dont elles jouiraient sans moi, que je leur fais tout le mal qui est en mon pouvoir, et cependant je ne puis ni ne veux cesser d'être criminelle. Ma tendresse pour toi triomphe de mes remords, Aza, que je t'aime! (316)

This persistent recourse to a symbolically loaded incestuous love gives Zilia the strength to disturb the peace of not just Déterville and Céline, but of certain mid-eighteenth-century assumptions about novels as well. Again and again, the incestuous nature of Zilia's relationship with Aza is underlined. Of her first meeting with Aza, Zilia writes:

Non, la mort même n'effacera pas de ma mémoire les tendres mouvements de nos âmes qui se rencontrèrent, et se confondirent dans un instant. Si nous pouvions douter de notre origine, mon cher Aza, ce trait de lumière confondrait notre incertitude. Quel autre que le principe du feu aurait pu nous transmettre cette vive intelligence des coeurs. (263)

Zilia emphasizes the bloodlines—"le principe du feu"—that she and Aza share: the "trait de lumière" assures them that they are both descended from their Sun-God father figure. In fact, the "trait de lumière" she experiences upon meeting Aza confuses the sexually inexperienced Zilia and leads her to believe she has been chosen through the mediation of Aza as mate to the Sun—who is interestingly enough the father figure. But this father–daughter dimension of incest in the novel is taken no further. Zilia discovers quickly that it is truly Aza whom she desires, and to whom she is destined.[42]

Earlier we examined Zilia's second letter, one of only two letters in the collection that actually respond to Aza's stated point of view—as opposed to his point of view as Zilia imagines it. We learn in that letter that Aza as a male ruler receives from the Spaniards a treatment very different from that accorded Zilia by the French. Firm indications already suggest that Aza's willing assimilation to Western culture lies ahead. After Déterville has made arrangements to ensure that Zilia's correspondence may finally reach Aza, a response arrives from the Spanish court—without a note from Aza. Zilia, shaken for a moment out of her faith in Aza's fidelity, writes him immediately:

Que manquerait-il à mon bonheur, si tu avais joint à la précieuse lettre que j'ai reçue quelques gages de tendresse! Pourquoi ne l'as-tu pas fait?

On t'a parlé de moi, tu es instruit de mon sort, et rien ne me parle de
ton amour. Mais puis-je douter de ton coeur? Le mien m'en répond. . . .
Cependant, tu as embrassé la religion de ce peuple féroce. Quelle est-
elle? Exige-t-elle que tu renonces à ma tendresse, comme celle de France
voudrait que je renonçasse à la tienne? non, tu l'aurais rejetée. (319)

Although Zilia refuses to see the obvious, it is clear to the reader by this point that Aza has become thoroughly Spanish. This assimilation is symbolized by his acceptance of the Catholic tradition, "la religion de ce peuple féroce," which forbids incest and therefore outlaws his relationship with Zilia. By contrast, Zilia resists assimilation and never gives up her attachment to incest as a religious or emotional precept.

Once again, a consideration of Graffigny's relationship to her primary source text for the "facts" of Peruvian culture proves illuminating. We thus far have considered two significant ways in which Graffigny transformed Garcilaso's history: first by positing the point of view of a woman instead of that of a man; and second by superimposing a love story onto the rigid hierarchical marriage system presented in Garcilaso's work. There is a third essential way in which Graffigny transforms her source material. Garcilaso, who is, in a sense, the protagonist of his own supposedly historical work, converted to Catholicism after the Spanish colonization of his country, and wrote his work ostensibly to help persuade other Peruvians to convert. In the preface to his *Histoire des Incas: Rois du Pérou*, he claims to have written his work "non pour mes intérêts particuliers, mais pour le service de toute la République chrétienne." Garcilaso continues: "Ceux qui prendront la peine de lire [mon oeuvre], ne peuvent que remercier Dieu, de ce qu'il a tiré tant de Peuples de l'abîme de l'idolâtrie pour les amener au giron de l'Eglise."[43]

In Graffigny's *Lettres*, Aza's trajectory recalls that of Garcilaso: both men arrive in Spain and make a pact with their colonizers that includes religious and social assimilation. Zilia's trajectory, on the other hand, is defined in opposition to that of the fictional Aza and the real Garcilaso. When first exposed to French religion during her stay in the convent where Madame Déterville has ordered her confined, Zilia is in fact pleased with what she finds, and struck by how similar the precepts of the Catholic church are to those of the Cult of the Sun. She writes of her first meeting with a priest: "De la façon dont il m'a parlé des vertus que [la religion de France] prescrit, elles sont tirées de la loi naturelle, et en vérité aussi pures que les nôtres . . ." (306). It is only when she learns that the Catholic tradition forbids incest that, through her commitment to Aza, she finds herself at odds with French law. (While there was a court that sought to protect marriages for love such as Céline's, certainly none existed to come to the rescue of an actually incestuous bond such as Zilia's to Aza.) After she tells the priest who has come to encourage her conversion to Christianity that she intends to love her brother for all eternity and that, in fact, she intends to marry him, we read:

> D'abord il prit une mine gaie, et paraissait douter de la vérité de mes paroles, il ne me répondit que des railleries, qui, tout insipides qu'elles étaient, ne laissèrent pas de m'offenser; je m'efforçai de le convaincre de la vérité; mais à mesure que les expressions de mon coeur en prouvaient les sentiments, son visage et ses paroles devinrent sévères; il osa me dire que mon amour pour toi était incompatible avec la vertu, qu'il fallait renoncer à l'un ou à l'autre, enfin que je ne pouvais t'aimer sans crime. (309)

Zilia has a strong emotional reaction to the news that she cannot love Aza:

> A ces paroles insensées, la plus vive colère s'empara de mon âme, j'oubliai la modération que je m'étais prescrite, je l'accablai de reproches, je lui appris ce que je pensais de la fausseté de ses paroles, je lui protestai mille fois de t'aimer toujours, et sans attendre ses excuses, je le quittai, et je courus m'enfermer dans ma chambre, où j'étais sûre qu'il ne pourrait me suivre. (309)

While Zilia frequently displays strong emotion in her letters, here she is more openly angry and disrespectful than at any other point in the novel. In Peru, when she was critical of the culture in which she lived (the "humiliant avantage" is an example of such criticism), she usually counterbalanced her criticism with praise. She was assimilated into the Peruvian culture in a way that she is not in France; her ability to remain an outsider is linked to this insistence on maintaining an allegiance to an incestuous bond: "je lui protestai mille fois de t'aimer toujours."

Zilia's situation in France is in many ways analogous to her previous situation in Cuzco. She is once again confined in a shadowy space of women, in accordance with, and at the symbolic center of, a patriarchal religion. She is once again being taught about the religion by a male power figure. But in France, even in the convent—a powerful symbol of patriarchal hierarchy—she has found a means of safeguarding her own physical and psychological space: "je le quittai, et je courus m'enfermer dans ma chambre, où j'étais sûre qu'il ne pourrait me suivre." In the Temple of the Sun, it was the Capa-Inca who controlled the doors and who therefore decided who could come and go and who was to marry whom. Zilia's explicit refusal to adopt Christianity because of its insistence on the incest taboo corresponds to her flight from the priest to her own room in the convent, a sanctuary in which she is protected from the priest's strictures and control. This room, described in Zilia's twenty-second letter, prefigures the house to which she will retire at the end of the novel, once again a space in which Zilia herself determines when the doors will open and shut, who may come and go, and whether she will marry.

In the Temple of the Sun she had no room (or house) of her own, but here in France, "Grâce aux Espagnols, elle n'est soumise à aucune autorité sociale, les cucipatas, amautas, et mamas (prêtres, philosophes, et duègnes, selon les notes du roman), sont au Pérou éloignés de plusieurs milliers de lieues."[44] In France, where Zilia's relationship with Aza is outlawed—"[elle] ne peut [l]'aimer sans crime,"—she is afforded a *new* space. While the French and Peruvian cultures presented in Graffigny's novel share many traits, it is precisely on this issue of incest that they diverge sharply. Within a culture that flirts with the idea of incest while always stopping short of condoning actual incest, Zilia's commitment to her "incestuous" love (according to French standards) for Aza allows, in fact forces, her to rebel. Graffigny presents incest in its literal form, thereby going beyond the imaginary relationship with intrafamilial love that, as Foucault points out, was an important factor in the shift from a strictly alliance-based system to another in which tenderness between family members played an essential role. Zilia's zealous obedience to the letter of Peruvian patriarchal law allows her to chart an unusual course within French patriarchy. Graffigny marshals an "acceptable" Peruvian incest to legitimize the imagination of alternative familial models. This ploy is at the heart of Graffigny's project to give women a new voice in the novel. She takes French patriarchy and, by playing it against its "Peruvian" mirror, opens up a distinct imaginative place for women.[45]

Nancy Miller emphasizes that this new space is inseparable from Zilia's mastery of French sign systems in France: "Zilia will develop from a destiny of love, union, and domestication to a symbolic 'individuation' through a mastery of social semiotics."[46] Julia Douthwaite too underlines the ways in which Zilia's writing, in particular, what she terms Zilia's "*prise de parole*," renders possible Zilia's French destiny:

> Zilia's coming to writing announces her acquisition of a voice and the possibility of articulating her ideas in a larger cultural arena. But a language contains more than a system of linguistic signs; it represents an entire body of maxims and prejudices—at once a world view and a system of values. . . . In learning to speak French, the heroine must also learn the operative rules of being French.[47]

True, when Zilia leaves Peru and settles in France, she enters into a new *language*, which, once mastered, gives her access to authority (in the literal sense of being able to write about and thereby legitimize her experience). Moreover, Zilia eventually enters, and masters, a particular system of economic exchange: Déterville arranges for a portion of the Inca booty that the French seamen had earlier captured from the Spaniards to be transformed into a lovely home in the country brimming with books and "une cassette remplie de pièces d'or à l'usage de France" (351).[48] She also becomes a landowner. Déterville uses the money received from selling the Inca goods he found on the Spanish ship to purchase for Zilia a lovely house in the country to which she eventually retires. Graffigny's heroine does not, however, enter the new *kinship* system. This is the means by which Graffigny presents a model of female subjectivity beyond the role assigned her within both the traditional familial paradigm and the emerging bourgeois nuclear family.

As an exchanger of words and of money, Zilia comes to have access to two of three of the Lévi-Straussian mainstays of social order. By not entering the new *kinship* system, she avoids becoming an *object* of the third. "Unmarriageable," the "Peruvian" gains access to the rights and privileges of a universal (male) subject in the emerging French (textual) economy and is not relegated to the home.[49] This partial, and only partial, integration into French society opens up the possibility of recuperating the feminist notion of "tendre amitié" introduced by the *salonnières* about a century earlier. Well before the novel has progressed toward exposing Zilia's idyllic love story with Aza as a fiction within Graffigny's fiction, Zilia has created another love story in her letters; the love story between Zilia and Déterville progresses through its own set of trials and tribulations and culminates not in marriage but in tender and supportive friendship. Katharine Jensen points out that it is Déterville who is entrusted with the letters and who sees to it that they are published at a point well beyond the end of the events recounted by the story. Again, the preface allows us to read beyond the ending and see the heroine's ongoing friendship (rather than marriage), which supports her vocation as writer. As Jensen has commented:

> The preface's presentation of Zilia as author of her book and of Déterville's role in its publication tells the reader what happened after the end of the novel. We will therefore realize that refusing Déterville in marriage is related to Zilia's desire for a writing life—a desire that has in fact already been fulfilled and that is actively supported by Déterville.[50]

Déterville, who already has indications from the Spanish court that Zilia's Aza may be unfaithful, makes his amorous intentions clear. When Zilia fails to respond in the appropriate way, he indicates that, while his love will make him an eternally faithful servant to Zilia and while he will do all in his power to reunite the young Peruvians, he cannot be available to Zilia as an intimate friend. Zilia, in her thirtieth letter, expresses her dismay at this state of events:

> Le penchant des Français les porte si naturellement aux extrêmes, mon cher Aza, que Déterville, quoique exempt de la plus grande partie des défauts de sa nation, participe néanmoins à celui-là. Non content de tenir la promesse qu'il m'a faite de ne plus me parler de ses sentiments, il évite avec une attention marquée de se rencontrer auprès de moi. (332)

As Zilia struggles with the difficulties of maintaining her friendship with Déterville in the face of his insistent desire, her hopes for consummating her passionate love for Aza are fading. Over the course of several letters, Zilia's doubts regarding her lover Aza become more apparent.

A pattern of lucidity and denial repeats itself several times before Zilia describes her discovery of the brutal truth. Confronted again with Déterville's vague insinuations that her lover Aza may not share her own unswerving fidelity, Zilia writes in her thirty-first letter:

> Je lui demandai la vérité avec les dernières instances, tout ce que je pus tirer de lui ne fut que des conjectures vagues, aussi propres à confirmer qu'à détruire mes craintes. Cependant les réflexions qu'il fit sur l'incon-

stance des hommes, sur les dangers de l'absence, et sur la légèreté avec laquelle tu avais changé de religion, jetèrent quelque trouble dans mon âme. . . . Non, c'est le désespoir qui a suggéré à Déterville ces affreuses idées. . . . Non, jamais tu ne pourras m'oublier. (336)

Despite her periodic doubts, Zilia's steadfast loyalty to her "incestuous" relationship with Aza plays an important role in defining her relationship with Déterville. Her refusal even to consider replacing Aza with Déterville frees Zilia to work out a new set of terms with Déterville, terms that contest the notion that, in the case of respectable young ladies, the only appropriate place for love is within the confines of marriage, be it arranged or companionate. In a letter directly following the one in which the tempestuous meeting with the priest is described, Zilia relates to Aza an important interaction with Déterville. Having finally learned enough French to distinguish between "to love" and "to love passionately" (*aimer* and *aimer d'amour*), she communicates to Déterville that, while she harbors strong feelings for him, they are not the *same* as those she has for Aza. She implies that the difference in her feelings is related to incest when she points out that in her relationship with her French friend it is "le hasard seul" that has brought them together, as opposed to the "trait de lumière" that links her with Aza. In response to Déterville's threats to leave her, to go far away where he may "adorer l'idée de [Zilia]," which will be "la nourriture amère de [son] coeur" (335), though "[sa] mort sera le prix du sacrifice" (312), the Peruvian responds with her very principled description of the difference between the (eternal) love she feels for Aza and the friendship she feels for Déterville:

J'aime [Aza] toujours de même, et je l'aimerai jusqu'à la mort: je ne sais . . . si vos lois vous permettent d'aimer deux objets de la même manière, mais nos usages et mon coeur me le défendent. Contentez-vous des sentiments que je vous promets, je ne puis en avoir d'autres. . . . (313)

This difference—Zilia cannot love Aza and Déterville "de la même manière"—structures the marriageless ending of Graffigny's novel. Zilia challenges those laws of Déterville's country, which apparently allow one to love two objects "de la même manière," with the laws of her country. As Paul Hoffmann points out: "Déterville, à la fin du roman, apparaît à la fois *presque* identique à Aza, dans le discours de Zilia, et comme absolument autre."[51] By having her heroine insist on an elusive but nevertheless fundamental difference between the Peruvian and the Frenchman, Graffigny sets the stage for Zilia's ability to avoid, on rational grounds, the general social obligation to marry (Déterville), even when it becomes clear that her relationship with Aza will not work out. Still, in the twenty-second letter, Zilia responds to Déterville's declaration that "des obstacles invincibles" will keep Aza from her by telling him that that would have no effect on the relationship she might have with Déterville: "Eh bien, lui dis-je, je ne le verrai plus, mais je n'en vivrai pas moins pour lui" (313).

Zilia, having once made her point, is free to channel the love and eroticism she feels for Déterville into a nonconjugal though nevertheless complexly intimate bond with the Frenchman. While there are indications in some of the later letters that although her relationship with Déterville is different from her relationship with Aza, it may not be entirely devoid of a pleasurable sensuality:

> Votre raison est presque celle de la nature; combien de motifs pour vous chérir! jusqu'à la noblesse de votre figure, tout me plaît en vous; l'amitié a des yeux aussi bien que l'amour. (334)

By the time we finally learn in the thirty-eighth letter that Zilia's worst fears have come true, that Aza has indeed been unfaithful, the stage has been set for Zilia's situation in the final pages of the novel, the ending that defies what Miller calls the heroine's "choice" among marriage, the convent, or death.

RECOVERING A TRADITION OF *Tendre Amitié*: Graffigny and Her *Précieuses* Predecessors

A consideration of female subjectivity defined outside of marriage is, of course, not without precedent. Over half a century earlier, in *La Princesse de Clèves* (1678), Madame de Lafayette had presented her famous protagonist who decides to live alone after the death of her husband rather than marry the man she desires. DeJean's work on seventeenth-century writers shows that the "tradition du refus" is present in women's writing even earlier. Throughout the seventeenth century, aristocratic women authors linked an avoidance (real or imagined) of marriage with the creation of a (real or imagined) space beyond the periphery of the court: "From the beginning of the seventeenth-century women's tradition, the interests 'retirement' and 'repos' are linked to the choice of private space over the space of public exposure, the court, and this choice is seen (logically) as possible for a noblewoman only if she refuses marriage and a place in the landed order."[52] While, from a Habermassian perspective, the notions of public and private spheres are not applicable to the period in question,[53] DeJean's comment invites us to consider Graffigny and her *salonnière* predecessors in relation to the development of a tradition of dissent.

The Habermassian model of social change in terms of an oppositional private sphere is posited in part on a historical *continuity* with certain representational structures of the old regime, that is, "the 'public use of reason' was historically rooted in the art of rational-critical debate which bourgeois intellectuals had learned from encounters with courtly-noble society."[54] While the oppositional private sphere was eventually posited *against* courtly culture, it was within courtly culture that the rational discourse on which it depended had its origins. In other words, the discourse formulated in salons where nobility and the bourgeoisie mixed within the confines of what Habermas calls "representative publicness"—which in principle regulated all words and deeds in accordance with the king's wishes and designs—eventually escaped the court's control and became the basis for a critical oppositional discourse, or, to borrow Richard Terdiman's useful term, a "counter-discourse."[55]

Erica Harth considers the role of female-dominated salons and exclusively male academies in the shift from discourse to counter-discourse. While Harth suggests that "the dissent shown in the academy . . . had far-reaching implications for the development of a discourse that was to outlive the Old Regime by at least two centuries,"[56] she is far less optimistic about the role of female-dominated salons. Their freedom "proved largely illusory," their "subversion unfruitful."

I believe that salons and salon-writing did, in fact, contribute much to a contestatory public sphere, though in a complicated way. Salon women like Madeleine de Scudéry and Anne Marie de Montpensier, in astonishingly feminist language even by today's standards, decried the traditional institution of marriage, which, in the seventeenth century and to a lesser degree continuing into the eighteenth, was characterized by loveless alliances and frequent childbirth. The impact of the *salonnière*'s condemnations of the physical and emotional pleasure denied women in marriage, and of the incessant childbearing that resulted from conjugal relations dutifully fulfilled (as required by the laws of the church), has been seen by many twentieth-century critics as a highly *particular,* and therefore nonstructural, critique of male-dominated old-regime institutions. As we learn more about the relationship between the development of new public and private lives, it becomes increasingly clear that the radical critiques leveled by the *précieuses* of the aristocratic tradition against the institution of marriage from within the space of the salon, contributed much to the protoforms of the Habermassian public sphere. Salon women, in their effort to carve out a space from which they might critique the patriarchal bases of the old regime, functioned as a pivot that, ironically, opened the way for the new gender reconfigurations, which, over the course of the following century, would *exclude* women from the right to a public voice.

As an alternative to an unhappy conjugal and family situation, the aristocratic *salonnières* had created the notion of *tendre amitié*: a kind of emotional sharing that might in some way compensate for the paucity of affection and the overwhelming child-care responsibilities that were the fundamental conditions of a married woman's existence.[57] Far from being a primarily erotic or even sentimental activity, extramarital tender friendship was for these women linked with a plethora of new intellectual and literary activities often crossing both class and gender lines. Women and men from the old nobility, new nobility, and bourgeoisie congregated on a regular basis in each others' homes, even in each others' bedrooms, the famous *ruelles,* to converse and to read one another's work in a spirit of respect for the (light-hearted) pursuit of knowledge.

By the late eighteenth century, however, these salon women had become, within many strands of discourse, "a convenient metonym for the worst sides of absolutist life."[58] Notions of *tendre amitié* emerging from the salon and salon-writing had not disappeared, but rather they were transformed. While *tendre amitié* had originally been imagined as taking place within a space beyond marriage, a space that posited itself against marriage, it was rechanneled over the course of the eighteenth century *into* marriage. This new affectionate model of marriage, complete with all of its libidinal complications, would eventually play a key role in the formation of the intimate core of the oppositional public sphere.

Since the salon women of the seventeenth century were also among the first to write modern psychological novels, their association with the evils of monarchical rule posed obvious problems for eighteenth-century women writers. By the simple fact of their gender, women writers risked being associated with the excesses of what Habermas calls the "representative publicness" of the court, even though they might be participating in an activity—novel-writing—that had, from its beginnings, contained elements subversive of the very bases of the court.

As the court, through its association with salon women, became feminized, the study of literature became increasingly masculinized. During the early part of the eighteenth century pedagogical anthologies appeared that played a central role in shaping tastes and national prejudices. These collections filtered out the strong tradition of women's writing coming out of the seventeenth century in the name of a new civic virtue. In 1747, when Graffigny first published *Lettres d'une Péruvienne*, Abbé Batteux, for example, published his *Cours de belles-lettres*, which, along with its companion volume, *Les Beaux arts réduits à un seul principe*, published the previous year, aimed to eliminate all literature deemed dangerous to civic virtue. Batteux includes no novels whatsoever, and the two women who do appear "achieve exemplary status solely as illustrations of the threat to 'vigorous' male Christian standards represented by the 'softening' and 'languishing' tendencies of female literary models."[59] Within this context, it becomes clear why women writers during a good part of the eighteenth century were in the awkward position of having to defend their right to a public voice without identifying themselves with their female literary predecessors (who themselves had, ironically, played such an important role in the creation of this public voice).

In the "marriageless" love story of Graffigny's novel, that is, the relationship between Zilia and Déterville, we see a recuperation of certain seventeenth-century notions of *tendre amitié* but in a post-Regency context. Within this social and literary milieu quite different from that of her seventeenth-century predecessors, Graffigny reclaims a notion of friendship outside of marriage to give a voice to her heroine, whom she defines as friend and writer rather than as wife. At the same time, Graffigny defines herself apart from her predecessors in important ways. While Zilia does use metaphoric language, her letters, seeped in eighteenth-century sentimentality, are a far cry from what Gutwirth calls the rococo style typical of seventeenth-century *salonnières*.[60] Moreover, the throne on which Aza was to sit, a symbol of monarchy and aristocratic privilege, has been melted down to assure Zilia's independence within a very different framework. In her "retreat," Zilia is in fact quite active in what Habermas calls the "public sphere," a space he defined in large part by the exchange of money and of books; Zilia, after having "translated" them from their "Peruvian" versions, has both at her disposal. The *quipos*, in the novel associated with aristocratic privilege of Inca royalty, have become published words, the throne transformed into exchangeable *ecus* and household linens.

Fauchery's research on the role of women in the eighteenth-century novel suggests that Graffigny's conclusion had elements in common with the endings invented by many other women writers of the period. In the meager twelve pages he devotes to "romancières" in his eight-hundred-and-fifty-nine-page *Destinée féminine dans le roman européen du dix-huitième siècle* (1972), Fauchery writes of the retreat ending:

> C'est là la conclusion canonique à la biographie de la femme désabusée; il est caractéristique que ce soit dans le roman féminin que ces aboutissements se proposent le plus fréquemment. On devine ainsi que le rêve autarcique (agrémenté ou non de satisfactions sexuelles) a dû effleurer bien des consciences de romancières.[61]

Fauchery may well be right in establishing some kind of connection between women writers' dissatisfactions with their lives, and the "canonical retreat" from the world at the close of the novel.[62] Graffigny's correspondence, as well as legal records from her eventually successful separation proceedings, document the extreme physical and psychological abuse the author endured. Fauchery concludes that such endings are merely the expression of personal, and therefore insignificant, rancor, that these women are exceptions:

> Sans doute n'est-elle [the woman writer] pas tout à fait une femme "comme les autres": écrivain, elle est donc quelqu'un qui a choisi de se distraire des actes quotidiens, des modes conventionnels de la vie, au moins une part de son temps; elle est aussi une femme que le train ordinaire des choses ne comble pas; elle semble donc devoir être plus sensible qu'une autre à ce qui, dans la condition des femmes, blesse l'équité, réprime des aspirations dont mieux qu'une autre elle sait le prix: il la faudrait supposer bien aveugle, ou de bien mauvaise foi, pour endosser sans examen l'appareil des idées reçues.[63]

In the eighteenth century, "des modes conventionnels de la vie," "le train ordinaire des choses," and "des idées reçues" were hardly givens. Rather, through a variety of discourses including the novel, they were in the process of being constructed. While the facts of Graffigny's bibliography and a more general *mentalité* are ultimately inseparable (as is the case for every writer, male or female), it is time to look at the ways in which the inclusion of recovered female voices both support and disrupt models that explore the relationship between literature and the emergence of modernity. As for Fauchery's mention of the "mauvaise foi" of women writers, I close this chapter with this passage as a reminder that the critical tradition with which eighteenth-century women writers like Graffigny had to cope has not been entirely overcome. In 1963 Georges May wrote that "l'histoire du roman reste à faire." As we approach the second millenium, in many ways this continues to be true.

❋ 2 ❋

The Mother–Daughter Plot in Isabelle de Charrière's *Lettres écrites de Lausanne*

> There can be no systematic study of woman in patriarchal culture, no theory of women's oppression, that does not take into account woman's role as a daughter of mothers and as a mother of daughters, that does not study female identity in relation to previous and subsequent generations of women, and that does not study that relationship in the wider context in which it takes place: the emotional, economic and symbolic structures of family and society.
> —Marianne Hirsch, "Mothers and Daughters:
> A Review Essay," in *Signs*, 1981

AFTER ROUSSEAU

In his well-known work, *Le Roman jusqu'à la Révolution* (1967), Henri Coulet designates 1760 as a turning point in the history of the French novel: "Aux environs de 1760, le roman traverse une crise grave et complexe."[1] Georges May, three years earlier, had also pointed to this moment as a crisis point in the evolution of the novel: "De façon à peu près universelle [après 1761], critiques et romanciers chantèrent à l'unisson les louanges du roman didactique, du roman sermon."[2] While neither Coulet nor May articulated their remarks in terms of an oppositional public sphere, they do suggest that over the course of the last third of the eighteenth century, the novel became the vehicle for expressing and reproducing an increasingly well-defined social and emotional vision of moral civic virtue. Based on the work of Habermas, we might extrapolate to suggest that this vision, by creating a shared sense of new identity among a broad spectrum of new readers, made possible effective dissent against the representative publicness of the monarchy.

May's choice of 1761 as the date of a shift from a rather chaotic "immorality" to an organized "morality" (like Coulet's mention of "une crise aux environs de 1760") is, of course, dictated by the publication date of two monumental works by Rousseau: *La Nouvelle Héloïse* (1761) and *Emile* (1761). Between the publication date of the final version of Graffigny's *Lettres d'une Péruvienne* in 1752 and that of Isabelle de Charrière's *Lettres écrites de Lausanne* in 1785, Rousseau had indelibly marked the mental terrain of France. A brief consideration of Rousseau's role in the changes underway is essential to the analysis in this chapter of the work of Charrière, who wrote both within and against the traces left by her influential predecessor.

In the years following the publication of *La Nouvelle Héloïse* and *Emile*, in the first documented instance of the modern phenomenon of fan mail, Rousseau received literally hundreds of letters from readers who, one after another, stressed the transformative role of his work in their lives. These letters, which Robert Darnton points to as the most important proof of the "reading revolution" that took place in Europe toward the end of the eighteenth century, provide us with a unique opportunity to consider how a wide range of people read and incorporated their reading into lived experience.[3]

There is, for example, the Scotsman who, even as he made his way to Rousseau's home, paused to put his feelings into words: "O cher Saint-Preux, Mentor éclairé, éloquent et aimable Rousseau, j'ai un pressentiment qu'une amitié bien noble va naître aujourd'hui."[4] The Scotsman's words typify what Jean-Marie Goulemot calls "une lecture intimiste," a sort of reading involving "un livre lu avec passion et qui appelle l'expansion lyrique envers son auteur, la communication intime avec l'écrivain."[5] In this case, it is almost as if the reality of the *epistolary* communication with his "ami" is more essential than, or at least as important as, the meeting itself. The words of the Scotsman's letter too suggest the domination of textual over extratextual realities. The fictional character ("Saint Preux") and the author ("éloquent et aimable Rousseau") together become the reader's single "Mentor éclairé."

It was not that readers like our Scotsman did not recognize the novel as a fictional creation. They simply were so emotionally taken by the fictional characters that the fictional reality felt more real to them than did anything in the "real" world. The words of another young reader, Bastide, provide a case in point:

> Ah permettez-moi de le dire, il fallait que vous sussiez tirer du sein d'une catastrophe horrible pour moi, les beautés dont vous l'avez couverte

ensuite, pour que je puisse vous pardonner de m'avoir enlevé Julie. . . . Mon coeur gémissait toujours de voir Julie infidèle à tant d'amour qu'elle m'avait donné.[6]

Rather than confuse author and character (as had the Scotsman), this reader writes to Rousseau as if he, Bastide, were Saint Preux. He so closely identifies with Rousseau's hero that he feels *personally* betrayed by Julie's marriage to the stern Wolmar. And yet, at the same time, Bastide willingly forgives Rousseau as the creator of "his" destiny. On the basis of Bastide's experience, one can certainly be persuaded by Claude Labrosse's comment that Julie "fait apparaître le fondateur [Rousseau] comme le concurrent possible des autorités reconnues et elles mêmes fondamentalement sacralisées (Etats et Eglises)."[7] As Grimm put it in his *Correspondance littéraire* some years later: "Jean Jacques has no admirers, only worshippers."[8]

In a letter to her husband, Françoise Charlotte Constant de Rebecque describes, in explicit terms, yet another kind of projection of text onto reality and vice versa.

> Je ne vous écrivis hier au soir, mon cher ami, parce que je lus en entier le premier volume de Rousseau dont je suis folle, mais vous n'y perdites rien, car je vis toujours votre figure à la place du héros et trouvant tous les sentiments de Julie dans mon coeur, il me semblait vous écrire en lisant ces lettres, elle dit tout plein de choses que j'avais pensé et senti avant elle mais que je n'avais su rendre. . . . En parlant de tout cela, je parle de vous et rapporte tout à vous et je n'aime et ne puis aimer que vous et pour toute ma vie.[9]

Rebecque both projects her reality onto the text ("je vis toujours votre figure à la place du héros") and sees the text as reflecting her own preexisting reality back to her ("[Julie] dit tout plein de choses que j'avais pensé et senti avant elle mais que n'avais su rendre"). Like so many of Rousseau's readers, Rebecque feels that she found her true self as she read *La Nouvelle Héloïse*. And yet, as Rebecque herself acknowledges, this is a self that she could never have expressed prior to reading Rousseau. One can find what is lost or find what is new. The magic of Rousseau was that his readers felt they were doing the former when all indications are that they were, in fact, doing the latter.

Habermas cites Rousseau's work (along with Richardson's) as having played an essential role in the development of modern subjectivity emerging from within the seemingly autonomous intimate sphere of the conjugal family:

> In the intimate sphere of the conjugal family privatized individuals viewed themselves as independent even from the . . . sphere of their economic activity—as persons capable of entering into "purely human" relations with one another. The literary form of these at the time was the letter. . . . When Rousseau used the form of the novel in letters for *La Nouvelle Héloïse* . . . there was no longer any holding back. The rest of the century reveled and felt at ease in a terrain of subjectivity barely known at its beginning.[10]

It is as though, after Rousseau, the French enjoyed a new sense of whom they "really" were, deep down, without regard to anything beyond their " 'purely human' relations." Rousseau's work struck a chord among the most primal passions in ways that drew readers into an identification with new models that somehow felt old. He made readers feel that they were at last *re*-finding their truest, most secret selves, his writings leading them *back* to their hearts and to the swell of virtue that there awaited them.

But, if we believe Habermas, in reveling in this "terrain of subjectivity," readers imagined themselves in ways that matched, and were indeed constitutive of, a *new* economic structure based on interdependent public and private spheres. The emotional center to which they "returned" depended on, and was the product of, the narration itself. Jean-Marie Goulemot describes the process:

> Tout se passe comme si l'intime échappait, avant la lecture, au sujet lui-même, ne pouvait être perçu que de l'extérieur par ce savoir fictionnel du roman, comme si l'intime, jusqu'ici caché à autrui, enfoui, ne pouvait naître à la conscience qu'en devenant lui-même narration transposée, relevant de schémas narratifs et culturels.[11]

An inner life in the modern sense of the word could only come into being with its publication. The epistolary web of publication created by the crossed letters among fictional characters, real readers, and the author himself, seemed to bridge the gap between the real and the fictional: "Roman et correspondance tentent de se mimer mutuellement: la fiction épistolaire mime les correspondances réelles et l'échange des lettres mime la fable romanesque."[12] The emotional investment of readers in their reading experience was sometimes so strong it would result in what LaBrosse calls "dé-lire," a process in which the reader would drop the book to give free reign to physical responses. This physically charged response to words on the page surely facilitated the willing suspension of disbelief: "Le plaisir, les larmes, le saisissement affectent le sujet jusqu'en son corps qui se trouve affectivement et esthétiquement capté par la chimère et par l'événement."[13] Private tears provoked by letters, confided in new letters, created a collectively shared pool of "private" emotion in which one's private sense of self responded to and reflected others' private sense of self.

From the medieval courtly romance to even the first modern psychological novels of the *précieuses* in the seventeenth century, the novel as love story had concerned love *outside* a rigid alliance-based marriage system. The person you loved was someone you could not ever marry. In his *Julie*, Rousseau wrote against what he viewed as the disarray of passions found in earlier novels, while, at the same time, appropriating their energy in ways that invited readers to participate in his social vision. Julie is the fallen woman in illicit love in the first half of the novel; by the second her libido has been rechanneled into the Clarens household (just as the water in the Elysium is rechanneled to sustain a "natural" garden). Joan DeJean writes: "[La Nouvelle Héloïse] is in actuality an immense indictment of the novel, an attempt to contain its 'violent passions,' and a condemnation of the novel as love story ('lettres de deux amans')."[14] In the words of Anne Attridge, "Despite the partial agony, the happiness of Clarens is very great, and it would not be so great if it did not come as a relief from the turbulent emotions of the earlier part of the book."[15] William Ray points out that Julie can embody virtue so powerfully "because she has sublimated her sexual desire to a desire for social order."[16]

Of course, the ambiguities in Rousseau's argument and the mystery of its balance between order and disorder have been the object of study and debate among political scientists, historians, and literary critics for the better part of two centuries. Indeed, just two of the several eighteenth-century rewritten versions of *La Nouvelle Héloïse* show that these were evident to many of Rousseau's contemporary readers as well. One year after Rousseau published his novel, a certain Formey created a new version that canceled out the "équivoques" of the original. *Julie* became a straightforwardly moral tale in which Rousseau's heroine is freed of the tarnish of illicit love. Over a decade later, as the debate over the morality of Rousseau's work simmered on, Milon published *La Nouvelle Héloïse dévoilée*. Like

Formey's version of Rousseau's story, Milon's canceled out the "équivoques" of the original letters, but did so in the *opposite* direction. Rather than cancel out all morally dubious elements, as had Formey, Milon excluded anything that might be considered morally uplifting. From being an ambiguously moral tale, *La Nouvelle Héloïse* became a straightforwardly evil one. A more detailed consideration of the relationship between morally dubious and morally uplifting elements in Rousseau's work goes far beyond the scope of this study.

I would simply stress that it was surely the uneasy combination of a love story with an anti–love story that made Rousseau's vision so palatable to masses of newly literate readers drawing forth a desire to be virtuous among the fallen as well as the exemplary. In his insightful analysis of *La Nouvelle Héloïse*, Tony Tanner underlines the precarious nature of the intrafamilial relationships in Rousseau's novel, the ways in which Rousseau's presentation is as much a condemnation of the bourgeois family as it is a support: "At the end, all the bonds have snapped; father, husband, cousin, children of misery without communication."[17] Of the eighteenth- and nineteenth-century novel more generally, he writes: "It writes of contracts but dreams of transgressions, and in reading it, the dream tends to emerge more powerfully."[18] Tanner is, of course, right that Rousseau's libidinal constructions are precarious. We saw how easily Milon transformed the novel into an overt condemnation of "family values." And yet, both despite and because of his novel's highly nuanced complexity, Rousseau provided readers within an emerging social order a resolution to difficult contradictions. As their letters attest, readers *were* seduced by his vision (no matter how hollow at its core), and they modeled their identities on those he presented in literature. At least to his contemporaries, one would be hard pressed to state that the subversive dream emerged more powerfully than the contract. As a *social event*, the post-Rousseauian (anti-)novel, far from disrupting the (new) family system, was a force that cemented it as the "natural" organizing principle of late eighteenth-century France.

Indeed, letter after letter to "l'ami Jean-Jacques" linked revelation and salvation to specific behavior within the conjugal family model. This was as true for readers of Rousseau's *Emile* as for those of his *Julie*. Ranson, a merchant from La Rochelle whose correspondence Darnton traces over the course of nearly a decade, is typical in this regard:

I send you my warmest thanks for your good wishes concerning my new estate. My wife is as touched as I am by what you wrote to me on her account. I hope it will not be difficult for me to fulfill my duties toward this dear spouse in the fashion that you prescribe and that I have prescribed for myself. If I have been able to do without women until the age of nearly thirty, though I have certainly never looked upon the fair sex with an indifferent eye, I am sure that one will be enough for me for the rest of my life. Everything that l'Ami Jean-Jacques has written about the duties of husbands and wives, of mothers and fathers, has had a profound effect on me; and I confess to you that it will serve me as a rule in any of those estates that I should occupy.[19]

Rousseau's vision of a virtuous life, separate from the decadent mores of Parisian high society, was rooted in the pleasures of passionate yet well-regulated domesticity.[20] Ranson envisions life after marriage in terms of series of sentimentalized gender-specific occupations, "the duties of husbands and wives, of mothers and fathers." At the symbolic center of this haven of nature and virtue, Rousseau envisioned "the one who will be enough" for all a man's life, a woman passionately devoted to her husband (though not necessarily in a sexual way), and to his children. This woman, legitimized and even rendered sacred, was to give up, and indeed give up any desire for, a voice in public affairs: "La véritable mère de famille loin d'être une femme du monde n'est guère moins recluse dans sa maison que la religieuse dans son cloître."[21]

Far from being the result of any sort of simple misogyny, this role for women played an essential part in his broader social vision. Patrick Coleman outlines how, already in the *Lettre à d'Alembert* (1758), Rousseau's project for public (male) life depended on the particularities of women at home. Women were to provide men with the individual sense of self denied them in the public sphere. Rousseau felt that the world of business tended to flatten out the particular and that the place to look for national particularities was in women: "When Rousseau compares the effect of business on men to the unmediated expression of moeurs in women, he assumes the existence of a national-type association, to which the social relationships of business are opposed."[22] In the Rousseauian schema, women in the private sphere provide a structurally necessary counterbalance to economic man. In Rousseau's later work, especially *La Nouvelle Héloïse*, these roles were textually transmitted to a much larger public. Rousseau is, to quote Ray, "the eighteenth-century author . . . most anxious about the role of women in the cultural economy as it intersects with the function of the novel in constructing subjectivity."[23]

While Ray's words are most applicable to Rousseau's best-selling novel, one finds a similar interpellation of gender-related subjectivities in his *Emile*. Rousseau, often addressing himself directly to his female readers, underlined their crucial role in the establishment of "natural" social order. He presented breastfeeding, for example, as the keystone upon which rested all hopes for a natural society:

> Quand la famille est vivante et animée, les soins domestiques font la plus chère occupation de la femme et le plus doux amusement du mari. Ainsi de ce seul abus corrigé resulteroit bientôt une réforme générale; bientot la nature auroit repris tous ses droits. Qu'une fois les femmes redeviennent mères, bientôt les hommes redeviendront pères et maris. . . . Voilà la règle de la nature. Pourquoi la contrariez-vous?[24]

We must remind ourselves that Rousseau's argument, even presented in such a direct and, to us, transparently manipulative way, was enormously influential.[25] In her *Sexual Politics in the Enlightenment: Women Writers Read Rousseau*, Mary Trouille describes Rousseau's appeal for eighteenth-century women:

> Rousseau's valorization of *la vie intérieure* (in the double sense of domestic life and affective experience) was enthusiastically adopted by his women readers. For many, *La Nouvelle Héloïse* came as a revelation, opening up hitherto unsuspected possibilities for emotional fulfillment by showing that conjugal fidelity was not incompatible with happiness—indeed that love and virtue could be combined. As their letters to Rousseau suggest, Julie seems to have filled an emotional gap for many of his readers by heightening the significance of their existing relationships or by helping them imagine a happier, more fulfilling life, which they might not otherwise have thought possible.[26]

Women enthusiastically adopted a discourse that drew them into new responsibilities within the domestic sphere. At the same time, this assured that patriarchal lineage and power escaped the threat of the powerful public women who had played a seminal role in cultural life during the earlier part of the century and who had been at the forefront of the earliest explorations of new relations between state and individual.[27] His portrayal of the contentedly domestic woman was constructed explicitly against women writers:

> Une femme bel-esprit est le fléau de son mari, de ses enfans, de ses amis, de ses valets, de tout le monde. De la sublime élévation de son beau génie, elle dédaigne tous ses devoirs de femme, et commence toujours par se faire homme.[28]

Rousseau makes a point of defining writing as a part of the exterior male world into which a woman can venture only if she is willing to jeopardize her femininity. To write is to become male.

We have seen that Rousseau's implied reader is frequently female ("Voilà la règle de la nature. Pourquoi la contrariez-vous?"). An examination of another brief passage from *Emile* demonstrates the ways that shifts in address interpellate women into his vision. In passages addressed to implied female readers, the author invites an identification between his readers and his model of natural and virtuous womanhood: "C'est à toi que je m'addresse, tendre et prévoyante mère . . ." (246). Sometimes, however, the narrator shifts his address to an implicitly male reader:

> Lecteur, je m'en rapporte à vous-même: soyez de bonne foi. Lequel vous donne meilleure opinion d'une femme en entrant dans sa chambre, lequel vous la fait aborder avec plus de respect, de la voir occupée des travaux de son sèxe, des soins de son ménage, environée des hardes de ses enfans, ou de la trouver écrivant des vers sur sa toilette, entourée de brochures de toutes les sortes, et petits billets peints de toutes les couleurs?[29]

In these passages, the author invites his male readers, with all "bonne foi," to prefer certain activities in women over others. The shift in gender of the implied reader invites women, particularly women who might have an inclination to express themselves in writing, to read themselves through the eyes of their spouses or potential spouses. Writing, an act proclaiming the self-shaping of the female writer, is transformed into an activity shaped by an outside gaze. Instead of envisioning herself as an active subject, the writing woman is invited to consider herself the object of the (disapproving) male gaze. In his insightful article, "Reading Women: Cultural Authority, Gender, and the Novel," Ray shows the ways in which Rousseau's text encourages two different and gendered readings, one for women that promotes a passive emulation of Julie's example, and one for men that, on the contrary, initiates them into a position of critical distance with regard to cultural narratives.[30] Much suggests that many women, especially the best educated, read Rousseau's texts from both positions. That is, while they may have been interpellated into female roles as mothers and wives through the example of Julie, these women nevertheless absorbed—sometimes much later in life—many of the lessons presented to his male readers. Despite the negative terms in which Rousseau presents women writing, for example, his work served as the self-proclaimed inspiration to an enormous number of women writers over the course of the following century. As we will see in chapter 3, Sand—like Ormoy, Staël,[31] and many others before her—revered Rousseau and leaned on his writings as a justification for her own (public) self-exploration.

Charrière's work too provides us a unique opportunity to listen to and better understand, from a female perspective, the "whole new terrain of subjectivity" inaugurated by Rousseau in the prerevolutionary decades.

THE WOMAN WRITER IN THE AGE OF ROUSSEAU: A CASE STUDY

Charrière wrote her *Lettres écrites de Lausanne* during the decade following Rousseau's death, a time during which his work received a tremendous amount of "official" attention. Charrière, like almost everyone else who could read, participated in heated discussions of Rousseau's work. In 1790, for example, she entered a contest sponsored by the French Academy, which, in the midst of the revolutionary period, took as its theme "l'éloge du citoyen de Genève."[32] Charrière's interaction with "le Genevois" actually began much earlier, well before Rousseau had died and before she (or he for that matter) had begun to write novels.[33] When she was fourteen she was introduced to Rousseau's early work by her governess and friend, Mademoiselle Prévost.[34] Charrière, or rather, Isabelle Agneta Elisabeth van Tuyll van Serooskerken van Zuylen, (or simply Belle de Zuylen as she was known until the day of her marriage),[35] was twenty-one when *La Nouvelle Héloïse* and *Emile* were published. Her first written reactions to Rousseau are recorded a few years later. In a letter to the Baron Constant d'Hermenches, she playfully compares herself to Rousseau's heroine Julie:

> Je viens de souper avec 90 paijsans et paysannes les paijsans avoient battu tout le jour une certaine graine dont je ne sai pas le nom, jugez comme ils avoient chaud, mais notre paysan, le maitre du logis etoit si aise de me voir là assise a coté de lui il posoit de si bonne foi ses mains suantes

sur les miennes, sa femme faisoit avec tant de plaisir les honneurs a mon frere et à moi, nos domestiques aussi trouvoient si plaisant d'etre a table avec nous que cette fête n'a pas laissé de me paroitre agréable; je me suis comparée un moment a Julie avec orgueil.[36]

Zuylen's wry identification with Julie in this passage is hardly an indication that she had adopted Rousseau's heroine as a model for her own life.[37] We have evidence that, on the contrary, even early on, the young Zuylen consciously took her distance from the domestic path that Rousseau paved for women. In another letter to Hermenches written just eight days after the one cited above, Charrière's words show that she imagined a very different married life for herself from that of Rousseau's Julie:

Pourvu qu'on me laisse aller mon train de leçons, de lectures, d'écritures comme je fais ici, un peu plus librement encore je serai contente. . . . Pour un throne je ne renoncerais pas a ce qui m'occupe dans ma chambre. Si je n'aprenois plus rien je mourois d'ennui au milieu des plaisirs et des grandeurs.[38]

This passage is included in a letter Charrière is discussing ways to introduce her parents to the possibility of her marriage to a marquis of Hermenche's acquaintance. In Zuylen's description of the conditions that would make marriage acceptable, she refuses Rousseau's dictum that a married woman not be a "bel esprit." She insists on her continued freedom to read and to write, to be Rousseau's decried "[femme] écrivant des vers sa toilette entourée de brochures de toutes les sortes, et petits billets de toutes les couleurs,"[39] as a *necessary condition* for marriage. She suggests that her eventual husband should not demand more and should, in fact, be grateful if her activities do not interfere with his own: "Mon esprit ni mon érudition ne l'incommoderont pas, que lui importe le reste?"[40]

Just five months after the above missive was written, the following poem was included in a collection of Zuylen's verse and musical compositions that James Boswell had copied and, against Zuylen's wishes, sent to Rousseau.[41] Here too the young Charrière shows an astute awareness of the position Rousseau conceives for women and especially its implications for women writers:

>   Du Lac Leman je connois les rivages
>   Cent fois mes yeux en ont admiré les appas.
>   Cent et cent fois mes pieds en ont foulé la plage.

> Mais vers ce peuple libre et sage
> Si je voulois porter mes pas
> Ami, l'on ne m'y voudroit pas.
> Un peu de vers et de Philosophie
> Avec Rousseau me brouilleroit.
> A tout venant il crieroit
> Non, ce n'est pas la ma Sophie
> Fille à brochures et Billets,
> Qui ne fit onc manchettes ni lassets,
> Ni Savonnage ni Purée
> Mais des Contes et des Portraits
> En un mot Fille un peu lettrée
> Doit rester Fille à jamais.[42]

At the eminently marriageable age of twenty-four, Zuylen was doubtless sensitive to Rousseau's prescriptions and on the defensive. Rousseau, whose works were among the biggest sellers of the century, was indeed crying out "à tout venant" that a woman like Zuylen was no Sophie, the idealized female companion of his Emile. The last two lines of Zuylen's poem—"En un mot Fille un peu lettrée / Doit rester fille à jamais"— are, in fact, a paraphrase of a line from the fifth book of *Emile*: "Toute fille lettrée restera fille toute sa vie, quand il n'y aura que des hommes sensés sur la terre."[43] The young Zuylen's "peu de vers et de Philosophie" had already made her an unacceptable candidate for the Rousseauian version of marriage.

Yet the tone of the young woman's poem is more rebellious than it is tragic. In her rewritten version of Rousseau's adage, Zuylen expresses her right to disagree. The region of Switzerland around Lake Leman symbolizes Rousseau's vision, a territory that has tempted her—"Cent fois mes yeux en ont admiré les appas"—but that she ultimately finds to be profoundly unwelcoming to a woman like herself: "Mais vers ce peuple libre et sage / Si je voulais porter mes pas / Ami, l'on ne m'y voudroit pas." Her hypothetical "Si je voulais" leaves open the possibility, in fact points to it, that she does not want to visit Rousseau's "peuple libre et sage." Zuylen uses the designation "Ami" for Rousseau just as do the writers of those fan letters considered above, but Zuylen uses the designation ironically. She addresses Rousseau, conveying to him the news that he would *not* welcome her into his vision, as she has not undergone the transformation demanded by his work.

The irony of the young Belle de Zuylen's poem is doubled by the real-life events that would transpire. The writer did eventually "direct her steps" to Rousseau's territory, and she did so to get married. At the age of thirty-one, she moved from Utrecht to Neuchâtel to set up household with a Swiss husband. Over twenty years after writing the above poem Charrière published the novel I consider in this chapter, *Lettres écrites de Lausanne* (1785). My point here is not to do a biographical reading of Charrière's work. A good deal has been done in this vein already.[44] Rather, I include these biographical remarks because they point to the issues that women writers in the age of Rousseau had to confront to do their work. They document an awareness on the part of a particular female writer of the role that literature plays in constructing the lives of women so as to deny them access to writing. Charrière's written responses to Rousseau indicate both his powerful influence and her capacity to resist his views, particularly those already associated with feminine "instinct" and "nature."

Charrière's *Lettres* both incorporate and put into question the post-Rousseauian position of woman. Charrière has recourse to strategies closely related to new familial discourses but which exploit contradictions in Rousseau's vision to justify dissenting behavior. In *Lettres d'une Péruvienne* Graffigny exploited anxieties associated with incest, and more particularly intersibling incest, to justify Zilia's choice to live independently as a writer. In the post-Rousseauian world, Charrière's narrator has recourse to a different means of escape from the limitations imposed on her by new codes of femininity.

Charrière dissects the modern marriage plot, exposing the violence done to the bodies of women by what the narrator of Charrière's novel calls "le romanesque," that is, the modern love match. In the first part of my reading, I explore the narrator's discussion of the marriage arrangements for her daughter Cécile. Thereafter I consider the importance of the mother's voice in the novel and the ways in which Charrière opens up a new imaginative space for women from *within* the bourgeois family. She gives the control of this narrative of *la vie intérieure* (again in the double sense of the word) to a mother figure who ultimately privileges the relationship between mother and daughter over those between mother and father or between daughter and suitor. Charrière thereby asserts a feminine maternal power central to Rousseau's vision of social stability which, in the absence of a father figure, opens up possibilities available to neither Julie nor Sophie.

The Mechanics of the Marriage Plot

> When I think of the mechanics of power, I think of its capillary form of existence, of the extent to which power seeps into the very grain of individuals, reaches right into their bodies, permeates their gestures, their posture, what they say, how they learn to live and work with other people.
> —Michel Foucault[45]

Charrière's *Lettres* is technically a monophonic epistolary novel, that is, a collection of letters written by one character. In this case that character is an anonymous widow living in Lausanne with her daughter, Cécile.[46] All her letters are addressed to her unnamed cousin who lives with her husband and daughter in Languedoc. While we are privy only to the letters of the woman in Lausanne, the narrator includes enough excerpts from her cousin's responses to suggest a lively discussion between the women on issues concerning the education of daughters and the institution of marriage. The narrator opens her first letter with the words: "Combien vous avez tort de vous plaindre!"[47] From what follows we learn that the narrator's cousin was largely excluded from the preparations of the marriage in question ("un établissement sur laquelle vous étiez à peine consultée"), and that she felt her daughter was being taken away from her ("On la sépare de vous, aviez-vous tant de plaisir à l'avoir près de vous?"). The narrator reinforces her initial "Vous avez tort de vous plaindre!" with the following advice:

> Laissez-vous gouverner par les circonstances, et trouvez-vous heureuse qu'il y ait pour vous des circonstances qui gouvernent, des parents qui exigent, un père qui marie sa fille, une fille peu sensible et peu réfléchissante qui se laisse marier. Que ne suis-je à votre place! (25)

The narrator seems to suggest that the appropriate way for a mother to behave when confronted with the prospect of an arranged marriage is to sit back and watch. And yet there are clear indications that all is not well in the marriage being plotted for her cousin's daughter. It is suggested that she, "[la] fille peu sensible and peu réfléchissante qui se laisse marier," will end up unhappy, as unhappy as her mother. Indeed, the narrator suggests that one of the advantages for the cousin in not participating in the marriage arrangements of her daughter is that she will be free of blame should things turn out less than ideally: "Si elle est malheureuse ne sera-ce pas un chagrin de moins que de n'avoir pas fait son sort?" (23). Despite these ominous signs, the narrator insists that her cousin cease her complaining and, instead, content herself with the fact that she has a definite position in society, even if it is one that relegates her to passivity.

Despite the narrator's glib exclamation to her cousin—"Que ne suis-je à votre place!"—it quickly becomes apparent that she is unwilling to risk the happiness of her own daughter Cécile. Her exclamation is, in other words, only in part sincere. While it is true that, because she is a widow, in her household no "père qui marie sa fille" is in sight, the narrator makes it clear that she herself could marry off her daughter Cécile quite as easily and as advantageously as could the husband of her unhappy cousin, "le père qui marie sa fille." She writes: "Il n'a pourtant tenu qu'à moi de la marier...." But she adds "non, il n'a pas tenu à moi; je n'aurais pu m'y résoudre, et [Cécile] elle-même n'aurait pas voulu" (29). Here the narrator is pointing to a difference between arranged marriages of the sort her cousin is (un)involved in and the love-based marriage plot in which the volition of the marrying parties plays a role. While novels throughout the century had criticized the former, Charrière tackles the latter, "scrutinizing [it] as lucidly as possible, [laying] [it] ... bare."[48]

Her half-sympathies with the situation of her cousin are in fact a springboard for her to talk about her own circumstances and more specifically the trials and tribulations she encounters in designing and observing the more modern marriage plot for her Cécile: "Aujourd'hui je me plains; je me trouve quelquefois très à plaindre" (25). The widow complains not because she is excluded from the marriage plans as is her cousin, but rather, in some sense because she is too much *included* in the plans (and, of course, because she is genuinely concerned about her daughter's happiness). The narrator occupies the positions of both father and mother in her household. Her ambiguous status plays an important role in the structure of the novel because it allows for transgressions of Rousseauian categories of gender relegating women to the domestic scene.[49]

The fact that the narrator is a widow, that there is therefore no "père qui marie sa fille," is only one of the ways that the narrator is not "à la place" of her cousin. Cécile and her mother are also less wealthy than their counterparts in Languedoc. When her correspondent asks her how she expects to succeed in finding a husband for Cécile when she has so little money, the narrator responds:

> La question est étrange. On se marie, parce qu'on est un homme et une femme, et qu'on se plaît; mais laissons cela, je vous ferai l'histoire de ma fortune. (28)

The story of the narrator's fortune turns out to be, in fact, the story of her (relative) poverty. She inherited money from neither her father nor her husband, and she lives on a modest pension inherited from her mother. The narrator is a pragmatic woman. If she is to make suitable marriage arrangements for Cécile, that is to say, arrangements for a marriage with someone who has some money and at least a semblance of a title, it is not because of her wealth or her nobility, an increasingly abstract quality with diminishing bargaining power in Swiss society at the close of the century.[50] The narrator claims, at first, that all of these things do not matter. After all, in the eighteenth century, love counts more than credentials: "On se marie parce qu'on est un homme et une femme et qu'on se plaît."

The irony of the epistler's declaration is revealed by her immediate shift to financial concerns: "Je vous ferai l'histoire de ma fortune." Her abrupt shift of attention from the *romanesque* love match to money betrays the close connection between the conjugal love and affection of privatized domesticity, and the bourgeois market economy, even for aristocrats like herself.[51] Cécile's pragmatic mother is aware that the notion of a woman's right to individual choice in the much-vaunted love match is to a great extent illusory. She knows that the love match is imbricated in a complex web of social relations and that to arrange a suitable marriage for Cécile she will have to depend on far more than love. But in this new marriage market of the late eighteenth century she has recourse to something else. She can arrange a "love match" by presenting her daughter to the world in a certain way, by molding her daughter's body to the demands of a marriage system linked to the emerging market economy. A few of the novel's earlier scenes suggest that this is just what she intends to exploit.

Much work now being done on the eighteenth century focuses on the ways in which the emancipatory side of self-expression and its potential for freedom was balanced by a new sort of discipline at the level of the body. In her discussion of Michel Foucault's work, Sandra Lee Bartky's words echo and expand on Althusser's and Gramsci's work considered in our discussion of Graffigny:

> The rise of . . . new conceptions of political liberty was accompanied by a darker counter-movement, by the emergence of a new and unprece-

dented discipline directed against the body. More is required of the body now than mere political allegiance or the appropriation of the products of its labor; the new discipline invades the body and seeks to regulate its very forces and operations, the economy and efficiency of its movements.[52]

Foucault suggests that it is through the patient study of details that the workings of power in modern culture may best be understood. Charrière, who, of all eighteenth-century novelists, is perhaps the most focused on the details of daily life,[53] provides us an opportunity to consider the small ways in which the body is made to participate in interlocking systems of control emerging with modern social organization. These intimate operations of power are inseparable from language and the field of representation. Foucault insists that "our subjectivity, our identity, and our sexuality are intimately linked . . . they do not exist outside of or prior to language and representation, but are actually brought into play by discursive strategies and representational practices."[54]

As noted in our consideration of Rousseau, the eighteenth-century novel plays a pivotal role in mediating between private subjectivity and a broader oppositional social system. In her work on woman-authored eighteenth-century novels, Joan Hinde Stewart points to "an inchoate realization of the opacity of the signifier and the degree to which everyday speech may sustain patriarchal arrangements—social, political and sexual."[55] Charrière's narrator is remarkably sensitive to the intricate and intimate relation between words, institutions, and identity at play in her world. In terms that display even more than "an inchoate realization" of the discursive foundations of her daughter's and her own reality, the epistler underlines and puts into question the ways in which particular configurations of words affect the lives of readers. Of the Rousseauian lessons that her brothers-in-law try to impose on her and her daughter Cécile, she writes, for example:

> Voilà comme, avec des mots qui se laissent mettre à côté les uns des autres, on fabrique des caractères, des législations, des éducations et des bonheurs domestiques impossibles. Avec cela on tourmente les femmes, les mères, les jeunes filles. . . . (24–25)

In contrast to Foucault, who two hundred years later concentrates primarily on male bodies—those of soldiers, prisoners, and school boys[56]—Charrière concerns herself with the link among discourse ("des mots qui se laissent mettre à coté les uns des autres"), politics ("des législations"), education ("des éducations"), domesticity ("des bonheurs domestiques impossibles"), and *female* bodies: "Avec cela on tourmente les femmes, les mères, les jeunes filles." While an awareness of the power of particular configurations of words to torment the bodies of mothers and daughters does not necessarily free the narrator or her daughter from their effects, it does suggest the possibility of alternative configurations, doubly oppositional paradigms, if you will (and here I am returning to Joan Landes's suggestion that, even after Rousseau, the oppositional public sphere was more multifaceted than Habermas would have us imagine).

We will come back to this, but I will first consider a few more passages in which Charrière's narrator points to the way that texts smooth over contradictions. From the first letter in the novel, the letter-writer puts into question novelistic and epistolary conventions, including those she herself uses. In the following passage she stops and puts into question the assumptions of a banal compliment that she herself is presenting to her cousin.

> A l'occasion de ce mariage on parlera de vous, et l'on sentira ce qu'il y aurait à gagner pour la princesse qui attacherait à son service une femme de votre mérite, sage sans pruderie, également sincère et polie, modeste quoique remplie de talents. Mais voyons si cela est bien vrai. J'ai trouvé que cette sorte de mérite n'existe que sur le papier, où les mots ne se battent jamais, quelque contradiction qu'il y ait entre eux. (24)

Again and again, the narrator rethinks what she at first presents as conventional wisdom: "Mais voyons si cela est bien vrai." The narrator's words to her cousin on the lack of congruence between words and life echo Charrière's brief foreword:

> A MADAME LA MARQUISE DE S...
> Si, au lieu d'un mélange de passion et de raison, de faiblesse et de vertu tel qu'on le trouve ordinairement dans la société, ces lettres ne peignaient que des vertus pures telles qu'on les voit en vous, l'Editeur eût osé les parer de votre nom, et vous en faire hautement l'hommage. (21)

The sincerity of the authorial preface is put into question by the fictional narrator's deconstruction of bland compliments of the sort one generally finds in dedications. The text of the novel thereby undermines the smooth-surfaced authority of the aristocratic woman being addressed. But the preface also does something else. It underscores the fact that the novel following it brings out contradictions—"le mélange de vice et de vertu"—instead of subsuming them into the workings of a seemingly seamless plot.[57]

We saw above that the narrator brushes off the bourgeois myth of romantic love with its prescription that men and women marry for the sole reason that they are attracted to one another. We noted too that if the narrator is to be successful in finding a husband for her daughter, it will not be for her money but for something else. This something else, linked to the circulation of money but at the same time outside of that circulation, is a tempered sexuality. A reconfigured eroticism plays an important role in the creation of the affectionate nuclear family, that intimate core of the public sphere opposed to monarchical authority. What Charrière makes clear is the cost to women of the idealization of such reconfigurations. In Charrière's novel we find an acute analysis of new workings of power at the level of the female body.

All the strategies of conjugal eroticism to which Cécile's mother has recourse are dependent on the male gaze: "Vous voyez bien que, si on l'épouse, ce ne sera pas pour avoir pensé, mais pour l'avoir *vue*" (25–26, my emphasis). The narrator presents her daughter to the world of suitors as a visually erotic object: "Il faut donc la montrer" (26). The daughter's body, rather than wealth or title, becomes the dowry in this kind of marriage. In an extraordinary passage, Charrière portrays with painstaking, loving exactitude, the game of hide-and-seek involved in successfully transforming the daughter into a suitably erotic commodity:

Il faut . . . la laisser danser. Il ne faut pourtant pas la trop montrer, de peur que les yeux ne se lassent; ni la trop divertir . . . de peur que les tuteurs ne me grondent, de peur que les mères des autres ne disent: "C'est bien mal entendu! Elle est si peu riche!" Que de temps perdu à s'habiller, sans compter le temps où l'on est dans le monde; et puis cette parure, toute modeste qu'elle est, ne laisse pas de coûter: les gazes, les rubans etc.; car rien n'est si exact, si long, si détaillé que la critique des femmes. Il ne faut pas non plus la laisser trop danser; la danse l'échauffe et ne lui sied pas bien: ses cheveux, médiocrement bien arrangés par elle et par moi, lui donnent en se dérangeant un air de rudesse; elle est trop rouge. . . . Figurez-vous un joli front, un joli nez, des yeux noirs un peu enfoncés ou plutôt couverts, pas bien grands, mais brillants et doux; les lèvres un peu grosses et très vermeilles, les dents saines, une belle peau de brune, le teint très animé, un cou qui grossit malgré tous les soins que je me donne, une gorge qui serait belle si elle était blanche, le pied et la main passables; voilà Cécile. (26)

The narrator's presentation of her daughter's participation in the supposedly romantic bourgeois marriage plot ("L'on se marie parce que l'on est un homme et une femme et l'on se plaît") emphasizes the demands placed on Cécile's body as it is commodified. Cécile's "teint" may be "animé," but every other aspect of her behavior is constrained within strictly defined limits. Cécile is presented as a series of precious—and some less precious—body parts.[58] Any actions that might express her *own* vitality are designed to fit into the marriage plot with the potential husband's gaze in mind. Dancing is fine insofar as it brings an appealing rosy color to Cécile's cheek, but in no case should she dance to the point of messing up her hair. Just as her hair must be constrained in particular patterns, so must every aspect of the young girl's body. There is even an effort to refashion the flesh of her neck to make her more presentable.[59]

Edward Shorter writes that, in the eighteenth century, "romantic love became a code word for female autonomy."[60] As I suggest elsewhere in this study, much more of a case could be made for this claim with regard to the seventeenth century, especially in the salon milieu within the court. Shorter's analysis may be accurate for certain late-eighteenth-century women who escaped the most horrible instances of alliance-based marriage, and it may be descriptive of the fantasies of many others, but Charrière's novel makes clear that "autonomy" is hardly the word for the life for which Cécile is being prepared. We find instead the presentation of an arduous training in the art of chaste eroticism (or, if you will, erotic chastity), which the mother dutifully passes on to the daughter. In strictly alliance-based models of marriage, women's bodies have always been exchanged between men to consolidate family wealth. But Cécile more than her predecessors is, to use Lévi-Strauss's formulation, "the supreme gift," both sign (as are words, she is still exchanged between men) and as a value *en soi*.[61]

The narrator of Charrière's novel does, at one point, imagine an alternative to the rules to which she and her daughter must submit: "Si j'étais roi, je ne sais pas si je serais juste, quoique je voulusse l'être; mais voici assurément ce que je ferais" (32). Her vision, while playful, is remarkable in several regards, not least significantly in that it coincides with the tripartite government that would be established by the imminent French Revolution. The epistler's vision is most radical, though, not in its exposition of class politics but rather in the role it allots women in the marriage market: "Tout homme, en se mariant, entrerait dans la classe de sa femme, et ses enfants seraient comme lui" (33).

As we recall, Rousseau's insistence on fidelity rests in part on the need to keep male bloodlines "clean." If a husband's infidelity is barbaric, a wife's is unforgivable:

> Tout mari infidelle . . . est un homme injuste et barbare: mais la femme infidelle fait plus, elle dissout la famille et brise tous les liens de la nature; en donnant à l'homme des enfans qui ne sont pas à lui elle trahit les uns et les autres, elle joint la perfidie à l'infidélité. J'ai peine à voir quel desordre et quel crime ne tient pas à celui-là.[62]

Rousseau betrays a fear of one aspect of the very quality that he so celebrates in women. While their capacity to reproduce is celebrated because women provide a continuation of the husband's name and bloodline, it is also potentially extremely destabilizing, for a woman is physically capable of conceiving a child by more than one man. As Patrick Coleman points out, the entirety of Rousseau's vision for a republican society of legitimate "frères" is based on female *pudeur*.

> The institutionalization of *pudeur*, to the extent that it restricts women's sexual initiative, is Rousseau's way of ensuring that fathers are never in a position to deny their children the legitimacy they deserve and which is as essential to the creation of a homogeneous citizenry as the abolition of class privileges in the Court of Honor set up to regulate duels.[63]

The narrator's fantasy of social order depends not on female *pudeur* but, rather, her potential lack of it:

> D'abord les enfants sont encore plus certainement de la femme que du mari. En second lieu, la première éducation, les préjugés, on les tient plus de sa mère que de son père. (33)

Cécile's mother claims to be putting this plan forward only because it would give her daughter better chances in the marriage market: "Vous voyez bien que, dans ce superbe arrangement politique, ma Cécile n'est pas oubliée" (33). But her justifications for her view are more than a manipulation of factors making her own daughter more "marketable." She presents a version of the Rousseauian celebration of women's maternal role—"La première éducation, les préjugés, on les tient plus de sa mère que de son père"—but she implicitly allots control of maternity to the mother. Rousseau writes that woman is "le lien entre le père et ses enfants." Charrière defines the connection between mother and child as more primary than the one between father and child: "Les enfants sont plus certainement de la femme que du mari." The narrator's vision of a different social order radically undermines patriarchy and any justification for controlling women's sexuality. Indeed, the narrator's stress on the maternal bond is strikingly similar to Luce Irigaray's valorization, in *Ce Sexe qui n'en est pas un*, of "le sang rouge," that is, the corporeal bond between mother and child, over "le sang blanc" (le semblant) of the symbolic relationship between father and child.[64]

The narrator's intention was probably not an actual overthrow of patriarchy. Nevertheless, her vision underlines the arbitrary nature of the marriage conventions of her day and suggests that, even at this time of Rousseau inundation, others are at least imaginable. Her fantasy allows both herself and her daughter an outlet for playing out scenarios impossible to fulfill in the real world where the king is a man—a world in which for a woman to express desire is to court danger. The narrator is not king, and she cannot change the marriage system. She is forced as a mother—just as Charrière is forced as a novelist—to work within a certain framework, the terms of which increasingly excluded the imagination of innovative marriage plots. Joan DeJean has written on the strangely diminished role of women writers once the novel had taken a socially agreed-upon form: "It is as if the French female tradition had come into existence [in the seventeenth- and earlier eighteenth-century novel] in order to create the modern novel. Once the genre had acquired the full range of its expression and the way had been paved for it to achieve in the nineteenth century what is now considered its canonical formation, women writers became far less prominent in its history."[65] Charrière's dissenting strategies need be made from within increasingly well-defined bourgeois plots.

The Chastity Lessons

[L'amour] reste pour [les romancières] quasiment l'unique sujet "romanesque." On ne saurait dire pourtant qu'elles en sont novatrices. Même si elles ont quelque chose de personnel à

dire à son sujet, on les sent avant tout soucieuses de rejoindre les voies tracées.
—Pierre Fauchery, *La Destinée féminine dans le roman du dix-huitième siècle*, 1972

Il n'est dans un premier temps, peut-être qu'un seul "chemin," celui qui est historiquement assigné au féminin: *le mimétisme*. Il s'agit d'assumer, délibérément, ce rôle. . . . Jouer de la mimésis, c'est, pour une femme, tenter de retrouver le lieu de son exploitation par le discours, sans s'y laisser simplement réduire. C'est se soumettre . . . à des "idées," notamment d'elle, élaborées dans/par une logique masculine, mais pour faire "apparaître" par un effet de répétition ludique, ce qui devait rester occulté: le recouvrement d'une possible opération du féminin dans le langage.
—Luce Irigaray, *Ce Sexe qui n'en est pas un*, 1977

In the narrator's assessment of her daughter for her suitors, Cécile's status as desiring subject was canceled out by her status as erotic object. The implicit silencing of Cécile's desire becomes explicit in the narrator's teachings once the young woman's desires are aroused by a particular suitor. Nothing is in these lessons of chastity of which Rousseau or his many followers would disapprove. In fact, in the realm of chastity, Charrière's Cécile and Rousseau's Julie and Sophie are provided with remarkably similar instruction.

A young Englishman, referred to simply as Milord, is staying in Lausanne with his tutor for an unspecified amount of time as part of a grand tour of Europe. The narrator learns that her daughter "a de la préférence" for Milord in the course of an afternoon she, Cécile, and Milord spend together in the drawing room. Cécile and Milord are playing a game of chess, an allegorical convention for the game of love. As Cécile reaches down to pick up a piece that has fallen to the floor, Milord takes her hand and raises it to his lips. Once Milord has departed, Cécile throws herself into her mother's lap and through her sobs asks: "Qu'est-ce qui se passe en moi? Qu'est-ce que j'ai éprouvé? de quoi suis-je honteuse? de quoi est-ce que je pleure?" (61). In accordance with her earlier descriptions of displaying Cécile, the narrator turns the conversation away from Cécile's experience to focus on Milord: "S'est-il aperçu de votre trouble?" (61).

At the first sign of her daughter's sexual confusion, the narrator is inspired to teach her Cécile the all-important "law" of female virtue:[66]

> Eh bien! Le moment est venu de pratiquer une vertu, de vous abstenir d'un vice dont vous ne pouviez avoir aucune idée. Si cette vertu vient à vous paraître, pensez aussi que c'est la seule que vous ayez à vous prescrire rigoureusement, à pratiquer avec vigilance, avec une attention scrupuleuse sur vous-même.—La seule! (62)

Cécile learns from her mother that a woman must watch herself even when she is participating in the socially condoned marriage plot. Indeed, if a woman is to succeed in achieving a "love match" she must make it at least seem that the love is felt more by the man than by herself. To do otherwise would be to expose herself to extremely harsh treatment: "Rien n'est si exact, si long, si détaillé que la critique des femmes."

Another event presents Cécile with an even more vivid lesson on the extreme vulnerability of a woman's good name and how guarded she must be toward men who have the power to "faire [son] sort." A distant relative, unhappily married, spends as much of his time as possible with Cécile and her mother. He thereby suffers less from being married "parce qu'il oublie qu'il le soit" (55). During one visit, this man cuts his thumb badly with a knife he had been using to sharpen a pencil. The narrator leaves in search of bandages, and Cécile hurries over to her guest to nurse his profusely bleeding wound. The man is not as close to being sick as he first claims—"C'est singulier, dit-il en riant, et ridicule; j'ai mal au coeur"—since, in the few moments they are alone, he uses his free hand to encircle Cécile's waist, draw her against him, and kiss her passionately. Cécile accepts the man's apology with an apology of her own: "Au fond, c'est ma faute. J'aurais dû être plus circonspecte, vous donner votre mouchoir, détacher mon tablier après en avoir enveloppé votre main" (76).

In response to Cécile's apology, her mother does not instantly jump to her defense and deny the truth of this statement. Given her previous words, her silence here makes an indelible impression on her daughter, who tells her later: "Je ne savais pas la conséquence de tout cela; me voici éclaircie pour le reste de ma vie" (80). The extreme fragility of a woman's good name, a lesson verbally and textually imposed on Cécile by her mother, is here again made real through concrete experience. While the blood that stains Cécile's dress flowed from the man's veins and not her own, she reads it as an emblem of the loss, or at least the partial loss, of *her* virginity.

These lessons that the epistler presents to her daughter are hardly radical. Rather, they are part of what had become conventional French wisdom about women in the decade following Rousseau's death. Indeed, we have seen much in Charrière's *Lettres* that would support May's contention that the novel was moralistically didactic during this period, as well as Habermas's contention that the genre played an essential role in the division between the public and private spheres of the oppositional public sphere. Cécile is being taught the same lessons as were most eighteenth-century girls. Again and again, however, this daughter poses questions that challenge and destabilize her mother's teachings. After the chessboard incident, for example, Cécile protests against the injustice of her mother's admonishments and points out that Milord was just as stirred up as she:

> Mais . . . s'il y a ici de quoi penser et dire du mal, il ne pourrait m'accuser sans s'accuser encore plus lui-même. N'a-t-il pas baisé ma main, et n'a-t-il pas été aussi troublé que moi? (61)

Cécile's questions undermine the notion that women are naturally more modest and less (sexually) sensitive than men ("N'a-t-il pas été aussi troublé que moi?"), a view that Rousseau instilled in his readers with his praise for the "natural" moral qualities of women. Moreover, Cécile's discomfort and dissatisfaction underline the fact that enforced female chastity is neither natural or pleasant. Even the reward for following the rules—that is, marriage to a man one loves—is far from compelling as it is presented in *Lettres écrites de Lausanne*. A few days after the above exchange, the narrator presents a rather cynical description of what a man really cares about in his wife:

> Un mari est une chose si différente d'un amant, que l'un ne juge de rien comme en avait jugé l'autre: On se rappelle les refus avec plaisir; on se rappelle les faveurs avec inquiétudes . . . car le désir d'une propriété exclusive est le sentiment le plus vif qui lui reste. Il se consolera d'être peu aimé, pourvu que personne d'autre ne puisse l'être. (65)

Charrière's novel never sentimentalizes women's subjection. Rousseau cloaks the more repressive aspects of his vision with an appeal to an emotionally charged natural order that must somehow be restored through curbing women's sexual appetite: "Montrez-leur dans les mêmes devoirs la source de leurs plaisirs et le fondement de leurs droits. Est-il si pénible d'aimer pour être aimée, de se rendre aimable pour être heureuse, de se rendre estimable pour être obéïe, de s'honorer pour se faire honorer? Que ces droits sont beaux!"[67] Both men and women experience sexual desire, but women control their desires through their *pudeur.* Charrière, through her narrator, offers the same lessons but, through Cécile, she expresses a great deal more ambivalence about this *pudeur* that, as we have seen, was so important in the Rousseauian vision.

In the first letter, we considered the passage in which the narrator emphasizes the relationship between words and "des éducations, des législations, et des bonheurs domestiques impossibles." We find a distorted echo of that notion in Cécile's comments to her mother after she has absorbed and put into practice the lessons her mother has taught her:

> Je n'ai pas tout compris, mais les mots sont gravés dans ma tête. J'expliquerai ce que vous m'avez dit par les choses que je verrai, que je lirai, par celles que j'ai déjà vues et lues, et ces choses-là je les expliquerai par celles que vous m'avez dites. (70)

In Cécile's words we find an astute, indeed an almost Gramscian, assessment of the way that ideology functions: reality ("les choses que je verrai", "celles que j'ai déjà vues"), literature ("[les choses] que j'ai déjà lues," "que je lirai"), and the discourses of mothers ("[les choses] que vous m'avez dites") all reflect and reinforce one another.

Stripped of the support of an overarching notion of nature, and with the inclusion of the narrator's unfavorable comments about husbands, the mother's arguments, not surprisingly, are not entirely persuasive. Before coming around to complete acceptance of her marriage lessons, Cécile wavers and asks her mother a crucial question:

> Un mot, maman. Si les maris sont comme vous les avez peints, si le mariage sert à si peu de chose, serait-ce une si grande perte? (68)

Apparently, even words that are "gravés dans [la] tête" (as well as in novels!) are subject to some change. Other currents flow with the "family-plot" elements of Charrière's novel. Cécile's question and her mother's immediate response to it function as a turning point in this work, a shift away from the moralism and didacticism of so many prerevolutionary novels:

Oui Cécile, vous voyez bien comme il est doux d'être mère. D'ailleurs, il y a des exceptions, et chaque fille, croyant que son amant et elle auraient été une exception, regrettera de n'avoir pu l'épouser comme si c'était un grand malheur, quand même ce n'en serait pas un. (68)[68]

The narrator presents two arguments in favor of marriage. The second is singularly unconvincing. The narrator suggests that if a woman does not marry she will regret the happiness that might, but probably would not, have been. The first reason presented, however, that marriage is worthwhile because of the pleasures of motherhood, bears further consideration.

Marrying Motherhood

Over the past few decades, many historians of the family have hailed the late eighteenth-century shift toward "good motherhood" as a step forward for civilization. Shorter, for example, writes of "an onward march of maternal breastfeeding."[69] He does so because breastfeeding is linked to a lower mortality rate but also because he privileges warm, affectionate relations between family members as signs of progress toward the "natural" codes of behavior that we as a society continue to valorize today and that therefore are rendered largely invisible as ideological constructs dating from a particular historical moment. But, as we have seen in our consideration of Rousseau, the eighteenth-century stress on maternal care of infants in both fiction and in practice was hardly a simple matter of advances in public and private health. Rather, it was inextricably linked to the emergence of modern social organization, that moment when, to use Gramscian terminology, ideology replaced force as the primary producer and reproducer of culture.[70]

By the time of the French Revolution, women in their new role as faithful wives and tender mothers had become the guarantors of the privatized family home-space from which might emerge modern male subjects with a new sense of their individualism. At the same time, this new womanhood served to soften the most threatening aspects of what Joan Kelly calls "selfish individualism":

> Maternal nurture awakened or instilled human empathy (pity) and love of virtue, the qualities that tempered selfish individualism; modesty at once equipped women to perform their roles and served as a corrective to their inability otherwise to restrain (sexual) desire. . . . The contain-

ment of voracious female sexuality was, in . . . Enlightenment theory, a prerequisite for the achievement of public virtue. And it required the restriction of women to the domestic realm, their exclusion from politics.[71]

Eighteenth-century conceptions of "natural" womanhood were thus inseparably linked to "universal" citizenship. Mary Jacobus, who has worked on the import of nursing imagery in revolutionary iconography, puts it succinctly: "The discourses of history and psychoanalysis meet . . . at the breast."[72] Jacobus's formulation is useful here, for it links the development of new conceptions of motherhood and femininity more generally ("the breast") with the development both of the unconscious structures that define modern subjectivity ("psychoanalysis") and of new political structures ("history"). While Jacobus focuses primarily on revolutionary imagery, her comment is equally apt with regard to novels in the prerevolutionary period, and her words are worth keeping in mind as we think about female roles in Charrière's *Lettres*.

We recall that when Cécile complains to her mother about the rules that so limit the proper behavior for women, the narrator responds with a defense of strictly divided gender roles. First she shows that the suffering they cause is not reserved for women:

> Croyez-vous, par exemple, que si la guerre se déclare, il soit bien agréable . . . d'aller s'exposer à être tué ou estropié, à prendre, couché sur la terre humide et vivant parmi des prisonniers malades, les germes d'une maladie dont on ne guérira jamais? (64)

Cécile is not convinced by this graphic presentation of the horrors of war. She points out that a soldier is a soldier by choice and, moreover, that he gains money and prestige from his profession. Her mother responds "C'est la profession de toute femme d'être sage" and adds a list of compensatory advantages that women in this "profession" enjoy:

> Une femme . . . est payée par cela seul qu'elle est femme. Ne nous dispense-t-on pas presque partout des travaux pénibles? N'est-ce pas nous que les hommes garantissent du chaud, du froid, de la fatigue? (64)

In the context of Charrière's *Lettres*, however, this conventional argument is rather ironic. In Charrière's novel, it is, after all, never men who shelter women from hot weather, cold weather, and exhaustion. Rather, it is the mother and the daughter who fulfill these roles for each other. The narrator tells her cousin that she and her daughter have been inseparable since Cécile's birth:

> Je l'ai toujours eue auprès de moi; elle a toujours couché dans ma chambre, et, quand il faisait froid, dans mon lit. Je l'aime uniquement. (41)

The narrator feeds her daughter, tends to her wounds, and generally provides for her a protective haven. And Cécile takes care of her mother as much as her mother does of her:

> Cécile m'a priée de rester au logis, et de faire les honneurs de sa journée, tant parce qu'elle est plus à son aise quand je suis auprès d'elle que parce qu'elle a trouvé l'air trop froid pour me laisser sortir. (45)

Whether the narrator of Charrière's *Lettres* breastfed her daughter—the question is left open—is less important than the nature of the mother–daughter bond.[73]

The extreme tenderness the narrator shows toward Cécile suggests the intimate, protective, and pleasurable relationship portrayed in novel after novel, in sentimentalized medical treatises, and in paintings of the late eighteenth century.[74] In letters to her cousin, the narrator emphasizes and reemphasizes the tenderness of her relationship with Cécile. Mother and daughter are constantly exchanging meaningful glances and notes or falling into each other's arms exuding loving affirmations: "—Que vous êtes aimable! . . . Que je suis contente et glorieuse de vous!" (80). We have seen that Charrière's narrator presented the requirement of female chastity as a necessary evil, a law to which one had to submit under some duress: "Ce qu'on appelle vertu chez les femmes sera presque la seule que vous puissiez ne pas avoir, la seule que vous pratiquiez en tant que vertu" (62). The narrator presents her own enjoyment, on the other hand, as natural, in fact the primary justification for marriage: "il est si doux d'être mère." It is here that the tenderness and love disallowed in the marriage plot are given free reign.

The tender mother–daughter bond was, of course, a key ingredient in the family system imagined by Rousseau, especially in his *Emile*. He encouraged mother–daughter intimacy in the extreme, especially regarding sexual matters. Rousseau's Sophie is told by her father: "Tant que vous serez de sang froid restez votre propre juge; mais sitôt que vous aimerez rendez à votre mère le soin de vous."[75]

Sophie's mother exclaims: "Ma fille, toi que j'ai portée dans mes entrailles et que je porte incessamment dans mon coeur, verse les secrets du tien dans le sein de ta mère." An intensely intimate, almost fusional type of relationship between mother and daughter is suggested by the mother's request that her daughter "verse [ses] secrets dans le sein de sa mère." *Verser* is something one does with a fluid, which we might read here as tears, of course, but in conjunction with the mother's comments about her "entrailles" (where Sophie used to be) and her heart (where she remains), it also suggests a relationship in which the boundaries between self and other are themselves fluid and hard to define.

In Rousseau, this physically charged confessional state of affairs serves an important social purpose by ensuring that the mother is in a position to effectively control the disruptive qualities of female desire so that her daughter will make an appropriate marriage. From the day a daughter sets her eyes on men until the day of her marriage, she is encouraged to tell all. The confessions of the daughter, in conjunction with the teachings of the mother, systematically and powerfully reinforce a girl's sense of dependence upon, and obedience to, a series of rules that the mother teaches but does not define.

In the Rousseauian scheme, despite, or perhaps precisely through her closeness with her children, a woman's primary role is to mediate between her children and her husband: "[La mère] sert de liaison entre [les enfants] et leur père."[76] Rousseau tells his female readers: "Forme de bonne heure une enceinte autour de l'ame de ton enfant: un autre en peut marquer le circuit; mais toi seule y dois poser la barrière."[77] Women are the guardians of codes—"toi seule y dois poser la barrière"—that are defined by someone else, presumably male—"un autre en peut marquer le circuit." Mothers play a pivotal role between the demands of the external world—from which they are excluded—and the fulfillment of these demands within the domestic sphere.

Like Sophie and her mother, Cécile and her mother are close; like Sophie, Cécile tells her mother everything. The mother encourages this confessional state of affairs—"Ne vous cachez jamais d'une mère qui vous adore" (68)—and she does so to impose the all-important law of female chastity on her daughter: "Profitez, s'il est possible, de mes conseils . . ." (68). Charrière's novelistic presentation of motherhood passed the moral litmus test administered by at least one critic:

> Nous conseillons la lecture [des *Lettres écrites de Lausanne*] à toutes les mères et toutes les jeunes personnes, qui pourront y puiser des forces contre l'impérieuse séduction des sens.[78]

The reviewer's enthusiastic approval of Charrière's *Lettres* recognizes the ways her story conformed to certain expectations regarding family relationships, especially the role mothers play in helping their daughters learn to fight "l'impérieuse séduction des sens."

While Charrière does seem to "follow the rules," she also shows her readers the ways in which good motherhood, even exemplary motherhood, has the potential to destabilize social roles. Rousseau writes:

> L'obéissance et la fidélité qu'[une femme] doit à son mari, la tendresse et les soins qu'elle doit à ses enfants sont des conséquences si naturelles et si sensibles de sa condition, qu'elle ne peut sans mauvaise foi refuser son consentement au sentiment intérieur qui la guide.[79]

A woman of "good faith" will follow her inner guide and thereby carry out her duties to her children *and* to her husband. What would happen if maternal duties came into conflict with conjugal duties? Devoted mothers in the late eighteenth century who scrupulously heeded Rousseau's (and others') strictures on the merits of breastfeeding, for example, would on occasion become less available to their husbands as sexual partners.[80] This concrete example points to a ubiquitous tension between two competing aspects of female domestic duties. Charrière's *Lettres* upsets the delicate balance between maternal love and "wifely" love, which, constantly under negotiation, plays a key role in the complicated system of desire and repression of the modern family romance.

Public and Private Transgressions

We have seen that Charrière's narrator scrupulously follows certain Rousseauian conventions when it comes to the necessity of premarital chastity, and at the same time shares with her daughter the passionate pleasures of motherhood. While she is careful in these areas, in others she strays further from conventional wisdom. She taught her daughter to read and write from the moment she could "prononcer et remuer les doigts" (42). Cécile studied Latin and music between her eighth and sixteenth birthdays. In addition to sewing, knitting and lace-making, she learned "autant d'arithmétique qu'une femme a besoin d'en savoir" (42). Aside from the fact that "[la narratrice] a laissé tout au hasard" (42), Cécile's education is not one fitting into Rousseau's dictum: "Elles doivent apprendre beaucoup de choses, mais seulement celles qu'il leur convient de savoir."[81] The narrator mixes the orthodox with the less orthodox.

We learn that the narrator's cousin's response to these descriptions of Cécile's education was less than enthusiastic. The narrator defends herself:

> N'y avait-il pas d'inconvénient, me dites-vous, à laisser lire, à laisser écouter? N'aurait-il pas mieux valu, etc.? J'abrège; je ne transcris pas toutes vos phrases, parce qu'elles m'ont fait de la peine. Peut-être aurait-il mieux valu faire plus ou moins, ou autre chose; peut-être y avait-il de l'inconvénient, etc. Mais songez que ma fille et moi ne sommes pas un roman comme Adèle et sa mère, ni une leçon à citer.(43)[82]

The unseen sentences of her correspondent recall the narrator's early reference to words being put next to one another to form systems that torment women: "avec cela on tourmente les femmes, les mères, les jeunes filles." Similarly, her cousin's sentences torment her: "Je ne transcris pas toutes vos phrases, parce qu'elles m'ont fait de la peine." The narrator refuses to let her own and Cécile's behavior be constrained by the plots of contemporary novels or by the new plethora of treatises on education. She is replacing one system of words with another that excludes the first, or in any case invests it with much less authority. The conventional wisdom of didactic novels (of which the cousin in Languedoc is the mouthpiece) is summarized by half-sentences and etceteras: "N'aurait-il pas mieux valu, etc. . . ." The absolute influence of novels and lessons is "wiped out" of the narrator's mind and from the letters that constitute Charrière's novel: "L'impression de votre lettre est presque effacée. . . . Ne me faites point d'excuses de votre lettre, oublions-la" (44).[83]

As evidence that she has done well with her daughter, the narrator describes the preceding afternoon spent with Cécile:

> Après la réception de votre lettre, je me suis assise vis-à-vis de Cécile; je l'ai vue travailler avec adresse, activité et gaieté. L'esprit rempli de ce que vous m'aviez écrit, les larmes me sont venues aux yeux; elle s'est mise à jouer du clavecin pour m'égayer. Je l'ai envoyée à l'autre bout de la ville; elle est allée et revenue sans souffrir, quoiqu'il fasse très froid.

> Des visites ennuyeuses sont venues; elle a été douce, obligeante et gaie. Le petit lord l'a priée d'accepter un billet de concert; elle a refusé de bonne grâce. (44)

The narrator offers Cécile's behavior as evidence of the success of her upbringing. The examples she offers all point to her daughter's obedience, kindness, and love, that is, to those characteristics that many prerevolutionary discourses cultivated in wives. But here the relationship being focused on is between mother and daughter rather than between husband and wife.

We have already seen that the importance of maternal responsibilities in the bourgeois family—emotional and pragmatic—set up a situation of potential rivalry between husband and child for the attentions of the woman of the house. The issue comes up in Charrière's novel, pointing to a different rivalry for Cécile's attentions between the mother and her daughter's potential husband. At one point the parallel between the loving relationship between mother and child and that between lovers is made implicitly: "Un enfant ne voit pas combien il occupe continuellement sa mère. Un amant ne voit et n'entend partout que lui" (47).[84] In the passage cited above, the narrator discourages Cécile from accepting Milord's invitation to a concert. Since she seems to want Cécile's happiness and since Cécile seems to be falling in love with the young Englishman, a trip to a concert would seem to be the perfect outing—particularly given the narrator's defense of her daughter's right to spend time alone with men. In tandem with her recurring "Vous avez tort" response, the narrator justifies the relative freedom she allows Cécile in her visiting habits by insisting that customs are different in Switzerland than in France ("En France, je ferais comme on fait en France: ici, vous feriez comme moi"):

> Vous êtes étonnée que Cécile sorte seule, et puisse recevoir sans moi de jeunes hommes et de jeunes femmes; je vois même que vous me blâmez à cet égard, mais vous avez tort. Pourquoi ne la pas laisser jouir d'une liberté que nos usages autorisent, et dont elle est si peu tentée d'abuser? (58)[85]

Perhaps her recommendation that Cécile refuse Milord's invitation harks back to her assertion that "il faut montrer [Cécile]" but "il ne faut pourtant pas la trop montrer" (26). Perhaps it is one more example of the strategies necessary to snare a husband. But we might also read it as being exactly the opposite. Let us consider for a moment the prospect of Cécile's marriage from the point of view of the mother in this family. What does the narrator herself stand to gain from Cécile's marriage? Earlier she gave Cécile two reasons for getting married. The second was, that if one did not, one would always wonder about missed opportunities. The narrator has already been married once, however, and she does not seem to miss having a husband. Indeed, the only reference she makes to him in the entire collection of letters concerns the position he held in his family and the relation this position had to the financial situation of the narrator (28–29). The first reason the narrator gave for getting married involved the pleasures of motherhood. These she knows well and can continue to enjoy—if she can hold on to Cécile.

The narrator's discouragements of Cécile's interacting with men in certain ways can be read as a means of assuring that Cécile *not* get married, her extreme selectiveness with respect to suitable suitors for her daughter a means of assuring that she *not* share the fate of her poor cousin in Languedoc. "On la sépare de vous. Aviez-vous tant de plaisir à l'avoir auprès de vous?," she asked her cousin in the opening lines of the opening letter. The question to her cousin seemed rhetorical, with the implied answer being in the negative. By the middle of the novel, however, it is clear that the narrator's own answer to the question would be in the most tender affirmative. All the mother's claims that she is working hard to arrange a good marriage for Cécile do not rule out the possibility that she would rather keep Cécile to herself. One is reminded of Lévi-Strauss's words in the final paragraph of his *Structures élémentaires de la parenté*: "Jusqu'à nos jours, l'humanité a rêvé de saisir et de fixer cet instant fugitif où il fut permis de croire qu'on pouvait ruser avec la loi d'échange, gagner sans perdre, jouir sans partager."[86] Lévi-Strauss imagines "un ciel où les femmes ne seront plus échangées, c'est-à-dire rejetant, dans un futur ou dans un passé également hors d'atteinte, la douceur, éternellement déniée à l'homme social, d'un monde où on pourrait vivre entre soi."[87] This vision, which Lévi-Strauss presents from the male perspective of one forced to exchange "his" women when he would rather keep them to himself, seems to be strongly at work as a wish in Charrière's novel, though in this case the hesitant exchanger is a woman rather than a man.

This epistler is allowed the unusual maternal privilege of loving her daughter with relatively little interference. Throughout the novel, mother and daughter lean on and protect each other emotionally and physically. In her presentation of her financial situation, the narrator writes, "La rente de nos vingt-six ou trente-mille francs suffit pour nous donner toutes les jouissances que nous désirons; mais vous voyez qu'on n'épousera pas Cécile pour sa fortune" (29). After all, if the interest on twenty or thirty thousand francs suffices to give Cécile and her mother "toutes les jouissances" they could desire, why should it matter whether the income is enough to attract a husband?

Béatrice Didier suggests that we may view this mother–daughter dyad as the fundamental couple relationship in Charrière's novel:

> Les *Lettres écrites de Lausanne* évoquent avec une tendresse toute particulière ce couple idéal que forment la mère veuve et la jeune fille.[88]

It is a fact that this relationship is more tender than any other evoked in the novel. It is moreover the relative absence of men in these women's lives that render their relationship possible:

> L'homme n'est pas absent, mais à l'état de prétendant, plus ou moins lointain; il ne vient pas troubler véritablement ce bonheur des femmes que la mère se plaît à évoquer dans [ses] lettres.[89]

While there are father substitutes in the persons of her deceased husband's brothers who are Cécile's tutors and who endeavor to impose their own views on mother and daughter, their attempts are generally foiled. Early on, the narrator decides not to rent out the second floor of her house to Cécile's English suitor and his tutor. She provides the following nonexplanation to her sister and brother-in-law: "J'ai dit pour toute raison que je n'avais pas jugé à propos de louer" (36). The brother-in-law becomes angry with the audacity of this reply, and Cécile comes to the rescue of her mother: "Cécile a dit que j'avais sans doute des raisons que je ne voulais pas dire; qu'il fallait les croire bonnes, et ne me pas presser davantage" (36). This mutual decision to keep Milord and William outside of their home-space allows for a continued private world of mother and daughter, which male guests may enter, but only upon invitation. In this household, women are not accountable to any male authority. Keeping the reasons for their decision not to rent out the apartment a secret provides a boundary between them and the larger community, represented in this case by the sister and brother-in-law.

While these visitors are in the living room, mother and daughter find themselves overwhelmed by the strength of their (private) commitment to each other:

> Je l'ai embrassée pour la remercier: les larmes lui sont venues aux yeux. Mon beau-frère et ma belle-soeur se sont retirés sans savoir qu'imaginer de la mère ni de la fille. (36)

Something about this relationship between mother and daughter seems a little odd when viewed by the outside world. The relationship between the two women is far more loving, and mutually respectful, than the conjugal models presented in the novel. These include that of her cousin in Languedoc, who is treated as a virtual nonentity, and a male relative who regrets being married just ten days after the ceremony: "On a si bien arrangé les choses, qu'arrivé ici le premier octobre, il s'est trouvé marié le 20. Je crois que le 30, il aurait voulu ne plus l'être" (55). The story of the narrator's relationship with her own husband never gets told, but if we are to judge from the narrator's comment "J'aimais Cécile uniquement," it would be hard to imagine that this marriage was particularly satisfying from her point of view.

A parallel must be drawn between the ways the narrator and her daughter protect their own nonmarital home-space and the way the narrator protects her textual space. Just as men are allowed to enter the narrator's home but on an invitational basis only, so the cousin's husband is allowed entrance into the text but only on terms set by the narrator. She addresses him directly for part of one letter, then returns to his wife: "Adieu mon cousin. Je retourne à votre femme" (41). In subsequent letters she continues her dialogue with him but always from within the feminine space of a correspondence between mothers ["Votre homme m'a enfin entendue . . ." (51), "Répondez-lui que . . ." (72), etc.]. She thereby valorizes the enclosure of the correspondence while at the same time moving out into a larger world of men and political discourse.

Resisting (En)closure: Charrière's Open Ending

> J'aurais peut-être encore moins de talent pour les dénouements que pour le reste. Les tristes sont tristes et les heureux sont fort sujets à être plats.
> —Isabelle de Charrière, *Correspondance*

Eventually the marriage plot in *Lettres* collapses entirely. It becomes evident that Milord has no intention of proposing marriage to Cécile. Cécile, in the meantime, refuses a proposal from another of her suitors. The narrator impresses on her daughter that her refusal of this marriage proposal may rule out marriage altogether for her. Cécile accepts this, albeit rather unwillingly.

> Vous m'avez demandé, maman, si je me consolerais de ne pas me marier. Il me semble que ce serait selon le genre de vie que je pourrais mener. (90)

Despite her disappointment, Cécile goes on to suggest a new chapter in her life with her mother:

> Si vous trouviez bon que nous allassions en Hollande ou en Angleterre tenir une boutique ou établir une pension, je crois qu'étant toujours avec vous et occupée, n'ayant pas le temps ... de lire des romans, ma vie pourrait être très douce. (90)

Cécile's mother hesitates before taking Cécile's suggestion seriously. "Nos paroles ont fini là, mais pas nos pensées" (90).

Some critics read the ending as tragic. Sigyn Minier, for example, conflates the ending of Cécile's story with that of Caliste in the "continuation" of Charrière's novel, which we will consider in the next section:

> Cécile et Caliste sont seules: elles le demeurent face à celui qu'elles aiment, ne formant jamais avec lui un couple capable de lutter contre les exigences du monde extérieur; elles finissent dans la solitude. La mère de Cécile nous offre le spectacle de son impuissance à soulager le malheur de sa fille.[90]

Cécile *is* sad, of that there is no doubt. But the ending need not be read in terms as tragic as Minier's.[91] Cécile is, after all, alive and well, a fate not allotted most eighteenth-century heroines. Her destiny clearly resists the tragic or idealized versions of experience presented in the novels that Cécile needs to avoid ("n'ayant pas le temps ... de lire des romans") if she is to find sweetness ("[sa] vie pourrait être très douce") in other realms.

Such a reading of the novel assumes that one of the purposes of the conjugal couple is to fight against the outside world. The tragedy, for Minier, is that Cécile does not find a man with whom to put up the good fight, "ne formant jamais avec lui un couple capable de lutter contre les exigences du monde extérieur." This couple is, on the contrary, precisely the one being *demanded* by the outside social and literary world in which Charrière writes. While this world continues to be oppositional (to go back to Habermassian terms), it is on the eve of becoming hegemonic. Critics have underestimated the cultural importance of stressing that mother–daughter dyad in ways that make for the startling destiny suggested by the conclusion to *Lettres*: a mother and a daughter working together in a small business in Holland or in England. Cécile does *not* end up alone (as Minier suggests); she still has her mother. Just as importantly, her mother, whose perspective we are invited to share throughout the novel, still has Cécile.[92]

In Charrière's novel the mother–daughter plot overtakes the marriage plot in such a way that a family not controlled by men is imagined. It is not that no men are involved in this household. On the contrary, rarely a day goes by in which male visitors do not share the living space of Cécile and her mother. And the men are not only there to see Cécile. In fact, the excuse of having to find a husband for Cécile provides the narrator opportunities for her own mildly flirtatious involvements with men. Cécile's mother, we learn in the opening letter, is still young. Her relationship with William, the tutor of Milord, while never fully explored, is ambiguous. We already have seen above that the narrator has Cécile and "peut-être le jeune lord" for herself. At another point during parlor games, Cécile, referring to one of her own suitors and the ubiquitous William, says to her mother: "L'un de ces deux hommes est amoureux de vous." Her mother replies: "Et l'autre de vous" (56). The marriage circuit actually provides mother as well as daughter a means of participating in a larger social world from which they would be excluded were a marriage of the sort desired by critics to take place.

Ultimately the mother–daughter plot in Charrière's *Lettres* allows for the imagination of female subjectivities, which, while incorporating certain aspects of the bourgeois plot and its definition of womanhood, resist such a plot's relegation of women to the private sphere. This is manifested in the resistance to the (en)closure of marriage, and a corresponding imagination of a life for women in the public sphere of the market. The two women are financially secure already, but they dream of making their fortunes through their own participation in the emerging economic system. Cécile tells her mother:

Je me flatterais de *devenir* assez riche pour acheter une maison entourée d'un champ, d'un verger, et d'un jardin. (90, my emphasis)

Cécile's proposal of a boutique run by women involves quite a leap of the imagination. Of women and work in the eighteenth century, Elizabeth Fox-Genovese writes:

> As the contours of capitalist France took clear shape during the revolutionary decade, discernible guidelines emerged for the appropriate relations of women to work in a new society. . . . At the upper levels of society, women would be discouraged from participation in the extra-domestic world of work. Many bourgeoises would work with their husbands in family enterprises ranging from crafts, to shops, to restaurants, to full-scale businesses; but all of these activities remained closely tied to family life and can be interpreted as an extension of women's role within the domestic economy. As the professions took shape, they would exclude women.[93]

Cécile and her mother are without a doubt among those Fox-Genovese refers to as being "at the upper levels of society." But while the narrator and her daughter are aristocrats, they are not wealthy aristocrats. Their status as emigrées emerging from old nobility actually places them outside the circle of what the Charrière refers to ironically in her note to the second edition as "les gens les plus distingués" (59). New definitions of nobility were based as much on recently acquired (and passed-on) wealth as on titles inherited from what, on the eve of the French Revolution, was a decidedly fragile ancien régime. Readers among the well-heeled bourgeoisie of Lausanne claimed to be scandalized by Charrière's presentation of characters belonging to and fraternizing with what they considered to be "une classe inférieure à la bonne compagnie."[94] In any case, whether Cécile's dream of a boutique in England or in Holland is plausible, its presence as an imagined alternative to marriage is highly disruptive of the rules of representation defined by new bourgeois social structures. In a satirical and genuinely funny pamphlet, a critic in Lausanne parodies Charrière's voice:

> Mais parlons encore de mon dernier ouvrage, je suis bien aise d'en faire sentir le mérite. N'est-ce pas un, par exemple, lecteur, de faire un roman sans but, sans intrigue surtout?[95]

The critic underlines the fact that Charrière's open-endedness was noted by her contemporaries. This critic goes on to mock Charrière's style as much as her content, linking in particular her word choice with her unwillingness to portray the most respectable strata of Lausanne society:

> Dans ma première lettre . . . j'avais quelqu'un en vue; je voulais l'*épiloguer*, et j'avais besoin de *me dégonfler*. Peut-être ce mot n'est-il pas français; et c'est en partie la difficulté d'écrire en français qui m'a engagée à prendre mes héroïnes dans une classe subalterne. . . ."[96]

This critic's tendency to condemn, in the same breath, Charrière's open plot, a certain *laisser-aller* in her style, and the presentation of marginal social classes implicitly points to what was expected from novels of the day, that is, bourgeois characters, a highly conventionalized style, and a neat close.

Reading beyond the Ending: Part Two

In 1787, no doubt encouraged by the success of *Lettres écrites de Lausanne,* Charrière republished it along with a "continuation," entitled *Caliste, ou Suite des Lettres écrites de Lausanne.*

The two parts of Charrière's project, radically different in content and tone, are thematically and structurally linked by the relationship between the original narrator (Cécile's mother) and William, the ubiquitous guest in the narrator's parlor throughout the first story. In the opening letter of the continuation, the narrator recounts to her cousin all that has happened since the closing letter of the original novel. In the second letter, which consists of the narrator's request that William confess the reasons for his great sadness, an important shift in narratee occurs. For the first time in the novel as a whole, a male interlocutor is invited—for what will turn out to be an extended visit!—into what has until then been a female-centered spatial as well as textual world. In two long epistles that make up the bulk of the novel, William shares with the narrator his own "histoire romanesque" (110), that is, the tragic tale of his relationship with his beloved Caliste, a virtuous if technically fallen woman.[97] In the final letters, we learn that William, encumbered with cultural prejudices and overwhelmed by his own lethargy, is incapable of reaching out to the woman he loves, and Caliste, heartbroken, dies. A fascinatingly complex work in its own right, Charrière's second story is much more in keeping with romanesque codes shaping and being shaped by republican notions of masculine selfhood.[98] Indeed, the representation of the relations between brothers, father figures, and women in *Caliste* is rife with the Oedipal symbolism informing that which in her book of the same name Lynn Hunt calls the "family romance of the French Revolution." In *Caliste*, one sees "the muting of sexual politics . . . in the choice of a suffering, Romantic male narrator who emphasizes those aspects of Caliste's story that denote a shared and bisexual plight."[99]

What are we to make of the presentation of William's romanesque story (narrated by a British man, sealed by the death of a saintly heroine) as a companion to the original letters (narrated by a pragmatic and decidely Swiss woman, refusing closure)? Elizabeth MacArthur suggests that Charrière's purpose in writing *Caliste* as the *suite* to the original letters was part of a well-calculated strategy. On the one hand, the Caliste story provided the often-criticized author an opportunity to show that she could write "universal" literature, thereby guaranteeing herself an audience.[100] While suggestive, this argument is undermined by the fact that Charrière's original *Lettres écrites de Lausanne* sold very well even before the addition of the Caliste story. In other words, Charrière already *had* an audience even without *Caliste*; if anything, I would argue that the *Lettres* served as a guarantee that the *Caliste* story would have an audience.

MacArthur's second argument is far more persuasive. By making *Caliste* a continuation of the *Lettres* rather than an independent piece, Charrière undercut its suppression of the highly particularized female voices (and open ending) of the narrator and her daughter by ensuring that they would continue be heard alongside William's. This reading is supported by the fact that the Caliste story, which we have access to in William's retrospective letters, is in fact unfolding as the narrator recounts her story in the day-by-day (or so) accounts of the original *Lettres*. The copresentation of the two stories underlines their simultaneity (in fictional time) and thereby stresses the *co*existence of the two very different kinds of narrative.

If, as suggested by her title *Caliste, ou Les Lettres écrites de Lausanne* it was Charrière's goal to have the narrator's story and William's story read as two parts of one work, she was successful up to a point. Until the middle of the nineteenth century, the two parts of her novel were published together either in one volume or as companion volumes. Sainte-Beuve even felt that the final version of the story should be called *Cécile* "car Caliste n'y fait qu'épisode, Cécile en est véritablement l'héroïne."[101] But he was the last critic in the nineteenth century to pay serious attention to the conarrative. In 1853 Madame Juste Olivier published *Caliste* without the narrator's letters, justifying her decision with the disclaimer that the early letters are "d'un intérêt médiocre."[102] She hails *Caliste* on the other hand as a subtle and tasteful masterpiece exploring a perfectly human "je ne sais quoi":

> A part la tache originelle de son histoire, Caliste est une des héroïnes qui réunissent au plus haut degré la simplicité, la passion, le naturel exquis des âmes élevées, l'attrait des esprits ornés, fins et doux, l'idéal enfin, avec un je ne sais quoi de parfaitement humain.[103]

Juste Olivier is fairly typical of critics who throughout the latter part of nineteenth century and well into the twentieth privileged William's story at the expense of the narrator's. Philippe Godet, for example, writes that in *Caliste*, Charrière "[nous] [donne] une idée plus haute de son talent délicat et profond, et [fait] succéder, à une piquante peinture de moeurs locales, une émouvante étude de passion, d'un intérêt général et humain."[104]

Even more recently, Jean Starobinski points to the narrator's story as a sketch elaborated on and rendered dramatic in *Caliste*:

> L'histoire de Caliste amplifie, porte au pathétique les éléments si discrètement dessinés dans l'histoire de Cécile. C'en est la version dramatisée.[105]

In reading the original *Lettres* as the less dramatic version of the Caliste story, Starobinski imposes on it a marriage plot that it in fact resists. Moreover, he reads the original *Lettres* once again as Cécile's story rather than her mother's (that is, the narrator's!) story. He entirely cancels out the mother's voice and the significance of her relationship with her daughter. His reading does not account for essential ways in which Charrière's *Lettres* defies the definitions of the modern family plot. Susan Jackson notes that an emphasis on *Caliste* "blurs the differences between Charrière's values and those of eighteenth-century men."[106] MacArthur remarks that "Caliste's foreign presence in the body of Cécile's history both draws more readers to that subversive, non-conventional narrative, and thoroughly overshadows it."[107]

In the remainder of my analysis, I too focus on the continuation, but rather than look in detail at William's Caliste story, I consider the ways in which the added letters very literally *continue* the story of

Cécile and her mother, the ways that they—much as did the preface to Graffigny's *Lettres d'une Péruvienne*—provide an opportunity to read beyond the original ending.

At the end of the original novel, we saw that one of the (pseudo)-arguments the mother presents against Cécile's suggestion that the two women set up household together on a permanent basis is that Cécile will be bored with her. In one of the two letters narrated by Cécile's mother in *Caliste,* the epistler writes to her cousin and informs her that her own fears concerning Cécile's well-being within the mother–daughter dyad were unfounded: "Nous voilà établies dans notre retraite, et Cécile n'a pas l'air de pouvoir s'y ennuyer; elle n'a pas eu recours encore à la moitié de ses ressources: les livres, l'ouvrage, les estampes sont restés dans un tiroir" (105). The two are involved in activities having nothing to do with Cécile's marriage plot, and we are not invited to view their mutual destiny as tragic.[108] While Cécile's sadness about Milord's behavior has lessened, her relationship with her mother has grown ever more passionate. At one point, the narrator recounts her daughter's efforts to persuade her to let Cécile come along to make the announcement to "le monde" that the two women are planning to leave town. Cécile says:

> A vos côtés, appuyée contre votre chaise, touchant votre bras ou seulement votre robe, je me sentirai forte de la plus puissante comme de la plus aimable protection. Vous savez bien, maman, combien vous m'aimez, mais non combien je vous aime, et que vous ayant, vous, je pourrais supporter de tout perdre et de renoncer à tout. (100)

At the close of the Caliste story, William's final words in the novel announce Caliste's death: "Me voici donc seul sur la terre. Ce qui m'aimait n'est plus. J'ai été sans courage pour prévenir cette perte; je suis sans force pour la supporter" (180).

William's announcement of Caliste's death does not close the novel. Cécile and her mother reemerge, albeit obliquely. Squeezed between William's words and those of Caliste's husband (whose letter addressed to William provides a more complete description of Caliste's saintly death) is a goodbye letter from Milord addressed to the narrator ("Ayant appris que vous comptez partir demain . . ."). We learn that mother and daughter are preparing to visit the narrator's cousin in Languedoc, the woman to whom the letters in the original novel were addressed. We leave mother and daughter in what Julia Douthwaite calls "geographic limbo."[109] Like Graffigny's

Lettres d'une Péruvienne, Charrière's *Lettres écrites de Lausanne* in this second (non)ending reaffirms its resistance to the "suitable" closure of marriage or death of the heroine. In the original letter the dangers of the romanesque were pointed to again and again. Recall the "que vous êtes romanesque" with which narrator opens the first of her letters to her cousin, who wants wedded bliss for her daughter, her emphasis that she and her daughter are not "un roman comme Adèle et sa mère," and finally Cécile's declaration that she will be happy with her mother "n'ayant pas le temps de lire des romans." The open ending of the mother–daughter plot, even referred to obliquely and in a brief penultimate letter, serves as an important reminder of the dangers of "novelistic conventions and their imposition on life."[110]

The lesson is reinforced in the last pages by William's transcription of a fragment of conversation he had with his charge, "Milord":

> Il m'a demandé si je croyais qu'elle eût du penchant pour quelqu'un. Je lui ai répondu que je l'avais soupçonné. Il m'a demandé si c'était pour lui. Je lui ai répondu que quelquefois je l'avais cru. —Si cela est, m'a-t-il dit, c'est bien dommage que mademoiselle Cécile soit bien née, car de me marier à mon âge on n'y peut penser. (179)

Milord's response to Cécile's interest is cynically unenthusiastic. His words imply that if Cécile were less well born he would be happy because, in that case, his chances of seducing her without a promise of marriage would be better.

Charrière's reaffirmation in the final pages of her project of female destinies resistant to the (en)closure of marriage and death, underlines that a woman's lived experience can still escape the destinies scripted in the sorts of novels described by Coulet and May. In William's "histoire tout romanesque" Caliste may be dead, but neither death nor marriage seem to be waiting in the wings for either Cécile or her mother in their continuing lives. That "real" lives continue beyond the ending (of both the open-ended Cécile story and the conventionally closed Caliste story) is suggested again by the preface to the *Caliste* story: "Supposé que cette seconde partie soit aussi bien accueillie du public que l'a été la première, nous tâcherons de nous procurer quelques-unes des lettres que les personnes que nous lui avons fait connaître ont dû s'écrire depuis" (97).

A decade after publishing *Les Lettres écrites de Lausanne* along with its companion *Caliste, ou La Suite des Lettres écrites de Lausanne*, Charrière writes:

Depuis la Révolution, je n'ai plus reconnu de public français qui dût nous imposer sur le style ou la langue, et déjà auparavant j'ai pensé que nous autres étrangers nous ne devions pas fléchir devant un tribunal en quelque sorte imaginaire ou composé de gens qui n'ont aucun titre que nous ne puissions prendre aussi bien qu'eux. Quand je fis réimprimer à Paris les *Lettres écrites de Lausanne*, un journal français avait relevé l'expression se dégonfler comme étant suisse, et non française. Je ne la changeai pas, et le journaliste put la trouver dès les premières lignes du livre. J'ai lu il n'y a pas longtemps des lettres encore manuscrites de Rousseau et de M. DuPeyrou. Celui-ci consultait l'autre sur une expression: Sachez ce que vous voulez dire, répond Rousseau, puis dites-le clairement sans vous embarrasser d'autre chose.[111]

In *La Nouvelle Héloïse*, Rousseau presents the events that transpire in what he calls "une petite ville au pied des Alpes." This town is probably very much like Neuchâtel, where Charrière's narrator and her daughter Cécile live. In *La Nouvelle Héloïse* Rousseau presented Switzerland and the Swiss as models from which the French should learn their lessons. And the French did, though not immediately. On June 2, 1762, the Parliament of Paris officially condemned Rousseau's *Emile* and issued a decree of a *prise de corps* against its author. Rousseau was forced to flee, an experience he recounts in his *Confessions*. By the time Charrière wrote her *Lettres*, Rousseau's works, however, were well on their way to being canonized.

The shift in reception of Rousseau's work tells us much about the major changes underway in both the literary and social landscapes of France in the last decades of the century and, to some degree, of Switzerland as well. Rousseau's influence is certainly felt in Charrière's *Lettres*. Many didactic and moralistic elements of the Rousseauian plot are there: the good mother, the chastity lessons, an impressionable girl, and the emotional and economic balancing act involved in the bourgeois marriage "love" plot.

While Charrière's novel may be Rousseauian in terms of these elements (which Coulet and May find to be typical of the novels of this period), there are also essential differences. By keeping the father figure out of her work, she creates a domestic sphere much less embedded in the patriarchal values that imbue the Rousseauian family. The mother–daughter dyad maintains a striking autonomy and resists its usual socially conservative function in novels, that is, assuring that a certain kind of marriage system be perpetuated. In Charrière's work this sort of marriage plot disintegrates. It does so without the heroine's death, the event in many eighteenth-century novels that effectively undermines contradictions inherent in the new family structure by drowning them in tragic pathos (as is the case in *La Nouvelle Héloïse*). Ultimately neither the husband of the mother nor the potential husband of the daughter has power to define the ways these women may lead their (continuing) lives.

The second major way in which Charrière's novel digresses from what I will refer to anachronistically as the Habermassian plot, is in its transgression of the gendered private sphere–public sphere divisions of the oppositional public sphere Habermas finds imagined in the novel, particularly after Rousseau. Cécile's mother repeatedly insists on her right and on her daughter's right to come and go as they please. Mother and daughter are free to move in and out of domestic space. The permeability of divisions is stressed: between inside and outside, between one house and another, between classes, between countries. Charrière imagines, in the novel form, female subjectivities that simultaneously incorporate and defy bourgeois norms, thereby radically breaking with the pact described by May among critics, authors, and readers at this point in the century. In 1785 Charrière, in the midst of Rousseau's country, reclaims Switzerland as a marginal space, a space from which she has the right to critique and rewrite what had become dominant (Rousseauian) discourses prescribing that women nurture and set free men's right to a public voice while suppressing their own.

❊ 3 ❊
After the Revolution(s): George Sand's *Indiana*

> O femmes! femmes, quand cesserez-vous d'être aveugles? Quels sont les avantages que vous avez recueillis dans la révolution?
> —Olympe de Gouges, *Les Droits de la femme,* 1791

Transitions

In his *Lettre d'un bourgeois de New Haven* (1788), Condorcet, one of the few revolutionaries who favored complete legal equality for women, writes:

> Depuis que Rousseau a mérité les suffrages [des femmes], en disant qu'elles n'étoient faites que pour nous soigner et propres qu'à nous tourmenter, je ne dois espérer qu'elles se déclarent en ma faveur. Mais il est bon de dire la vérité, dût-on s'exposer au ridicule....[1]

Condorcet's words point to just how deeply entrenched gendered notions of "nature" and "virtue" had become in the French imagination on the eve of the French Revolution, especially among women. At the same time, they suggest something terribly amiss in this phenomenon.

Of course, not all women were as willing to accept these gendered notions of key republican terms as Condorcet claimed. Just as Charrière had been, many *citoyennes* were clearly aware, and increasingly so, that such definitions of femininity necessarily barred them from having a voice in the new political system. Taking advantage of the shock of the revolution with its ubiquitous slogans proclaiming freedom for all, they worked hard to be included in the social experiment of "Liberté, égalité, and fraternité." Some women did this by joining political organizations devoted to spreading the gospel of virtuous motherhood within a republican framework. Others, in their effort to be included in the last term of the tripartite republican slogan, donned red bonnets and pantaloons. Women from both classes took to the streets en masse in October 1989 to protest food shortages, claiming that "men didn't understand anything about the matter and they wanted a voice in public affairs."[2] While women within the new revolutionary government in Paris were never allowed to vote or to hold office, they were frequently present in the galleries of the halls in which the affairs of the new republican government were conducted.[3]

In her *Droits de la femme* (1791), Olympe de Gouges made an eloquent plea for a notion of nature that would include men and women on equal terms. She did so by pointing to the organic world of plants—so dear to Rousseau—and showing that nothing was *natural* about the very different roles he prescribed for men and women:

> Homme, es-tu capable d'être juste? . . . Remonte aux animaux, consulte les éléments, étudie les végétaux, jette enfin un coup d'oeil sur toutes les modifications de la matière organisée; et rends-toi à l'évidence quand je t'en offre les moyens; cherche, fouille et distingue, si tu le peux, les sexes dans l'administration de la nature. Partout tu les trouveras confondus, partout ils coopèrent avec un ensemble harmonieux à ce chef-d'oeuvre immortel.[4]

Gouges's words gave a theoretical foundation to women's attempts to be included as participants in the republican process, and, as such, they incited a great deal of anxiety among "les hommes" she addressed in her essay. The new republic had been symbolized from the beginning by the image of a woman to escape any association with royal (paternal) power. Over the next two years, the demeanor of Liberty was changed in ways to emphasize that "she" represented an abstract notion rather than any actual woman actively involved in the new experiment of government by the people. In 1793, as France entered the Reign of Terror, the Convention voted to replace Marianne with an image of Hercules. And on November 2 of the same year, just a few days after women's political clubs were outlawed and a few days before women were barred from attendance in the galleries of the Convention, Gouges was sentenced to death.

The words of Pierre Chaumette, the president of the General Council, admonished women to be content with their supremacy in the domestic realm and to leave the public sphere to men:

Well! Since when is it decent to see women abandoning the pious cares of their households, the cribs of their children, to come to public places, to harangue in the galleries, at the bar of the senate? Is it to men that nature confided domestic cares? Has she given us breasts to breast-feed our children? No, she has said to man: "Be a man: hunting, farming, political concerns, toils of every kind, that is your appanage." She has said to woman: "Be a woman. The tender cares owing to infancy, the details of the household, the sweet anxieties of maternity, these are your labors; but your attentive cares deserve a reward. Fine! You will have it, and you will be the divinity of the domestic sanctuary; you will reign over everything that surrounds you by the invincible charm of the graces and of virtue."[5]

In this remarkable passage recorded in the *Ancien Moniteur*, Chaumette links law (he is president of a legislative body, and its members are discussing a recently passed law) with Rousseauian gender roles. In emphasizing that it was in the interest of the women present to adopt this notion of "nature," Chaumette alluded to the fates of the recently guillotined Gouges and Marie-Jeanne Roland. Gouges and Roland had been condemned to death for the crime of being royalists. Chaumette's presentation of their fates to the women patriots before him (who were clearly *not* royalists) must have been felt as a threat by his listeners, women who had gathered to protest their exclusion from government halls. Whatever their political beliefs, they were being told to behave as "women" or to suffer the consequences.

Chaumette's words that day inaugurated a bleak outlook for women's rights in the century ahead. The Napoleonic civil code, drawn up between 1800 and 1804, declared civil rights for all citizens—"Tout Français jouira des droits civiles"—even as it excluded women's access to citizenship. Women could not vote, nor could they witness state documents or be *notaires*. Married women were excluded from participation in the economic realm as well. Husbands controlled all property jointly held, and wives could not dispose of even their own property without the permission of their husbands. In 1816 divorce was prohibited (after having been legalized in 1792), but separation continued to be legal. The terms for legal separation, however, were highly inequitable. A husband might seek a separation should he discover that his wife had been unfaithful. A woman, on the other hand, had to prove that her husband's mistress actually resided in their home. If a woman moved out without proving this, she was in violation of the law. As in prerevolutionary days, the criminal penalties for adultery were likewise inequitable. While an adulteress could be imprisoned for her crime, the maximum punishment for an adulterer was a fine.[6]

By the time George Sand took up her pen, the private sphere, a novelty a century earlier, had become formally established among almost all classes of society. Republicans, Bonapartistes, and royalists found a sense of stability in a shared agreement that the family was "the basic cell of an organic social order."[7] Indeed, in terms of familial economies, the difference between aristocrats and bourgeois continued to lessen as gender to some degree replaced class as a fundamental organizing principle of society. Even staunch royalists legitimized themselves by insisting on the need for "bourgeois" family values.[8] For them a celebration of "chez soi" was a means of differentiating their political vision from the rejected (feminized) excesses of the old regime. The division between gendered public and private spheres had become a stabilizing constant in this time of continuing social unrest and shifts in political and economic power structures.

This rigid division between masculine and feminine spheres proved especially vexing for women writers. In the *Courrier Français* of December 18, 1827, a critic wrote: "Il y a déjà longtemps que sous la plume des écrivains habiles le roman a perdu son caractère frivole."[9] While not explicitly stated, the implications were clear. "Ecrivains habiles," i.e., male authors, had cleansed the genre of its "caractère frivole," i.e., a historical association with women. In her fine study of reviews and prefaces of nineteenth-century novels, Leyla Ezdinli shows that the term *roman de femme* became a way to systematically disparage the productions of women. We saw the beginnings of such a tendency with Rousseau, who had already invited his readers, male and female, to view the woman writer as sexually undesirable. In the post-revolutionary period, this sort of denigration of the woman writer became commonplace. Journalists frequently presented women writers as unnatural, lonely, or sexless creatures. Take Jules Janin who wrote of "[. . .] la race toute moderne, des malheureuses créatures féminines qui, renonçant à la beauté, à la grâce, à la jeunesse, au bonheur du mariage, aux chastes prévoyances de la maternité, à tout ce qui est le foyer domestique, la famille, le repos au-dedans, la considération au dehors, entreprennent de vivre à la force de leur esprit."[10] Stendahl and Balzac too had unkind words for women writers. Almost none of the new journals of any political persuasion accepted work by women writers or critics.[11] Women found themselves locked out of the sorts of alliances being forged between professional writers and powerful editors of journals and publishing houses.

At the same time, women within the works of the Romantic movement were invariably displayed as angelic symbols of redemption, their virginity fetishized.[12] The male *culte du moi* in literature, with its insistence on freedom of the individual and of his poetic creations unfettered by social constraints, did little to undermine a division between public and private spheres or to allow for the imagination of new female subjectivities. The joys of the domestic interior, a haven to which men might retreat and be sheltered from the outer world, constituted a major theme in Romantic literature, particularly in the decade during which Sand wrote *Indiana*: "L'élégie romantique modulera sans relâche les joies du foyer, et l'intimisme connaîtra une glorieuse décennie, après 1830, à la suite des *Consolations* (1830) de Sainte-Beuve ou des *Feuilles d'automne* (1831) de Hugo."[13]

As authorship and publishing became masculinized, women were increasingly presented as symbols playing a part in masculine destinies, rather than as the subjects of their own destinies. To be included at all, women writers were forced to play the literary game according to the rules set up by male writers and critics. Loathe to be associated with the shunned *roman de femme*, they inevitably downplayed, at least superficially, the specificity of their point of view as women writers, often publishing under assumed masculine names or, if under their own names, with the addition of a series of disclaimers.[14]

When George Sand published her first independently written novel, she too had recourse to these defensive strategies. She chose to publish under an assumed masculine name and used a consistently male-gendered authorial voice. Indeed, *Indiana* (1832) was thought to have been written by a man for several months after it appeared. I will examine the ways in which Sand uses male "camouflage" as more than a way to be included in a world from which she would otherwise be excluded. Sand used a "masculinized" authorial voice to address issues of specific concern to women from within an increasingly masculinized genre—both in terms of the literary market and in terms of acceptable plots. I will examine the role that Sand's adoption of a male authorial voice plays in her prefaces to *Indiana* before looking at the role this voice plays in the novel as a whole. Thereafter, I will consider her critical integration of traditional love plots and their juxtaposition with new plots, paying close attention to the role played by Saint-Simonian ideas. Finally, I will consider Sand's highly ambivalent relationship to gendered public and private spheres, especially in her presentation of the Ralph–Indiana love story presented in the final pages of her novel.

Cross-voicing in *Indiana*

> L'auteur d'*Indiana*, cet écrivain hermaphrodite. . . .
> —Unsigned review of *Heures du soir, livre des femmes*,
> *Figaro*, May 20, 1833

George Sand, like the most colorful revolutionary women of fifty years earlier, favored trousers and boots over dresses and feminine shoes.[15] She writes in *Histoire de ma vie* (1855) that her preference for male attire, and in particular for boots, stemmed from the freedom they afforded her to walk easily in the streets of Paris, an activity that provided the young woman with a heady sense of her independence:

> Je ne peux pas dire quel plaisir me firent mes bottes: j'aurais volontiers dormi avec. . . . Avec ces petits talons ferrés, j'étais solide sur le trottoir. Je voltigeais d'un bout de Paris à l'autre. Il me semblait que j'aurais fait le tour du monde.[16]

Sand's decision to wear male attire is intriguing on a number of levels. Her male costume, in which, she tells us, she resembled "un petit étudiant de première année," enabled her to pass from the private into the public sphere defined as accessible to one gender only.

Likewise, in the literary world, the adoption of a male persona allowed Sand forays into the public sphere of the market that, given the literary establishment's general hostility toward women, would otherwise have been impossible.[17] It was only by using the name of her friend and sometime collaborator Jules Sandeau, that Sand was able to write and have her articles published in *Le Figaro*, *La Revue de Paris*, and *La Mode*. Sand had also published two novels in collaboration with Sandeau before changing their joint pseudonym "J. Sand" to "G. Sand" and devoting herself to establishing an independent career.[18]

Indiana was an immediate bestseller. The novel went through three editions within four months and received warm praise from the critical establishment. A critic in *La France Littéraire*, for example, wrote that *Indiana* was "digne d'être distingué parmi les meilleurs romans de notre époque." Another critic commented that "Monsieur" Sand had "un talent d'observation et d'analyse morale très distingué."[19] For several months after the publication of *Indiana*, critics generally assumed that its male authorial voice corresponded to a male author. It was not long, however, before the question of the author's real gender became a matter of great speculation. Even after they knew that Sand was in fact a woman, some critics fueled the guessing game by presenting their readers with an almost flirtatious game of peek-a-boo with the real authorial body. Sand capitalized on her ambiguous gender identity, privately female, publicly male, to create for herself a highly marketable literary persona.[20]

Sand successively wrote three different prefaces to *Indiana* for the 1832, 1842, and 1852 editions of her novel. The first was written at the behest of her editor, who, concerned with the public's response to certain sensitive points in the novel such as female sexuality and adultery, requested a little "padding." This padding takes three forms. First, Sand disassociates herself completely as a woman from the authorial voice of the preface. Sand creates a *préfacier* who is not only male, but who is referred to exclusively with distancing third-person forms ("il," "l'historien," or "le narrateur"), as though he were simply another character in the work. The "je" in this preface is masked.

Secondly, we find in the preface a disassociation of the male authorial voice from any notion that the novel it precedes deals with issues of specific concern to women. Sand's narrator makes a single reference to her female protagonist of the novel and then only to present *Indiana* as an abstract symbol of (unbodied) repressed emotion:

> Indiana, si vous voulez absolument expliquer tout dans ce livre, c'est un type; c'est la femme, l'être faible chargé de représenter les *passions* comprimées, ou si vous l'aimez mieux, supprimées par les lois; c'est la volonté aux prises avec la nécessité; c'est l'amour heurtant son front aveugle à tous les obstacles de la civilisation.[21]

Sand's narrator hereby associates Indiana with what has become a trope in romantic fiction. Rather than specifically female sentiment, she symbolizes "human" passions unrecognized by the increasingly rigid structures of bourgeois bureaucracy. This notion of an ungendered, or rather, double-gendered humanity is underlined by Sand's oscillation between male and female grammatical genders in the above passage. "La femme" is "l'être faible" (masculine), "*la* volonté," "l'amour" (masculine). This lack of gender specificity and tendency toward abstraction is true as well of Sand's references to other characters in the novel. The *préfacier* refers, for example, to "des plaintes arrachées à ses personnages par le malaise social dont ils sont atteints," and to "quelques cris de souffrance et de colère épars dans le drame d'une vie humaine." Sand's play with gender markers leads to a vagueness that refuses clear divisions between masculine and feminine. The reader would certainly not guess from this preface that the novel that follows treats the woes and passions of an unhappily married woman.

Finally, this authorial persona distances himself from the subject matter that follows by claiming a passive role vis-à-vis his subject:

> Si quelques pages de ce livre encouraient le grave reproche de tendance vers des croyances nouvelles, si des juges rigides trouvaient leur allure imprudente et dangereuse, il faudrait répondre à la critique qu'elle fait beaucoup trop d'honneur à une oeuvre sans importance. (37)

He is simply "une machine qui . . . décalque, et qui n'a rien à se faire pardonner si ses empreintes sont exactes, si son reflet est fidèle." Sand's refuge behind the notion that literature is the reflection of society, a classic ruse during this period for male as well as female writers, serves as an extra distancing measure from issues of specifically female concern.

When Sand wrote her second preface in 1842, her prefatory strategy changed. By this time, the reading public was well aware she was a woman. The fact that she continued to use her male literary persona long after it had outgrown the function of disguise suggests a new relationship to cross-voicing. Sand intersperses third-person references to her "narrateur" with an occasional "je," which suggests a more direct link between author and reader. While adjectival endings still signal a masculine(ized) identity, this "je" identifies himself with female categories (even though they may be gendered male):

> J'ai cédé à un instinct puissant de plainte et de reproche que Dieu avait mis en moi, Dieu qui ne fait rien d'inutile, pas même les plus chétifs êtres, et qui intervient dans les plus petites causes aussi bien que les grandes. (46)

Given gender stereotypes prevalent in the literary world of the nineteenth century, "les plus chétifs êtres" and "les plus petites causes" may be assumed to refer to women and their concerns. It is among this feminine group that the male authorial voice places him/herself. Moreover, that the "chétifs êtres" and "les petites causes" referred to above signal women and their concerns becomes explicit as the narrator continues:

> Mais quoi! celle que je défendais est-elle donc si petite? C'est celle de la moitié du genre humain, c'est celle du genre humain tout entier; car le malheur de la femme entraîne celui de l'homme, comme celui de l'esclave entraîne celui du maître. (46)

Sand's authorial voice, which in the first preface tended to disassociate itself from women, here becomes feminized (despite the fact that it continues to be grammatically male), and it allies itself far more directly with the importance of women as subject matter in *Indiana*. Rather than refer to women as abstract symbols of human suffering as had been the case in the first preface, the narrator here speaks of women as a specific segment of society. While woman's cause is associated here with the suffering of a generalized humanity, she is no longer the symbol of that suffering. Rather her suffering is painted as one part of a larger system. The narrator reinforces and renders specific "his" alliance with women when "he" makes reference to a deep concern about "l'injustice et de la barbarie des lois qui régissent encore l'existence de la femme dans le mariage, dans la famille, et dans la société" (46–47). Sand's cross-voicing has gone from disguise to what Naomi Schor has aptly called "bitextuality," a kind of writing that plays with language and its role in the construction of gender. Sand implicitly suggests that gender, the great dividing line of the nineteenth century, is finally a set of external signs subject to manipulation. She, as a woman who controls masculine forms of language, maintains an outside perspective within officially recognized modes of discourse. As a cross-voiced writer, she can be man and woman at the same time.

In Sand's short third preface, written after her literary career had become well established, she maintains the use of a masculine "je" ("Je fus étonné au dernier point . . ."), but her tone has shifted far from the conciliatory tones of the first preface. She takes on the "race de critiques . . . qui [portent] non seulement sur les oeuvres, mais encore sur les personnes" (35), and insists on the right to create storylines that defy reigning bourgeois standards of morality.

Let us move backward from Sand's prefaces—for all of them were written after the novel itself—to the text of *Indiana*. Many of the issues raised in the prefaces play an important role in the novel itself. I now consider the ways in which cross-voicing within the novel allows for an exploration of the complex interrelations between public and private worlds in the post-revolutionary period, and in particular, the place of women within this structure.

To be sure, in *Indiana*, none of the cast of Sand's characters cross-dresses or takes on cross-gendered names to gain access to worlds from which access would otherwise be denied. On the contrary, Sand's characters seem to follow Chaumette's implicit prescription to the revolutionary women before him, to whom he "taught" the desires of nature ("She has said to man: 'Be a man: hunting, farming, political concerns, toils of every kind, that is your appanage.' She has said to woman: 'Be a woman. The tender cares owing to infancy, the details of the household, the sweet anxieties of maternity, these are your labors.' ") The men in Sand's novel have positions in the larger world; the women are confined to the private sphere where they obey, serve tea, and have nervous spells. Sand's characters—a father-figure husband, a willowy wife, a sexy chambermaid, a rake, and a restrained handsome Englishman—are stock characters by this point in the trajectory of the novel genre. But while Sand's characters are in some ways quite conventional, we will see that they are also put into question. Sand writes her novel within and against a tradition of "romans à l'usage des femmes de chambre," sentimental, gothic, and fantastic novels whose drama depends on the relationships between manly men and womanly women. One of the ways this is achieved is through the use Sand makes of her male narrator.

Sand's novel opens with a domestic scene. We are introduced to the Delmare family on a dark and rainy night as they sit in a circle around the hearth. What might be a romantic view into the domestic interior of the "familles très unies" that dominated the nineteenth-century French imagination is, in Sand's novel, something else entirely.[22] The characters present, Monsieur Delmare, his young wife Indiana, and her cousin Ralph, are all manifestly bored and miserable, "gravement occupés . . . à regarder brûler les tisons du foyer et cheminer lentement l'aiguille de la pendule" (49). The painting-like stillness of the family scene is broken by M. Delmare, who rises and begins to pace back and forth through the shadows all the while glaring at his young wife (Indiana) and her cousin

(Ralph). From the beginning, M. Delmare is treated pitilessly by the narrator. M. Delmare, who, in many respects, holds a position equivalent to that of the venerated M. de Wolmar in La Nouvelle Héloïse, is presented as pathetic and ridiculous, a caricature of the respectable head of the bourgeois family:

> Il quitta enfin sa chaise, évidemment impatienté de ne savoir comment rompre le silence, et se prit à marcher pesamment dans toute la longeur du salon, sans perdre un instant la roideur convenable à tous les mouvements d'un ancien militaire, s'appuyant sur les reins et se tournant tout d'une pièce, avec ce contentement perpétuel de soi-même qui caractérise l'homme de parade et l'officier modèle. . . . Il était l'époux d'une jeune et jolie femme, le propriétaire d'un commode manoir avec ses dépendances, et, de plus, un industriel heureux dans ses spéculations. (50)

Delmare is defined by his private life ("l'époux d'une jeune et jolie femme, le propriétaire d'un commode manoir") and his public life ("un homme heureux dans ses spéculations").[23] While, as Habermas has shown, the eighteenth-century novel played an essential role in the emergence of such a subjectivity, it did so in a somewhat indirect way. Rather than portraying the family as a unit within a larger system, it instilled the illusion of a private life independent of the outer world, a "natural" world independent of the artificial world of commerce and politics. In fact, the whole system was dependent on people living their lives in this "natural" way. Sand, especially in the early portion of her novel, instead *emphasizes* the link between the private family and a larger ideological system, and thereby undermines its seeming naturalness. Rather than hide it, she underlines the ways in which public structures support private individuals, and vice versa. Already in the opening pages, the narrator uses his/her masculine gender status to gaze upon both the private and the public worlds with a distinctly female critical eye.

We saw above that the Napoleonic code translated the division between public and private spheres into legislative rules by allotting men increased power in the household while decreasing women's in both the home and in political and economic matters. Delmare's notion of honor depends on just such Napoleonic notions: "Toute sa conscience, c'était la loi; toute sa morale, c'était son droit" (134). His bourgeois insistence on individual economic rights according to abstract laws is coupled with an insistence of his right to a private life in which no outsiders have the right to interfere:

> Pourvu qu'il respecte religieusement la vie et la bourse de ses concitoy-
> ens, on lui demande pas compte d'autre chose. Il peut battre sa femme,
> maltraiter ses gens, ruiner ses enfants, cela ne regarde personne. . . .
> Telle était la morale de M. Delmare. Il n'avait jamais étudié d'autre con-
> trat social que celui-ci: Chacun chez soi. (132)

Sand shows a remarkable awareness of the interrelation between public and private. Delmare needs a sense of being a private person, "chez soi," to function as an individual in the world of the bourgeois market "où il respecte la vie et la bourse de ses concitoyens." Here this link between the two worlds is made explicit and criticized.

Delmare lived his glory days during Napoleon's empire. He is physically strong, with a tendency toward violence, "il avait de larges épaules, un vigoureux poignet" (132). In the first chapter of Sand's novel he threatens to kill both a dog and shortly thereafter an intruder on his property, the latter of whom he does, in fact, shoot in the hand. He is a hunter, and on two separate occasions he physically abuses his wife; on others he imagines hurting her. This presentation of the bourgeois as a brutish character was not ununusual in novels of the first half of the nineteenth century. In *The Battle of the Bourgeois*, Clark shows that, on the contrary, "from whatever angle he might be viewed, the bourgeois appeared as the enemy."[24] But such an explicit presentation of the link between public and private spheres and an exploration of the resulting abuse *was* unusual. Even before it was generally known that Sand was a woman, she was chastised for her introduction into the narrative of this unorthodox kind of socioeconomic commentary. Charles Rabou wrote in *Le Nouvelliste*: "Faisons descendre l'auteur d'*Indiana* de sa chaire d'économie sociale et réduisons-le à n'être qu'un puissant peintre de passions."[25] When this critic insists that the novel should be a forum of passions to the exclusion of "l'économie sociale," no matter what his declared political position, he is defending a particular (bourgeois) ideology that depends on an unquestioned division between public and private spheres.

In *Indiana* the male authorial voice is undermined in a subtle way by Sand's use of cross-voicing. All the male characters in *Indiana* have deprecatory thoughts or make derogatory comments about women. Delmare says, "Ah comme la ruse est innée chez cesêtres-là" (69). Ralph, Indiana's cousin, thinks "Ces deux femmes sont folles. . . . D'ailleurs . . . toutes les femmes le sont" (61), and Raymon complains about "un amour de femme" (221). Despite the narrator's harsh criticism of Delmare (and, as we will see, Raymon as well), "he" himself occasionally slips into the kind of language one hears in the mouths of *Indiana*'s male characters. Cross-voicing allows Sand to explore territory unavailable to a female narrator; like cross-dressing, it can also function as a parody of the assumed gender, in this case the male gender. When the narrator exclaims, "La femme est imbécile par nature" (251), "he" is parodying male assumptions about women. By undermining his own voice, he undermines the power of a more generalized male authorial voice.[26]

The narrator's voice functions parodically because it makes more blatant the kinds of assumptions about women more generally present in fiction. But the narrator does more than simply parody the male authorial voice. He also subtly introduces ideas that counter the views of this authorial voice. In the continuation to his comment regarding the imbecility of women, we find the following words:

> Il semble que, pour contrebalancer l'éminente supériorité que ses délicates perceptions lui donnent sur nous, le ciel ait mis à dessein dans son coeur une vanité aveugle, une idiote crédulité. (251)

The narrator includes himself in the general category of men ("nous") in a shared assumption that women are stupid, proud, and gullible. But he also slips in a comment on the superiority of women in terms of their abilities in the matter of "délicates perceptions." This quality, recognized to be essential for any writer of fiction, is, significantly, attributed to women. Sand thereby introduces a subtle association between women and writing novels.

Sand's cross-voiced narrator alternates between identification with male models—sometimes serious, sometimes parodic, and a female position critical of these models. The reader is invited to read doubly, on the one hand, in terms of dominant models—male authorial voice, conventionally gendered characters—and, on the other hand, in terms of that which is neglected by those models—female perspectives, a critique of conventional gender roles.

Old Plots

The male narrator's focus on public life allows for a consideration of a series of plots depicting the relationships between men and women, within the broadest possible variety of settings. In *Indiana* we find two of what had become classic plots of sentimental fiction: the marriage plot and the passion plot ending with the death of the heroine. Both of these are treated critically in Sand's novel, before she moves on to a consideration of new plots in which new female subjectivities are imagined. The first of the "classic" female plots we will consider is Indiana's (post-)marriage plot. Sand begins her novel where most novels of the period end. Marriage, the goal in so many eighteenth- and nineteenth-century novels, is the baseline condition in *Indiana*. Indeed, Indiana and Delmare have been married and submerged in the bourgeois domestic family for three years by the time the novel opens. They live within a well-defined domesticity clearly demarcated by the high walls surrounding the "parc" of the Delmare property.[27] We learn little concerning the details of the Delmare (pre)marriage plot other than that the ceremony occurred on the île Bourbon and that shortly thereafter Delmare decided for economic reasons to move to France with his young wife. In Sand's novel, the details leading up to this bourgeois marriage plot are less important than the state of marriage itself. *La Nouvelle Héloïse*, the prototypical bourgeois plot of the later eighteenth century, likewise focuses on life after, rather than before, marriage. In Rousseau's work, the stability of the family plot depends on a precarious resolution of contradictions involved in shifting from one kinship system (aristocratic, alliance-based) to another ("classless," dependent on the creation of a new domestic unit). Sand too presents an "after marriage plot" but, in rewriting Rousseau, she dispenses with his sentimentalization of the domestic interior.

In accordance with the Napoleonic code, Indiana is entirely dependent, both legally and economically, on her husband.[28] Sand presents us with a heroine who manifests, in an exaggerated, almost parodic form, the degraded status of women in "la famille très unie" of the nineteenth century. Within her marriage, Indiana behaves like the unpaid laborer that, according to French law, she is:

> Parfois [Delmare] donnait chez lui un ordre mal exprimé, ou bien il dictait sans réflexion des ordres nuisibles à ses propres intérêts. Madame Delmare les faisait exécuter sans examen, sans appel, avec l'indifférence du cheval qui traîne la charrue dans un sens ou dans l'autre. (208)

Indiana's exaggerated respect for the legal and economic stipulations of marriage is coupled with a refusal to make any concessions to the notion of bourgeois intraconjugal affection demanded by the myth of the privatized family: "Elle n'aima pas son mari, par la seule raison peut-être qu'on lui faisait un devoir de l'aimer" (88–89). The bourgeois family in the eighteenth century had depended on the notion of conjugal love as a means of defining a new family unit against the preexisting family tradition of the old regime.

By the time Sand was writing, the bourgeois family had become the dominant, albeit not uncontested, model. While it still depended *symbolically* on the notion of conjugal affection, it in fact depended increasingly less on love and increasingly more on financial concerns; a beautiful wife was still desirable, but as a prize rather than as a companion. Delmare thinks of his wife as "un trésor fragile et précieux" (50). Through her overblown acceptance of her slavish role, Indiana fights back against the family in a passively aggressive way: "Indiana était roide et hautaine dans sa soumission.... Sa résignation, c'était la dignité d'un roi qui accepte des fers et un cachot, plutôt que d'abdiquer sa couronne et de se dépouiller d'un vain titre" (207). Indiana's submission is critical, disdainful, and provocative.

Indiana's strict adherence to her legally defined duties brings out a parallel exaggeration of Delmare's husbandly characteristics as they are defined by the law. He resents Indiana's refusal to behave like a "real" wife in accordance with the myth of the loving family. His position of power becomes ridiculous without the crutch of his wife's reverence and love: "Si son amour-propre eût souffert de n'être pas le maître absolu, il souffrait bien davantage de l'être d'une façon odieuse ou ridicule" (208). When, in response to Delmare's irritation, Indiana points out that "elle n'avait fait qu'obéir strictement à ses arrêts" (208), Delmare responds in a manner that makes visible the violence usually latent in the nuclear family: "Il était tenté de l'étrangler, de la traîner par les cheveux, de la fouler aux pieds pour la forcer de crier merci" (209).

Indiana insists on her ability to resist absorption into the mask she wears. In a manner reminiscent of Laclos's Madame de Merteuil in *Liaisons dangereuses* (1782), Indiana makes a great effort to preserve another subjectivity beneath the mask of wifehood:

> Résister mentalement à toute espèce de contrainte morale était devenu chez elle une seconde nature, un principe de conduite, une loi de conscience. (89)

Unlike Merteuil, however, Indiana is a virgin, and she does not seek out the sexual pleasures that Merteuil's mask afforded her. When we are introduced to Indiana she is not in good health. In the opening scene, her condition stops her husband's abusive words short:

> Il remarqua l'air de souffrance et d'abattement qui, ce soir-là, était répandu sur toute sa personne, son attitude fatiguée, ses longs cheveux bruns pendants sur ses joues amaigries, et une teinte violacée sous ses yeux ternis et échauffés. (55)

Indiana is feverish, her blood flows irregularly, and she is subject to fainting spells and nervous spasms that last for hours. In fact, she is described through all of her time with Delmare as hovering in a space between life and death:

> Un mal inconnu dévorait sa jeunesse. Elle était sans force et sans sommeil. Les médecins lui cherchaient en vain une désorganisation apparente, il n'en existait pas; toutes ses facultés appauvrissaient également, tous ses organes se lésaient avec lenteur; son coeur brûlait à petit feu, ses yeux s'éteignaient, son sang ne circulait plus que par crise et par fièvre; encore quelque temps, et la pauvre captive allait mourir. (89)[29]

Freud tells us that hysterical symptoms are hieroglyphs needing to be decoded. If we accept this, what might be the hidden meaning of Indiana's body language? We might interpret Indiana's symptoms as an exaggerated, corporeal inscription of social power relations in which women's bodies are treated as the object of a complicated set of social/sexual disciplines.[30] We might read them too as a refusal of the libidinal economy that prescribes fulfillment for women within the role of wife and mother. We are told:

> La nuit avait pour cette femme rêveuse et triste un langage tout de mystères et de fantômes qu'elle seule savait comprendre et *traduire*. (my emphasis, 59)

In *La Jeune Née*, Catherine Clément and Hélène Cixous debate whether the hysteric should or should not be celebrated/romanticized as a resisting heroine. The debate could be continued at length with respect to Indiana and her role in the family. I would like to have it both ways. I see Indiana's symptoms as the translation of a repressed "langage de mystères et de fantômes," that is, a language that refuses the definitions of "enlightened" men and laws, a language of protest against the role allotted women in the family and in literature; it is also a language eventually retranslatable into something less self-destructive and more communicable than bodily suffering. Sand's novel provides the beginnings of such a retranslation. I will return to this in the next section but, before doing so, we will consider the second "classic" female plot included in Sand's multiply plotted novel: the passion plot ending in the death of a heroine.

Within the first few pages of *Indiana*, we are introduced to the rake of the novel, Raymon de Ramière, an aristocratic neighbor who penetrates the Delmare bourgeois interior. Our introduction to Raymon takes place in the Delmare living room, where he has been brought after being shot in the hand while scrambling across the wall surrounding the Delmare property. Indiana tends to his wounded hand while Raymon, in a feigned state of semi-consciousness, takes in the scene. We learn, though Indiana does not, that before Raymon's dramatic entrance into Indiana's life, the better part of another seduction plot has been played out. By the time he enters Sand's novel, Raymon has already met, been enchanted by, and seduced Indiana's extremely sensual childhood companion (*soeur de lait*) and chambermaid, Noun. This plot comes to a traditional ending in the body of the text when Noun discovers that Raymon has betrayed her by falling in love with her mistress, Indiana. In despair, she drowns herself in the river flowing through the Delmare property.

The death of the heroine, especially the sexualized heroine, was certainly not anomalous in the nineteenth century. In fact, this cathartic resolution served a social function:

> Qui trouvera-t-on autour du lit de l'agonisante? . . . Tous ceux qui ont fait cortège à sa vie. . . . Mais il semble que toute malveillance, toute nocivité les ait abandonnés par miracle; en eux, le "public" se fait soudain faste et pieusement attentif, le monde des hommes rend enfin hommage à l'être exceptionnel qu'il n'a pas pu conserver. L'agonie est l'heure de toutes les réconciliations, de tous les ralliements.[31]

Fauchery points out that the death of the heroine is usually conservative, a ritualistic way of confronting social contradictions and resolving them novelistically through pathos rather than ideological change.

Noun's tragic plot might easily fill an entire "roman à l'usage des femmes de chambres," planting in the hearts of readers like Noun the longing for a love that would transcend class differences and sweep them into blissful security with a man their social superior. But Noun, who is sensual, dark, and exotic, drowns herself in an "appropriate" manner so that her lover may continue to live a peaceful and socially acceptable existence in the future.[32] Noun's death is rendered unromantic and unacceptable by the very starkness of its presentation:

> Un cri déchirant attira en ce lieu les ouvriers de la fabrique; madame Delmare était évanouie sur la rive, et le cadavre de Noun flottait sur l'eau, devant elle. (119)[33]

We are not grateful for a good cathartic cry here. Moreover, the death-of-the-heroine ending is only the beginning of Sand's novel. Indeed, Noun's story is condensed into the first of the four books that make up *Indiana*. In the second book we are told that the causes of Noun's death were silenced in the Delmare household to shelter Indiana from the true story and thereby to avoid further aggravating her symptoms: "Il y eut une convention tacite de ne jamais en parler devant Indiana, et bientôt même on n'en parla pas du tout" (125). While Ralph and Delmare may stop discussing Noun, Sand's novel does not. *Indiana*, its plot constantly looping back on itself in a series of echoes and dissections, constitutes, finally, the undoing of both the marriage plot (in which the heroine suffers the woes of hysteria) and the passion plot (in which the heroine ends up dead).

New Plots

It seems at first glance that Indiana's story simply replays Noun's relationship with Raymon, that she steps in to replace the gap left in Raymon's life by Noun's absence. But the plots of the two women are entangled in complicated ways well before Noun drowns herself. Indeed, it is Raymon's involvement with Indiana that motivates Noun's decision to end her life. For Raymon, the two women, both Créole, represent two extremes of womanhood: on the one hand, Noun, the hypersexualized, lower-class woman, and, on the other, Indiana, the desexualized, angelic, upper-class woman. The doubling of Raymon's plot, once with the sexualized "sister," once with her angelic "sister," allows for some ingenious play with literary views of women.

While it is Noun's frank sensuality that attracts Raymon when he first sees her at a social event, he soon grows tired of this woman who has surrendered sexually to him: "Pour lui une grisette n'était pas une femme" (75). It is not long before he is able to desire her only by imagining her as something she is not: "Noun, en déshabillé blanc, parée de ses longs cheveux noirs, était une dame, une reine, une fée; lorsqu'il la voyait sortir de ce castel de briques rouges" (74). It is precisely these qualities that lead to his passionate attraction to Indiana. She seems really to be all the things that he has had to project onto Noun. She is wealthy, delicate, and, above all, she is fairylike. At the ball where she meets Raymon for the second time, Indiana is actually described as a vision straight out of "les contes fantastiques [qui] étaient à cette époque à toute la fraîcheur de leur succès":

> Le blanc mat de son collier, celui de sa robe de crêpe et de ses épaules nues, se confondaient à quelque distance, et la chaleur des appartements avait à peine réussi à élever sur ses joues une nuance délicate comme celle d'une rose de Bengale éclose sur la neige. C'était une créature toute petite, toute mignonne, toute déliée; une beauté de salon que la lueur vive des bougies rendait féerique et qu'un rayon de soleil eût ternie. En dansant, elle était légère sans vivacité, sans plaisir. (80)

At the ball, Raymon and this rosebud are considered a perfect romantic pair, especially in the the view of one "femme *artiste*," who whispers to her neighbor:

> N'est-ce pas qu'auprès de cette jeune personne si pâle et si menue, le ton *solide* de l'un fait admirablement ressortir le ton *fin* de l'autre? (81)

Sand's readers, familiar with Noun's story, know to read this romanesque couple more skeptically than does the woman at the ball. The narrator, by way of the same sort of ironic distance we have already considered in his presentation of Delmare, has made certain that we view Raymon as a less-than-admirable man: we know (although Indiana does not) that Raymon has already seduced and is in the process of abandoning Noun by the time he sweeps Indiana off her feet at the ball. The narrator has already described for us how Raymon "honorably" decides to break off his relationship with Noun:

> Oui, sur mon honneur! il avait songé [au mariage]; mais l'amour, qui légitime tout, s'affaiblissait maintenant; il s'en allait avec les dangers de

l'aventure et le piquant du mystère. Plus d'hymen possible; et faites attention; Raymon raisonnait fort bien et tout à fait dans l'intérêt de sa maîtresse. (75)

Such passages recounted by the narrator in Noun's story invite us to read Indiana's story with a good deal of critical distance.

Raymon "reads" his mistresses in terms traditionally provided in literature, i.e., the fallen woman or the madonna. For him, Noun represents the sexualized heroine, while Indiana represents the virginal heroine. Sand's novel shows the ways in which these terms are hurtful to women. This becomes even more clear in perhaps the most frequently cited passage in *Indiana*, a bedroom scene in which Raymon melds the two relationships into one. As he continues his "courtship" of Indiana, Noun's pregnancy becomes more apparent and her terror more pressing. To spend time in the Delmare household, Raymon has had to juggle his relationship with Indiana along with that of Noun in such a way that neither woman is aware of his relationship with the other. He finally resolves to send Noun away with money so that he can be free of her. Noun greets Raymon at the arranged time and place, but she is unexpectedly dressed in Indiana's clothes. She leads Raymon into Indiana's virginal chambers. In the presence of Noun draped in Indiana's white lace, his resolve fades. Despite the fact that Noun's disguise is only partially successful—she is "belle comme une femme et pas comme une fée"— he gives in to her seductions and makes passionate love to her on Indiana's narrow white bed:

> Elle l'entourait de ses bras frais et bruns, elle le couvrait de ses longs cheveux; ses grands yeux noirs lui jetaient une langueur brûlante, et cette ardeur du sang, cette volupté tout orientale qui sait triompher de tous les efforts de la volonté, de toutes les délicatesses de la pensée. Raymon oublia tout, et ses résolutions, et son nouvel amour, et le lieu où il était. Il rendit à Noun ses caresses délirantes. (104)

There is something profoundly egalitarian in the shared eroticism of this scene. But in Raymon's imagination, this experience of submission to women's sexuality is frighteningly dangerous. He can only conceptualize Noun's forthright sexuality in terms of what he sees as Indiana's angelic lack of sexuality. Coming back to his "senses" and addressing his thoughts to Indiana, Raymon bemoans his encounter with Noun and casts it and her in a demonic light:

> Quels songes impurs, quelles pensées âcres et dévorantes ne viendront pas à ton cerveau pour le dessécher? Ton sommeil, pur comme celui d'un enfant, quelle divinité chaste voudra le protéger maintenant? N'ai-je pas ouvert au démon de la luxure l'entrée de ton alcôve?... L'ardeur insensée qui consume les flancs de cette créole lascive ne viendra-t-elle pas... s'attacher aux tiens pour les ronger? (106)

Raymon's tendency to pit the two women against each other results in an inability to see either of them. Earlier he had been unwilling to read the letter that Noun sent him ("C'était peut-être un chef-d'oeuvre de passion naïve et gracieuse; Virginie n'en écrivit peut-être pas une plus charmante à Paul lorsqu'elle eut quitté sa patrie.... Mais M. de Ramière se hâta de la jeter au feu" [77]). Likewise, Raymon's expressed regrets show a profound *mis*reading of Indiana's situation. We know that what he assumes to be Indiana's tranquil innocence, "[son] sommeil pur comme celui d'un enfant", is a far cry from the actual sleepless and pain-filled nights she experiences regularly, nights that contribute to the "feminine" frailty Raymon finds so tantalizing.

In Raymon's imagination, the two women shift into and out of the whore/madonna roles. On occasion, Indiana becomes the sexualized heroine, and Noun the submissive angel. This is the case when Raymon witnesses Indiana's remarkable behavior on horseback:

> Il ne se doutait pas que, dans cette femme si frêle et en apparence si timide, résidât un courage plus que masculin.... Raymon fut effrayé de la voir courir ainsi, se livrant sans peur à la fougue de ce cheval qu'elle connaissait à peine, le lancer hardiment dans le taillis, éviter avec une adresse étonnante les branches dont la vigueur élastique fouettait son visage, franchir les fossés sans hésitation, se hasarder avec confiance dans les terrains glaiseux et mouvants, ne s'inquiétant pas de briser ses membres fluets, mais jalouse d'arriver la première sur la piste fumante du sanglier. Tant de résolution l'effraya et faillit le dégoûter de madame Delmare. Les hommes, et les amants surtout, ont la fatuité innocente de vouloir protéger la faiblesse plutôt que d'admirer le courage chez les femmes. L'avouerai-je? Raymon se sentit épouvanté de tout ce qu'un esprit si intrépide promettait de hardiesse et de ténacité en amour. (162)[34]

Indiana's impressive maneuvering on horseback attests to her capacity for sensual experience *other* than bodily pain. In Raymon's imagination, these momentary signs of life shift Indiana into what had previously been Noun's role. Confronted with Indiana expressing vitality and pleasure, he compares her in negative terms to the now-dead Noun, whom he has transformed in his imagination into a timid creature: "Ce n'était plus le coeur résigné de la pauvre Noun, qui aimait mieux se noyer que de lutter contre son malheur" (162). For Raymon, which role the woman occupies ultimately seems less important than that she occupy one or the other.

As was the case with Delmare, Raymon's behavior in his personal life is inseparable from his behavior in public life. He is a glib journalist with an ability to convince his listener/reader of almost any position on any issue. While he claims his views are based on principles, these shift incessantly according to the needs of particular individuals within a particular power structure, in this case the constitutional monarchy:[35]

> Dispensé par sa fortune d'écrire pour de l'argent, Raymon écrivait par goût et (disait-il) par devoir. Cette rare faculté qu'il possédait, de réfuter par le talent la vérité positive, en avait fait un homme précieux au ministère. (130)

Indeed, Raymon in his public and private lives is a storyteller, a teller of fictions. And yet, again and again, Raymon accuses the women in his life of behaving as if *they* were characters in a novel when they make demands on him or show surprise at his behavior. In these moments, he implies that novels are simply women's foolishness rather than an integral part of the world *he* inhabits.

Shortly into Indiana's (unconsummated) love affair with Raymon, Delmare suddenly loses his wealth and announces to his wife that they must return to île Bourbon. On the eve of their planned departure, Indiana breaks out of her house (where her husband has literally locked her in) and goes to the Ramière residence. She waits for Raymon in his chambers, thereby losing all claim to public respectability. Raymon has already foreseen "qu'un instant viendrait le mettre aux prises avec cet amour de femme, qu'il faudrait défendre sa liberté contre les exigences d'une passion romanesque" (234). When he arrives home after a long and festive night to find Indiana waiting for him, he cries out: "Dans quel roman à l'usage des femmes de chambre avez-vous rêvé l'amour, je vous prie?" (221).

But the romanesque project to live together outside the law that Raymon attributes to Indiana's imagination and to novels is actually a project that Raymon and Indiana conceived together on the evening of their second meeting. Sand's prose blends the perspectives of the two participants on the evening of the ball. The narrator moves from reporting the thoughts of one character in the *style indirect libre* to reporting those of the other with no clearly defined transition between the two:

> Elle ne pensa pas non plus que cet homme pouvait être menteur ou frivole. Elle le vit comme elle le désirait, comme elle l'avait rêvé, et Raymon eût pu la tromper, s'il n'eût pas été sincère. Mais comment n'eût-il pas été auprès d'une femme si belle et si aimante? Quelle autre s'était jamais montrée à lui avec autant de candeur et d'innocence? Chez qui avait-il trouvé à placer un avenir si riant et si sûr? N'était-elle pas née pour l'aimer, cette femme esclave qui n'attendait qu'un signe pour briser sa chaîne, qu'un mot pour le suivre? Le ciel, sans doute, l'avait formée pour Raymon, cette triste enfant de l'île Bourbon, que personne n'avait aimée, et qui sans lui devait mourir. (90)

The first portion of the passage describes Indiana's perspective ("Elle ne pensa pas . . . rêvé"), and the second Raymon's perspective ("Raymon eût pu la tromper . . . si sûr"). Finally the third passage once again presents Indiana's perspective ("N'était-elle pas née pour l'aimer . . . mourir")—for how could Raymon, meeting her unexpectedly at this ball after only the encounter in which she had nursed his wound, know that she was from the île Bourbon and that she had never been loved? Thanks to the omniscience of the narrator, we find in this remarkable passage an agreement between the two on the terms of a still-unspoken project.[36] *Both* characters imagine devoting themselves to each other in a joyously secure future.

In fact, it is clear that Raymon takes the more active role in initiating the romance plots into which he encourages both Noun and Indiana to enter. To cite but one example, Raymon sneaks into the Delmare residence following the evening of the ball and falls at Indiana's feet with the following rush of words:

> Ce ne sont pas des circonstances vulgaires qui nous ont réunis, vois-tu; ce n'est ni le hasard ni le caprice, c'est la fatalité, c'est la mort, qui m'ont ouvert les portes de cette vie nouvelle. . . . Reste là, Indiana, reste contre mon coeur, c'est là ton refuge et ton abri. Aime-moi, et je serai invulnérable. (96)

He continues to participate in and to encourage the coauthorship of this romance plot even when he has given up any relationship between the fiction and the events of his life: "Il se retrancha dans l'opinion où il était que [Indiana] appliquait maintenant à sa situation l'exagération des sentiments qu'elle avait puisée dans les livres. Il s'évertua à l'éloquence passionnée, à l'improvisation dramatique, afin de se maintenir au niveau de sa romanesque maîtresse, et il réussit à prolonger son erreur" (205). When Indiana enters into his story without making distinctions between what happens in books and what happens in life, enters his story with her heart and her soul, Raymon accuses *her* of being *romanesque*. Indiana and Noun, as his trusting "readers," are left dead or abandoned when he fails to make good on his *romanesque* promises. Raymon presents the women's stories in the same manner as he writes his articles, to assure himself immediate gratification without true concern for the fates of his readers.[37] In this way, Sand's novel points out how dangerous it is for women to take at face value the ubiquitous love plots of sentimental fiction, be they passion plots or bourgeois marriage plots.

After Raymon's refusal to take her under his wing, Indiana, stunned and desperate, comes close to repeating Noun's passion/death plot by drowning herself in the Seine. Indiana's plunge is cut short, however, by Ralph and his dog Ophélia, who come upon Indiana ankle deep in the river. After rubbing her numbed feet, Ralph accompanies her home. This felicitous twist in the traditional passion plot—Indiana survives—opens the way for the presentation of a new plot. In fact, the protagonist emerges from her disastrous experience with Raymon to assume a stronger position than she had held before she met him. Indiana is able to articulate her resistance to her husband more forcefully and directly than earlier, when her only communication had taken the form of hysterical symptoms. When her husband's violence takes concrete rather than abstract form, Indiana finds her tongue:

> Je sais que je suis l'esclave et vous le seigneur. La loi de ce pays vous a fait mon maître. Vous pouvez lier mon corps, garrotter mes mains, gouverner mes actions. Vous avez le droit du plus fort, et la société vous le confirme; mais sur ma volonté, monsieur, vous ne pouvez rien, Dieu seul peut la courber et la réduire. (232)

When Delmare refers to Indiana's words as "des phrases de roman," he is not referring to the same sentences that defined the plots we have thus far considered. Here they refer to sentences that subvert dominant plots. Just what these plots composed of such "phrases de roman" might consist in, is articulated in a long letter

Indiana writes to Raymon after she has returned to île Bourbon with her husband. She is responding to a letter from Raymon in which the clichés of what I have been referring to as the "old plots" stand out. Raymon writes:

> Je vous l'ai dit souvent Indiana, vous n'êtes pas une femme, et, quand j'y songe dans le calme de mes pensées, vous êtes un ange. Je vous adore dans mon coeur comme une divinité. . . . Pourquoi, pur esprit, avais-tu pris la forme tentatrice d'une femme? Pourquoi, ange de lumière, avais-tu revêtu les séductions de l'enfer? Souvent j'ai cru tenir le bonheur dans mas bras, et tu n'étais que la vertu. (240)

After this reduction of Indiana once again into a bipolar being, at once angel and demon, he congratulates himself, and her too, for not giving in to the temptations of the flesh: "Dieu nous récompensera d'un tel effort; car Dieu est bon. Il nous réunira dans une vie plus heureuse" (242).

Raymon's words, which have always assured him success in both public and private affairs, are here refused by Indiana. Indiana begins her response to Raymon with an apology for disturbing him and a claim that she is writing to ease his mind. She urges him to forget her, and assures him she is well: "Soyez heureux, soyez insouciant; oubliez-moi; je vis encore, et peut-être vivrai-je longtemps. . ." (245). But from this passive, forgiving posture, she moves quickly to less docile tones, particularly in her response to Raymon's earlier charge that she has imagined her life in terms typical of "des romans à l'usage des femmes de chambre." Rather than denying the charge, Indiana embraces it and defines the ladies' novel as a potential means of resistance to the social limitations placed on women like herself. She turns Raymon's accusation that she is overly *romanesque* back on him by suggesting that it is he who is not *romanesque* enough:

> C'est que, selon votre expression cynique, j'avais appris la vie dans les romans à l'usage des femmes de chambre, dans ces riantes et puériles fictions où l'on intéresse le coeur au succès de folles entreprises et d'impossibles félicités . . . j'ai puisé dans l'exaltation de mes sentiments la force de me placer dans une situation d'invraisemblance et de roman, et que vous, homme de coeur, vous n'ayez pas trouvé dans votre volonté celle de m'y suivre. (247)

Indiana associates novels here with sentiment and implausibility.

In "Vraisemblance et motivation," Gérard Genette describes the relationship of plausibility to ideology:

> C'est-à-dire un corps de maximes et de préjugés qui constitue tout à la fois une vision du monde et un système de valeurs. . . . Ce qui subsiste, et qui définit le vraisemblable, c'est le principe formel de respect de la norme, c'est-à-dire l'existence d'un rapport d'implication entre la conduite particulière attribuée à un tel personnage, et telle maxime générale implicite et reçue.[38]

Indiana's refusal to behave "plausibly" represents then a refusal to adhere to certain maxims governing feminine behavior within a particular political structure. Indiana undermines this particular world view by showing how it rests on a specific conception of God, the guarantor of truth and of legitimacy within it:

> Ne m'exhortez pas à penser à Dieu; . . . Pour moi, j'ai plus de foi que vous; je ne sers pas le même Dieu, mais je le sers mieux, et plus purement. Le vôtre, c'est le dieu des hommes, c'est le roi, le fondateur et l'appui de votre race; le mien, c'est le Dieu de l'univers, le créateur, le soutien et l'espoir de toutes les créatures. . . . Vous vous croyez les maîtres du monde; je crois que vous n'en êtes que les tyrans. . . . Toute votre morale, tous vos principes, ce sont les intérêts de votre société que vous avez érigés en lois et que vous prétendez faire émaner de Dieu. (248–249)[39]

Indiana, the survivor of both the marriage plot and the passion plot, here defends her right to imagine and inhabit an entirely different social structure from the one in which Delmare and Raymon wield such power. Her hysterical symptoms have found a way into the language of dominant culture, a way into the words of novels, at least for a short while.

ALL IN THE (SAINT-SIMONIAN) FAMILY

> Mes soeurs, ma mère! vous serez obéies, vous serez aimées par delà tous les siècles! Car le règne de Dieu commence et le règne de Dieu n'aura pas de fin, et là où toute puissance, tout amour sont enlevés à la force brutale, vous avez des droits à la gloire aussi bien qu'à l'amour.
> —Anonymous exhortation to Saint-Simonian "family" gathering, circa 1830

Sand, in the preface to the 1852 version of *Indiana*, writes: "Du temps que je fis *Indiana*, on criait au saint-simonisme à propos de tout" (36). Her evocation of the Saint-Simonians, even in the form of an implicit denial of their influence, points to the importance of utopian socialist ideas during the period in which she began writing. "On criait au saint-simonisme à propos de tout" because the Saint-Simonians were in fact a significant presence in the social and intellectual landscape of the early 1830s.[40] The Saint-Simonians began to give public lectures in the late 1820s, and by 1832 their meetings were drawing significant public attendance.[41] Despite her disclaimers, Sand does refer to the Saint-Simonians in her correspondence in the early 1830s, sometimes quite favorably.[42] We have no way of knowing whether Sand was sincere in her denials of Saint-Simonian influence, although in 1852 she certainly had reason to distance herself from a movement whose ideals were given up after the 1848 revolution. What concerns me here is not Sand's sincerity or lack thereof, but rather the ways in which utopian socialist ideas, borrowed consciously or unconsciously, function in *Indiana*.

The Saint-Simonians were not a literary movement, but rather a social and religious movement. The "père" Enfantin who headed the movement from the late 1820s through the early 1830s, "rejected radical individualism in favor of a harmonious association of differentiated classes and . . . sexes."[43] In accordance with this vision, Enfantin imagined a family that extended beyond the boundaries of the nuclear family to include members linked by cooperation and mutual support—what the utopian socialists termed "association"—rather than by blood.

We find a rendition of this anti-individualistic notion of family in *Indiana*. Let us return for a moment to the opening scene in the Delmare salon. The only sign of tenderness and vitality is presented in animal rather than human form. Ralph's dog, the bright-eyed, furry Ophélia, "heureuse et caressante" (51), enters the room and, after being reprimanded by her master, approaches Indiana. The dog's presence provides an outlet for Delmare's pent-up frustrations. As M. Delmare pulls out his hunting whip and approaches the cowering dog, Indiana holds on to the dog protectively and begs her husband to show pity: "De grâce monsieur, ne la tuez-pas!" (54). In the argument that ensues—to which the narrator ironically refers as a "conversation conjugale"—, we learn that Indiana has good reason to expect the worst: Delmare has already killed Indiana's beloved spaniel. Some moments later, a servant announces that he suspects an intruder on the Delmare premises, probably a coal thief. Delmare claims that "[il] le tuera comme un chien" (56). In response to his wife's protests he adds disdainfully: "Si vous connaissiez la loi, madame, vous sauriez qu'elle m'y autorise."

Sand immediately sets up a coalition of sorts among Indiana, Ophélia, and the intruder, who is assumed to be a poor wretch (but who in fact turns out to be Raymon de Ramière) all united in the face of Delmare's violence and the law that legitimizes his behavior. Over the course of the novel, the number of members of this "family" expands through a system of echoes and analogies. Noun is related to Indiana through their shared childhood as well as their exploitation at the hands of Raymon. Noun's death by drowning is echoed by Indiana's near-drowning in the Seine and by Ophélia's eventual death as well.[44] In Sand's novel, the bonds between these beings unrelated by blood undermine the validity of the Delmare "family" by showing its destructiveness to all involved. They set up an ideal that transcends the nest version of the family to move toward a broader conception of fraternity (and sorority)—which challenges notions of bourgeois individualism rooted in the nuclear family.

One of the last engravings in the illustrated version of Bernardin de Saint-Pierre's enormously successful *Paul et Virginie*—a work that plays an important role in *Indiana*—depicts the virginal heroine Virginie rising angelically, her finger pointing toward the distant glow of heaven. The Saint-Simonians conceived of heaven as something quite different from this apotheosis of domestic bliss. Saint-Simon wrote in 1824: "L'âge d'or n'est pas dans le passé, il est dans l'avenir."[45] According to Saint-Simonian doctrine, the new familial economy of "association," less private and less selfish than its bourgeois counterpart, would be realized in a future paradise on earth. Saint-Simonian thought brought heaven down to earth in a utopian vision of the future. Adherents believed that this golden age of egalitarianism and cooperation would be overseen by a benevolent and socially concerned God.

This idea of a providential history is frequently evoked in *Indiana*. We see it in the narrator's repeated references to the instability of historical processes in passages such as the following: "Je vous parle d'un temps bien loin de nous, aujourd'hui que l'on ne compte plus par siècles, ni même par règnes, mais par ministères" (128). Several times, Ralph refers to this condition of instability as a precursor to a stable and more just social organization. In reference to Raymon, for example, we read:

C'étaient des hommes d'un grand talent, en effet, que ceux qui retenaient encore la société près de crouler dans l'abîme, et qui, suspendus eux-mêmes entre deux écueils, luttaient avec calme et aisance contre la rude vérité qui allait les engloutir. (130–131)

The utopian socialist aspect of this future "rude vérité" becomes even more explicit in Indiana's letter to Raymon from île Bourbon in which she discusses her very utopian socialist notion of God, "le Dieu de toutes les créatures":

Vous pensez que Dieu vous protège et vous autorise à usurper l'empire de la terre; moi, je pense qu'il le souffre pour un peu de temps, et qu'un jour viendra où, comme des grains de sable, son souffle vous dispersera. (249)

Significantly, it is during the time on île Bourbon when Indiana is, so to speak, between couple plots—that is, when she is thinking less about Raymon in France ("elle s'habituait à penser moins à Raymon" [274]) and has not yet been introduced into Ralph's plot—that Indiana is the most forward-looking in her vision and independent in her actions. Ophélia, her beloved dog, is still alive, and Ralph figures as a comforting presence, but he keeps his distance. Indiana is free to explore the island and to dream. In her letter to Raymon from île Bourbon, Indiana has already described her dreams:

Voilà mes rêves; ils sont tous d'une autre vie, d'un autre monde où la loi du brutal n'aura point passé sur la tête du pacifique, où du moins la résistance et la fuite ne seront pas des crimes, où l'homme pourra échapper à l'homme, comme la gazelle échappe à la panthère, sans que la chaîne des lois soit tendue autour de lui. (250)

Sand's descriptions of her reveries during her solitary forays in the wilderness suggest a link between her social vision as described above and a new sexual economy:

Suspendue à une grande élévation au-dessus du sol de la côte, et voyant fuir sous ses yeux les gorges qui la séparaient de l'Océan, il lui semblait être lancée dans cet espace par un mouvement rapide.... Dans ce rêve, elle se cramponnait au rocher qui lui servait d'appui; et pour qui eût observé alors ses yeux avides, son sein haletant d'impatience et l'effrayante expression de joie répandue sur ses traits, elle eût offert tous les symptômes de la folie.... Chez elle tout se rapportait ... à une ardente aspiration vers un point qui n'était ni le souvenir, ni l'espoir, ni le regret, mais le désir dans toute son intensité dévorante. (254)

The combination of a new social vision with this frankly erotic evocation of female extramarital desire contributes to making this "in-between plot" the richest and most subversive of all Sand's subplots. The narrator refers to Indiana's reveries as "[des] projets romanesques et [des] projets extravagants" (273), pointing toward a new novel that might truly subvert the family romance. But Sand is writing in 1832, and she has to make a living. The Ralph-and-Indiana romance is waiting in the wings.

AFTER THE FALL (AT BERNICA): INDIANA AND SIR RALPH'S "NATURAL MARRIAGE"

> Les femmes n'ont encore rien à dire, ce me semble. Que feront-elles par la révolte? Quand le monde mâle sera converti, la femme le sera sans qu'on ait besoin de s'en occuper.
> George Sand, *Correspondance*

Thus far, I have given little attention to Indiana's cousin and faithful friend, Ralph. He is a constant if restrained presence throughout Sand's novel, his life story (also Indiana's life story) recounted in short passages between what I have referred to as the marriage plot and the passion plot. In these passages we learn that Ralph, like Indiana, was rejected as a child from the house of his father, and that he and Indiana, along with Noun, spent all their days together exploring île Bourbon's plethora of hills and valleys. This seemingly blissful state of affairs continued until Ralph, called upon to marry his brother's widow, moved to England. He is ten years older than Indiana, seven years older than Noun. By the time he returned to the island—after the death of his wife—Indiana was married to Delmare, and the couple was preparing to leave for France. Ralph, unable to bear his solitude on île Bourbon, bought himself a piece of land near Lagny, the Delmare property, and introduced himself into the Delmare household with the following proposition to Indiana's husband:

> Monsieur, j'aime votre femme; c'est moi qui l'ai élevée; je la regarde comme ma soeur, et plus encore comme ma fille.... Quand je vous

aurai donné ma parole que je n'eus jamais d'amour pour elle et que je n'en aurai jamais, vous pourrez me voir avec aussi peu d'inquiétude que si j'étais réellement votre beau-frère. N'est-il pas vrai monsieur? (159)

At that time, Delmare, convinced that Ralph posed no danger to his marriage, honorably accepted the offer. Indiana, equally convinced, considered Ralph to be a passionless and egotistical presence in the household. He has been living at Lagny for several years when we are introduced to the Delmare family in the opening pages of Sand's novel.

Throughout the novel, Ralph's position in the social structure is presented as different from that of the other male characters. Both Delmare and Raymon hold well-defined roles in the public sphere. Delmare represents a bourgeois who has made, and then lost, his fortune according to the competitive laws of the market. Raymon represents a class of opportunistic aristocrats who use their influence and connections (in Raymon's case through his pen) to balance themselves on the edge of precarious reigning political systems in such a way that their own comforts are consistently assured. The presentation of both Delmare and Raymon makes clear that their public lives are inseparable from their private lives. As we have seen, Sand seems to undermine the notion, prevalent even among the most critical romantics, that personal life takes place in some private psychological realm outside society. Sand provides no comparable role for Ralph in public life. He is associated with a political view, but it is not one linked to a series of routine daily activities, as are the political views of Delmare and Raymon. In the political arguments that become ever more frequent among the men in the Delmare household once Raymon has entered the picture, Ralph consistently supports what is nominally a republican point of view:

> Ralph allait donc toujours soutenant son rêve de république d'où il voulait exclure tous les abus, tous les préjugés, toutes les injustices, projet fondé tout entier sur l'espoir d'une nouvelle race d'hommes. (167)

Ralph's "rêve de république" and his "nouvelle race d'hommes" seem to be consistent with Indiana's dream of "une autre vie, un autre monde où la loi brutale n'aura point passé sur la tête du pacifique" (250). Ralph's position recalls the forward-looking vision prevalent among utopian socialists and especially among the Saint-Simonians as much as it does a past revolutionary ideal. This vision, however, is complicated by its association with the works of Bernardin de Saint-Pierre, and in particular with his *Paul et Virginie*.

Paul et Virginie is a topos throughout Sand's novel. The first reference to the work is in Noun's passion plot with Raymon. Noun's letters—which never have much of an effect on Raymon—are compared by the narrator to those that Virginie might have written: "Virginie n'en écrivait peut-être pas une plus charmante à Paul lorsqu'elle eut quitté sa patrie . . . mais M. de Ramière se hâta de la jeter au feu, dans la crainte de rougir de lui-même" (77). We find a second reference to Bernardin's work in Sand's descriptions of Indiana's bedroom, its walls adorned with lithographs depicting scenes from the lives of Paul and Virginie:[46]

> Le goût exquis et la simplicité chaste qui présidaient à l'ameublement; ces livres d'amour et de voyages, épars sur les planches d'acajou; ce métier chargé d'un travail si joli et si frais, oeuvre de patience et de mélancolie; cette harpe dont les cordes semblaient encore vibrer des chants d'attente et de tristesse; ces gravures qui représentaient les pastorales amours de Paul et de Virginie, les cimes de l'île Bourbon et les rivages bleus de Saint-Paul; . . . tout révélait madame Delmare. (101)

Sand's interweaving of themes from Bernardin's well-known novel into *Indiana* is certainly more than simple pastoral decoration. The juxtaposition of Paul and the Créole Virginie's "pastorales amours" with Raymon's seduction of the Créole Noun in the Créole Indiana's bed invites comment. We might read the lithographs as the myth of romantic (familial) love in contrast to the much less palatable reality of romantic love represented in Raymon's passion plots first with Noun and then with Indiana. These plots might serve as critiques then of the *Paul et Virginie* plot. But this reading would lead us far astray in the consideration of Sand's novel as a whole. Despite the critiques we have thus far considered, *Indiana* is not readily classified as an antiromantic novel. On the contrary, in the final love story between Ralph and Indiana, Sand exalts romantic love, and Bernardin's vision plays an important role in this exaltation.

To come to some understanding of Sand's return to Bernardin, it is helpful to take a brief detour through *Paul et Virginie*. Bernardin published his novel in 1788, on the very eve of the French Revolution. The novel went through thirty editions between 1789 and 1799, more than any other novel during the same period and, as was the case with *La Nouvelle Héloïse*, resulted in hundreds of fan letters to the author.[47] Bernardin, like Rousseau, preached a "return" to nature and virtue. In the preface to *Paul et Virginie*, he states: "Notre bonheur consiste à vivre suivant la nature et la vertu."[48] His novel tells the story of two children who grow up in a feminized paradise far removed from the world of France and of kings, where they taste the delights of intrafamilial love and sensuality. Blissfully ignorant of political or economic events, they live with their single mothers (one is a widow, the other was callously abandoned by a nobleman), each day reveling in nature and mutual tenderness:

> Ils croyaient que le monde finissait où finissait leur île, et ils n'imaginaient rien d'aimable où ils n'étaient pas. Leur affection mutuelle et celle de leurs mères occupaient toute l'activité de leurs âmes.[49]

In case of any doubt that what is being portrayed is a new ideal of the family, Bernardin points it out explicitly in his repeated references to this small group of individuals as "les familles heureuses" or "ces familles si unies." Additionally, we find a strikingly explicit lesson on the naturalness of the small loving family in the following exclamation adressed to Paul by Virginie:

> O mon frère! les rayons du soleil au matin, au haut de ces rochers, me donnent moins de joie que ta présence. J'aime bien ma mère, j'aime bien la tienne; mais, quand elles t'appellent mon fils, je les aime encore davantage. Les caresses qu'elles te font me sont plus sensibles que celles que j'en reçois. Tu me demandes pourquoi tu m'aimes; mais tout ce qui a été élevé ensemble s'aime. Vois nos oiseaux: élevés dans les mêmes nids, ils s'aiment comme nous; ils sont toujours ensemble comme nous.[50]

Amidst the economic and political changes underway in France, Bernardin proposed what *seemed* to his readers an escape from the turmoil. In fact, far from being an escape, his vision was intimately linked to events in France. He, like Rousseau, presents a naturalized, private, affectionate family from which emerge the self-conscious individuals demanded by capitalism.[51] *Paul et Virginie* celebrates privacy and domesticity in a utopian world where the public sphere is so remote as to be nonexistent. While this may seem incompatible with the *embourgeoisement* of society, where the two spheres are interdependent, and where the public sphere justifies its existence by producing material abundance, I would argue that in fact it is not. One of the qualities of the new intimate sphere was that it *seemed* entirely independent from outside forces. Goulemot makes this point:

> Je suis Paul ou je suis Virginie; ce que le livre raconte, c'est mon histoire; ce qu'éprouvent les héros, ce sont mes sentiments, mes aspirations, mes émotions. Le livre agit comme un révélateur et la lecture comme une reconnaissance de soi et un déchiffrement. Ce que je ressentais en moi et n'arrivais pas à exprimer, cette intimité profonde, ce caché spécifique, voilà qu'un livre lu par hasard, assis sur un banc, à l'ombre d'un arbre, me permet soudain de le comprendre et d'en avoir une conscience claire.[52]

The "je" thus interpellated is precisely the one demanded by the public sphere. Focusing on women in the home, Bernardin's presentation of an isolated feminine utopia is entirely in keeping with the imagination of the private sphere, which, with its complementary opposite of the public sphere, was defined as a whole against the structure of absolute monarchy.

While Bernardin focuses on the private realm, discussions of the social and political complement to his familial vision occasionally creep in. He opposes one social structure, symbolized by the loving "family," against another in the following passage, which transcribes the words of Paul's mother, Madame de La Tour, to her companion, Marguerite (who is also Virginie's mother): "J'ai goûté plus de consolation et de félicité avec vous, sous ces pauvres cabanes, que jamais les richesses de ma famille ne m'en ont fait même espérer dans ma patrie" (66)[53]. Here Madame de La Tour (note the aristocratic particle) expresses to her bourgeois friend how happy she is to be part of a loving family and how relieved to be free of her previous aristocratic existence. The monarchy, historically the protector of the aristocracy, is also presented in negative terms as a system in which it is impossible for most individual subjects to achieve well-being: "Le roi est un soleil que les grands et les corps environnent comme des nuages; il est presque impossible qu'un de ses rayons tombe sur vous."[54]

Just as Paul and Virginie are feeling their first pubescent sexual pangs within the family, Virginie is called upon to leave for France to stay with a rich aunt who has promised to make the young girl her protégée. Bernardin's France, represented by Virginie's great aunt, is overly invested in old-regime values, including some semblance of education for women and arranged marriages. This France scorns

Virginie's bourgeois aspirations of becoming a good housewife. Virginie writes to her mother from France:

> Ma grand'tante fut bien surprise à mon arrivée, lorsque, m'ayant questionnée sur mes talents, je lui dis que je ne savais ni lire ni écrire. Elle me demanda qu'est-ce que j'avais donc appris depuis que j'étais au monde; et, quand je lui eus répondu que c'était à avoir soin d'un ménage et faire votre volonté, elle me répondit que j'avais reçu l'éducation d'une servante. Elle me mit, dès le lendemain, en pension dans une grande abbaye auprès de Paris, où j'ai de si faibles dispositions pour toutes les sciences, que je ne profiterai pas beaucoup avec ces messieurs. (87)

Bernardin's heroine, almost certainly modeled on Rousseau's Sophie, is willfully inept at any kind of learning not linked to her role in the domestic realm. She has no ambition to participate in any activities other than those preparing her for her place within the confines of the bourgeois family. Her domestic (and sexual) purity, untarnished by public matters, is elevated to mythical heights by the conclusion to Bernardin's novel. When Virginie refuses the marriage her great aunt arranges for her in the traditional mode of the old regime, Virginie is sent back to her family across seas made turbulent by winter storms. Any sympathies the reader might have had with this aunt's position are hereby extinguished. Bernardin makes it clear that the timing of Virginie's return to her "family" was calculated to assure the highest degree of danger. His novel in hardly veiled terms puts the blame for Virginie's eventual death squarely in this aristocratic woman's hands, underlining Rousseau's theory that aristocratic (public) women were a menace to society. The boat that carries Virginie homeward sinks in sight of the shoreline from which Paul, helpless, watches his beloved Virginie drown. She might have been saved but, unwilling to undress for the swim across the waters, she is doomed. Virginie's elaborate funeral is attended by all the islanders, and the reader is invited to interiorize her image as the essence of true womanhood.

Bernardin's novel continued to be read well into the nineteenth century. In fact, the work was read more widely during the Restoration than before.[55] Some of this can be explained by advances in printing technology, but certainly other reasons prolonged the novel's success. Arguably, Bernardin's presentation of familial issues reaffirmed readers' views of themselves as privatized individuals within the politically tumultuous post-revolutionary society; that is, it served as a conservative rather than disruptive force. His myth of a natural private life provided psychic stability within a culture rocked by the broad array of post-revolutionary, post-empire political positions.

Let us return to *Indiana*. After Ralph has saved Indiana from the boarding house where she lies destitute and dying after Raymon's second rejection, the two return to île Bourbon where they plan to commit suicide together.[56] On a moonlit night the two "promeneurs solitaires" make their way through fragrant foliage to Bernica, a steep-walled valley in which they spent many days together as children.[57] There have already been hints regarding Ralph's true feelings for Indiana: certain glances, his near-suicide when he fears that Indiana may have died, the fact that he kisses her on the lips, and so forth. But it is only in the final pages of the fourth (and last) book, as Ralph and Indiana prepare for the leap into the shared deliverance of suicide *à deux*, that Ralph finally makes explicit his story. Ralph, whose verbal clumsiness has been contrasted throughout the novel with Raymon's verbal facility, is at last able to speak. Through his tale, imbued with passion finally set free, we learn that he suffered as much as did Indiana from what he calls the "simulacrum légal" (323) of the Delmare marriage.[57] Ralph's story, the true marriage plot as opposed to this simulacrum, is laden with references to *Paul et Virginie*.[58] Above the cataracts crashing into the abyss below, he tells Indiana:

> Quand je vous lisais l'histoire de Paul et Virginie vous ne la compreniez qu'à demi. Vous pleuriez, cependant; vous aviez vu l'histoire d'un frère et d'une soeur là où j'avais frissonné de sympathie en apercevant les angoisses de deux amants. . . . Moi, je relisais seul les entretiens de Paul et de son amie, les impétueux soupçons de l'un, les secrètes souffrances de l'autre. Oh! que je les comprenais bien, ces premières inquiétudes de l'adolescence, qui cherche dans son coeur l'explication des mystères de la vie, et qui s'empare avec enthousiasme du premier objet d'amour qui s'offre à lui. (318)

Ralph's description of falling in love with Indiana, "le premier objet d'amour qui s'offre à lui," echoes Virginie's "tout ce qui a été élevé ensemble s'aime." Again and again Ralph, a cousin by marriage to Indiana, emphasizes a more immediate familial relationship with his beloved:

> Je fis de vous ma soeur, ma fille, ma compagne, mon élève, ma société. . . . Vous n'étiez que mon enfant, ou tout au plus ma petite soeur; mais

j'étais amoureux de vos quinze ans quand, livré seul à l'ardeur des miens, je dévorais l'avenir d'un oeil avide. (316–317)

Like Paul and Virginie, the two lovers in this "natural" marriage are presented as symbolically linked by blood, their desire incestuous.

Thus far, my reading of *Indiana* has suggested that Sand was highly *critical* of bourgeois domesticity and the position in which it placed women, that she *de*romanticizes the domestic interior by showing its complicity with oppressive economic and political positions. She also imagines an alternative realm in her incorporation of utopian socialist notions of progress toward a less competitive, more egalitarian society. If, as I have suggested, Bernardin's novel constitutes an extended hymn to bourgeois domesticity, what are we to make of Sand's weaving its themes through her novel, and in particular through descriptions of the relationship between Indiana and Ralph? How are we to resolve Sand's critique of the private domestic sphere with her celebration of Bernardin? These questions point to fundamental ambiguities in Sand's relationship to the myth and the reality of gendered public and private spheres. Up until this point, Sand's novel constitutes a scathing critique of both the nuclear family and the free-market economy based on individual competitiveness. In the final pages of her novel, however, she looks nostalgically toward the vision of domestic bliss that Bernardin provides. After opening the possibility of new conceptions of public and private lives, Sand in the final marriage scene and the following conclusion presents what has become a conservative vision.

Indeed, the marriage ceremony between Indiana and Ralph is entirely compatible with bourgeois notions of romantic love. Indiana is dressed in white at Ralph's request: "Si j'ai mérité d'être sauvé, j'ai mérité de te posséder. C'est dans ces idées que je t'ai priée de revêtir cet habit blanc; c'est la robe de noces" (329). (Significantly, the custom of bridal whites was inaugurated in the mid-eighteenth century while the bourgeois family was emerging.) Any suggestion of the adulterous nature of Indiana's relationship with Ralph is doubly offset; first by the fact that her legal husband is dead, secondly by the fact that Indiana is still a virgin when she "marries" Ralph at the "altar" above the waterfall. Moreover, Ralph, who himself has fathered a child with another woman, puts great stock in Indiana's purity: "J'eusse souffert de voir un autre homme vous donner une parcelle de bien-être, un instant de satisfaction, c'eût été un vol que l'on m'eût fait" (327).

As in Françoise de Graffigny's *Lettres d'une Péruvienne* and Isabelle de Charrière's *Lettres écrites de Lausanne*, we are invited to read beyond the ending. In Sand's brief conclusion, we learn that the planned suicide turns out instead to be a rebirth, the marriage a baptismal rite. In a sense, we are provided with a second, miniature "after-marriage plot." The narrator, now a flesh-and-blood participant in the events recounted, comes across Ralph and Indiana on a remote part of the island. The couple live alone together in a rustic cabin enjoying the same sort of timeless bliss depicted in the early portions of *Paul et Virginie*. The Saint-Simonian elements of their respective visions play no role in this after-plot. Indeed, both Noun and Ophélia, the other members of the Saint-Simonian family, are dead. Ralph and Indiana's isolation from the rest of the islanders is emphasized; the family folds back in on itself in a way that precludes Indiana moving out of the confines of domesticity. We are told: "Quant à madame Delmare, sa retraite avait été si absolue, que son existence était encore une chose problématique pour beaucoup d'habitants" (334). So much for Saint-Simonian notions of fraternity! Indiana speaks only to encourage her husband to do so and thereby, with a touch of coquetterie worthy of a Sophie, to invite the visitor to admire Ralph's great wisdom:

> Elle est avide d'apprendre ce que les préoccupations de sa vie l'ont empêché de savoir; et puis peut-être y eut-il un peu de coquetterie de sa part à questionner sir Ralph, afin de faire briller devant moi les immenses connaissances de son ami. (337)

While Indiana is presented as learning more than she was able to in her other plots, and presumably more than her counterparts Sophie and Virginie, this fact is softened by the narrator's suggestion that her questions may well be more for Ralph's sake than for her own. Indiana, in other words, is bound up in an old role.

The narrator tells Ralph:

> Quelques moralistes blâment votre solitude; ils prétendent que tout homme appartient à la société, qui le réclame. On ajoute que vous donnez aux hommes un exemple dangereux à suivre. (343)

This myth, presented as dangerous or subversive, in fact fully coincides with prevailing notions of privacy and individualism. Against the often robust critique found in the rest of the novel, we find posited a conservative rendition of the privatized "natural" family.[59]

I am not trying to prove here that Sand is somehow finally an antifeminist, that her work, because of its occasional nostalgia for a reromanticized version of the privatized family and the bourgeois elements of its conclusion, is *ultimately* complicitous with the romantic visions of domesticity that limited the emotional and intellectual horizons of a century of women.[60] For reasons we considered in the introduction to this chapter, one would imagine that Sand would be particulary sensitive to the hazards involved in transgressing certain conventions while writing her first independent work, particularly in the area of gender politics. Sand is the only nineteenth-century woman writer who has become canonized, and certainly this is linked to her concessions to certain romantic tropes, including the exaltation of the private sphere.

In her analysis of Sand's *Lettres à Marcie*, Naomi Schor suggests that Sand is ultimately unable to imagine a life not defined by gendered public and private spheres:

> Ce qui est non pas l'impensé mais l'impensable pour Sand c'est le franchissement par la femme (comme par l'homme) de la barre qui sépare les deux sphères. Pour Sand la séparation des sphères est sacrée, inscrite dans la nature, et doit être maintenue, car l'ordre social en dépend. (31)

My reading of the conclusion to *Indiana* supports Schor's view. Sand does indeed take the married romantic couple as a basic building block, confined within a household from which only the man may venture freely. I hope to have shown, however, that Sand's relationship to the division between public and private spheres is more complicated than Schor suggests. Sand's final glowing presentation of Indiana and Ralph's marriage hardly supplants completely the criticism of the institution we find in the rest of the novel. One critic's comment that *Indiana* constituted "un long cri contre le mariage" would seem to support this view.

If we move our focus away from Ralph and Indiana and toward the narrator in the volcanic landscape beyond the cabin, we discover a questioning of the public/private divide even in the conclusion to Sand's novel. I began my study of Sand with a consideration of her cross-voicing as a rhetorical strategy for transcending the barrier between public and private realms. The narrator in Sand's conclusion is both cross-voiced and cross-dressed (since he is now voice *and* body). "He" directs his words to Jules Neyraud, a naturalist whose work Sand draws on in her descriptions of île Bourbon: "Le sol avait conservé l'empreinte de vos pas" (331). Now the narrator's boots (presumably) like the ones Sand herself liked to wear are leaving their own impressions in the landscape. He is free to explore and record the private life of Indiana and Ralph but will return to the public world of France. Ralph tells him: "Allez jeune homme, poursuivez le cours de votre destinée; ayez des amis, un état, une réputation" (343).

Before arriving at Ralph and Indiana's cabin, the narrator comes across an intriguing phenomenon amidst the lavishly described tropical flora:

> Ces pierres volcaniques offrent souvent le même phénomène. Jadis leur substance, amollie par l'action du feu, reçut, tiède et malléable encore, l'empreinte des coquillages et des lianes qui s'y collèrent. De ces rencontres fortuites sont résultés des jeux bizarres, des impressions hiéroglyphiques, des caractères mystérieux, qui semblent jetés là comme le *seing* d'un être surnaturel, écrit en lettres cabalistiques. (332–333)

The narrator stands transfixed in front of the incomprehensible language transcribed in the volcanic rock:

> Je restai longtemps dominé par la puérile prétention de chercher un sens à ces chiffres inconnus. Ces inutiles recherches me firent tomber dans une méditation profonde pendant laquelle j'oubliai le temps qui fuyait.

We might see in these hieroglyphs, as in Indiana's earlier hysterical symptoms, a female language that, in the nineteenth century, could be included in the narrative, only by moments, or in coded form.[61]

Conclusion

THE HISTORY OF THE NOVEL GENRE AND OF THE FAMILY ARE INSEPARABLY linked. In a sense the novel is the space that psychologically made possible the emergence of the privatized affectionate family in the mid-eighteenth century. The genre allowed for intricate negotiations concerning new definitions of privacy linked to new subjectivities. These subjectivities accommodated the massive economic and political shifts underway in France before, during, and after the French Revolution. The novel, with its focus on the minute details of domestic life, reinforced the notion of a *chez soi*, and it was from this privatized home life that a self-consciously individualized "je" emerged into (and thereby made possible) the early public arena of free enterprise. Over the course of the eighteenth and nineteenth centuries the contours of this privatized family became increasingly well defined and at the same time highly impermeable to women who might try to cross the gender divide. By the nineteenth century the notion of a private life, now supported not just by novels but by a host of etiquette books, medical doctrines, and even laws, had effectively replaced the preexisting aristocratic family tradition. Even aristocrats adopted the bourgeois family style in an effort to differentiate themselves from what were perceived to be the excesses of the old regime.

The nest in which men achieved a new sense of individuality was defined in large part by the role it allotted women. Especially after Rousseau, women were encouraged to find fulfillment in the creation of the domestic interior. This new role of loving wife and mother—defined to some degree against the role of aristocratic women in the seventeenth century, who enjoyed a significant influence in intellectual and literary circles—demanded that women sacrifice their own public ambitions to those of their husband and children. Certainly many women embraced this new role and the status it conferred upon them. The fact that, especially during the early part of the eighteenth century, women wrote novels that, while participating in various ways in the creation of the emerging bourgeois social structure, also negotiated new female subjectivities other than those of wife and mother proves that some women, particularly women writers, were acutely aware of the limitations placed on them by the emerging system of gendered public and private spheres. They plotted ways out of the bourgeois family in its various stages of development by subverting the "family romance."

Of the three writers I treat, Graffigny wrote during the period in which the bourgeois family was the least well defined. The novel, at this point still considered a disreputable and disruptive form, was the sole domain in which women could claim a voice in public matters. Graffigny, in the context of an ethnographic novel, posits a "Peruvian" romantic love story in the spirit of the modern love match. The marriage plot is destined to "failure," however, because the European culture into which the lovers are introduced forbids incestuous unions. Graffigny exploits a contemporary anxiety with respect to incest to imagine an escape from the plot she herself sets up in the novel. She presents a woman able to realize her ambitions while still participating in the romance of the marriage plot. After Graffigny's heroine is abandoned by Aza, the Frenchman Déterville continues to be her devoted (and romantic) friend, despite the fact that Zilia refuses his proposal of marriage.

Zilia's most ecstatic moment takes place while traveling. She marvels at the wonders of the French landscape in terms that prefigure those of Rousseau in his *Rêveries d'un promeneur solitaire*. By the time Charrière wrote her *Lettres écrites de Lausanne*, Rousseau's celebration of nature had become a persuasive argument for well-defined gender roles in the privatized affectionate family. Women, discouraged from any public activity including writing, were presented as naturally suited to their responsibilities in the home. With Rousseau, gendered private and public spheres became an established part of the French imagination. In many ways, Charrière works within the terms provided by Rousseau. She presents a domestic interior in which a mother teaches her daughter the lessons of the world. Like Rousseau's Sophie, Charrière's Cécile is taught to deny her existence as a desiring subject and to protect her chastity at all costs. The mother puts a great deal of energy into grooming Cécile in such a way that she will be appealing to an eventual husband. In Charrière's novel, however, the projected love marriage never materializes because Milord, presented early on as the ideal lover, turns out to be nothing of the sort. He has no interest in marrying Cécile. Instead of arranging her novel exclusively around the marriage plot,

Charrière exploits the new focus on good motherhood to present an autonomous mother–child dyad. She ultimately celebrates the love story between the narrator and her daughter over that between spouses and between potential spouses. By exaggerating one of the aspects of the Rousseauian model, Charrière destabilizes it. She shows that what has become a conservative domestic role may be translated into something subversive of bourgeois family values.

Sand writes *Indiana* after two political revolutions and the revolution in family structure embodied in Rousseau's works. In the midst of the great political instability of the first decades of the nineteenth century, the divisions between public and private were a generally unquestioned part of daily life. Even those romantics who most loudly criticized bourgeois public life continued to celebrate the joys of a private life idyllically separated from the public world of politics and economic issues. Sand was not immune to this tendency. She too waxes nostalgic over a myth of bourgeois domesticity in which public life is kept out and private life kept within the walls of a small family unit. The depiction of the "natural" marriage of Ralph and Indiana in the conclusion to her novel also harks back to an idealized vision of the private sphere. But coinciding with this typical Romantic celebration of domestic bliss, we find a vehement critique of the nonmythified position of women in the real bourgeois interior of post-revolutionary France. The novel genre by this time had become a male bastion. The stakes of presenting a woman's subjectivity defined outside of the private sphere had become publicly unimaginable. Sand's subversion of the family romance takes the form of a questioning of categories of gender, not in terms of the characters she presents, but rather in terms of an ambiguously gendered narrator who freely shifts from public to private affairs, underlining the links between the two, and sparing criticism for neither. Sand's frequent allusions to the mysterious symptoms of hysteria, like those to hieroglyphs, suggest too another (repressed) (female) story that exists but cannot be expressed directly in the nineteenth-century novel.

Notes

Introduction

1. Roger Chartier, *Les Origines culturelles de la révolution française* (Paris: Seuil, 1990), 87.

2. See Georges May, *Le Dilemme du roman au dix-huitième siècle (1715–1761)* (Paris: Presses universitaires de France, 1963). In his classic study, May charts the passionate early eighteenth-century debates among men of letters on the uses or dangers associated with the rapid rise of the novel genre, which turned again and again to the following questions: Was the novel's focus on sentiment and the details of private life dangerous or beneficial to society? Did novels encourage licentiousness or contain it? Who should and who should not read novels? What were the implications of the important role played by women (as both characters and authors) in the genre? The debates point to a realization on some level that what was happening in the novel was inseparable from definitions of what would henceforth constitute the "natural" order of society.

3. The term "bastard genre" is appropriate on several levels. The novel as a genre did not have a clear literary heritage. Moreover, novels were frequently published anonymously, that is, without acknowledged "parentship." Finally, the term works on a thematic level when one considers the large number of "enfants naturels" inhabiting eighteenth-century novels. As Marthe Robert claims: "There are but two ways of writing a novel: the way of the realistic Bastard who backs the world while fighting it head on; and the way of the Foundling who, lacking both the experience and the means to fight, avoids confrontation by flight or rejection." Cited in Lynn Hunt, *The Family Romance of the French Revolution* (Berkeley: University of California Press, 1992), 28.

4. Jean-Marie Goulemot, "Tensions et contradictions de l'intime dans la pratique des Lumières," *Littérales* 17 (1995): 13, 15.

5. Marc de Launay's French translation of Habermas's *Strukturwandel der Öffentlichkeit: Untersuchungen zu einer Kategorie der bürgerlichen Gesellschaft* (1962), published under the title *L'Espace public: archéologie de la publicité comme dimension constitutive de la société bourgeoise* (Paris: Payot, 1978), contributed to the diffusion of Habermas's ideas among many scholars of French literature. There has been a resurgence of interest in Habermas studies since the publication of an English translation, *The Structural Transformation of the Public Sphere: An Inquiry Into a Category of Bourgeois Society* (Boston: Massachusetts Institute of Technology Press, 1989).

6. See, for example, Sara Maza, "Only Connect: Family Values in the Age of Sentiment," *Eighteenth-Century Studies* 30.3 (1997): 208.

7. Habermas, *Structural Transformation*, 38.

8. Ibid., 27.

9. There has been a tendency in some applications of Habermas's theory of the development of the public sphere to oversimplify the relationship between public and private. This is due, at least in part, to the ambiguities in Habermas's own use of the terms. Sometimes he refers to the bourgeois "public sphere" that opposes itself to the "representative publicness" of state authority. At other times the sphere of the market is referred to as "private": "The sphere of the market we call 'private'; the sphere of the family, as the core of the private sphere, we call the 'intimate sphere' " (*Structural Transformation*, 55). The important thing to keep in mind is that in his model the sphere of the market and the sphere of the privatized family opposed themselves as an economic and political whole against the existing state authority. Habermas uses the example of the single-family house with its own public and private spaces as a metaphor for this whole: "The line between the public and the public sphere extended right through the home" (45). Whereas urban nobility, especially in Paris, "still kept an open 'house' and despised the bourgeois family turned in on itself" (44), architectural records show that the bourgeois household was split into private areas for family members on the one hand, and a salon for social activity on the other: "The privatized individuals stepped out of the intimacy of their living rooms into the public sphere of the salon, but the one was strictly complementary to the other" (45). It has been pointed out that Habermas's distinction between "urban nobility" and the "bourgeois household" is too strongly drawn. Marie-Antoinette was the owner of perhaps the most complete set of eighteenth-century novels and, in the years directly preceding the revolution, one of the most feverish defenders of new notions of good (bourgeois) motherhood.

That the court itself was making emotional concessions to the new vision of civic virtue in the prerevolutionary years does not change the fact that these values would be the eventual undoing of the French monarchy. These indications of changes of "mentalité" *within* the court offer us a fascinating view of the extremely complicated ways in which the control of representation shifted from one group to another. As Carol Blum points out: "To the extent that the royal family or members of the aristocracy had internalized Rousseau's concept of virtue, it could only serve to undermine a social or functional self-representation which was already weakened by external attack from the left" (*Rousseau and the Republic of Virtue: The Language of Politics in the French Revolution* [Ithaca: Cornell University Press, 1986], 139).

10. Habermas discusses other new institutions such as coffee houses and salons. They, like the novel, existed on a divide between a new private life that created self-consciously individual subjects and a public life based on exchange systems participated in by these self-consciously individual subjects. For a treatment of the role played by salons in the evolution of the bourgeois public and private spheres, see Dena Goodman, "Seriousness of Purpose: Salonnières, Philosophes, and the Shaping of the Eighteenth-Century Salon," in *Proceedings of the Annual Meeting for the Western Society for French History* 15 (1988): 111–21.

11. Habermas, *Structural Transformation*, 55.

12. See Jürgen Habermas, "Further Reflections on the Public Sphere," in *Habermas and the Public Sphere*, ed. Craig Calhoun (Cambridge: Massachusetts Institute of Technology Press, 1992), 421–61.

13. Joan Landes, *Women and the Public Sphere in the Age of the French Revolution* (Ithaca: Cornell University Press, 1988), 7.

14. Madelyn Gutwirth, *Twilight of the Goddesses: Women and Representation in the French Revolutionary Era* (New Brunswick: Rutgers University Press, 1992), 195–96.

15. Nancy Fraser, "What's Critical About Critical Theory? The Case of Habermas and Gender," *New German Critique* 35 (1985): 98.

16. In his 1908 essay "The Family Romance," Freud describes the neurotic's fictional narrative of his origins. In this story, the neurotic's actual progenitors are replaced by the fantasy of another, more desirable and usually more socially prestigious set of parents:

> The later stage in the development of the estrangement from his parents, begun in this manner, might be described as "the neurotic's family romance." . . . The child's imagination becomes engaged in the task of getting free from the parents of whom he now has such a low opinion and of replacing them by others, occupying, as a rule, a higher social station. (Sigmund Freud, "Family Romances," in *The Standard Edition of the Complete Works*, ed. James Strachey, vol. 9 [London: Hogarth Press, 1964], 235–41)

I am among the many scholars who use the term "family romance" as a convenient designation for Freud's general model of the unconscious passion and conflict that order the nuclear family. This appears at first to be a misborrowing, but a closer look at Freud's essay suggests it is not. While the neurotic's story seems to represent an escape from experiences within the nuclear family, Freud tells us that the narrative in fact represents the repressed story of childhood experiences within the family. It reenacts a generalized domestic psychodrama, one that ultimately exalts the father:

> If we examine in detail the commonest of these imaginative romances, the replacement of both parents or of the father alone by grander people, we find that these new . . . parents are equipped with attributes that are derived entirely from real recollections of the actual and humble ones; so that in fact the child is not getting rid of his father but exalting him. Indeed the whole effort at replacing the real father by a superior one is only an expression of the child's longing for the happy, vanished days when his father seemed to him the noblest and strongest of men and his mother the dearest and loveliest of women. (240–41)

One need not extrapolate far to read Freud's comments as being applicable to literature more generally.

17. Laurence Stone, *The Family, Sex and Marriage* (New York: Harper and Row, 1979), 115.

18. Habermas, *Structural Transformation*, 47. While Habermas's statement does make a link between his project and psychoanalysis, he stops short of looking at the question in any depth and in fact—despite the argument he sets up—his brief reference to Freud does not suggest that the "mechanism of the internalization of paternal authority" might change over time or, indeed, that it might be the product of the flourishing textual products he describes.

19. Claude Bonnet, "La Malédiction paternelle," *Dix-huitième siècle* 12 (1980): 208; Paul Pelckmans, *Le Sacre du père: fictions des Lumières et historicité d'Oedipe, 1699–1775* (Amsterdam: Rodopi, 1983), 542.

20. Gayle Rubin, "The Traffic in Women," in *Toward an Anthropology of Women*, ed. Rayna R. Reiter (New York: Monthly Review Press, 1975), 165.

21. Pelckmans does consider a few works by women, though even then he focuses on the development of male models of subjectivity. As we see in my second chapter, this leads to a highly problematic reading of Graffigny's *Lettres d'une Péruvienne*.

22. "La Malédiction paternelle," 208.
23. Marie Fleming, "Women and the Public Use of Reason," in *Feminists Read Habermas*, ed. Johanna Meehan (New York: Routledge, 1995), 120. Dena Goodman writes: "If Habermas' framework is used properly, it can help to explain why the *salonnières* in particular played such a prominent role in the shaping of the authentic public sphere in the eighteenth century. To do so, however, requires first making a distinction between the role of women in this public sphere and that of women in the public sphere of the state" ("Public Sphere and Private Life: Toward a Synthesis of Current Historiographical Approaches to the Old Regime," *History and Theory* 31 (1992): 17). Her comment about *salonnières* and the importance of distinguishing between those *salonnières* associated with the authentic public sphere and those associated with the public sphere of the state is helpful because it underlines the ways in which the development of the public sphere benefited and was exploited by women. I think, however, that with *salonnières* as with women novelists, the division between those upholding aristocratic values and those propounding oppositional values remains difficult to pin down.
24. See Joan DeJean, *Tender Geographies: Women and the Origins of the Novel in France* (New York: Columbia University Press, 1991), for a discussion of the ways in which early women's writing, even that emerging from the court, was subversive of the patriarchal tradition upon which the court rested.
25. Goodman, "Public Sphere and Private Life," 14.

Chapter 1: Françoise de Graffigny's *Lettres d'une Péruvienne* and the Privatization of the Family

1. For a more detailed account of the publishing history of the novel, see David W. Smith, "The Popularity of Madame de Graffigny's *Lettres d'une Péruvienne*: The Bibliographical Evidence," *Eighteenth-Century Studies* 3 (1990): 1–20.
2. Louis Etienne, who discusses Graffigny's novel in the nineteenth century, is a notable exception ("Un Roman socialiste d'autrefois," *Revue des deux mondes* 94 [1871], 454–64).
3. Françoise de Graffigny, *Lettres d'une Péruvienne et d'autres romans d'amour par lettres*, eds. Bernard Bray and Isabelle Landy-Houillon (Paris: Flammarion, 1983); *Lettres d'une Péruvienne*, eds. Joan DeJean and Nancy Miller (New York: Modern Language Association, 1993).
4. Between the publication dates of Montesquieu's *Lettres Persanes* (1721) and Graffigny's *Lettres d'une Péruvienne*, a plethora of "spy novels" were written, including: *Lettres turques* (1730); *Lettres chinoises* (1739–1740); *Lettres cabalistiques* (1737); *Lettres juives* (1738) (Henri Coulet, *Le Roman jusqu'à la Révolution* [Paris: Armand Colin, 1967], 393).
5. Armand-Pierre Jacquin, *Entretiens sur les romans* (1755; reprint, Geneva: Slatkine Reprints, 1970), 101.
6. Cited in English Showalter, "*Les Lettres d'une Péruvienne*: composition, publication, suites," *Archives et Bibliothèques de Belgique* 54 (1983): 27.
7. Cited in Georges Noël, *Madame de Graffigny: Une "Primitive" oubliée de l'école des "coeurs sensibles"* (Paris: Plon, 1913), 199.
8. Jacques Rustin, "Sur Les Suites des *Lettres d'une Péruvienne*," in *Vierge du soleil/*

Fille des Lumières: La Péruvienne de Mme. de Graffigny et ses suites, ed. Travaux du groupe d'étude du dix-huitième siècle (Strasbourg: Université de Strasbourg II, 1989), 124.

9. Rustin, "Sur les Suites des *Lettres d'une Péruvienne*," 126.

10. See Robert Darnton, *The Literary Underground of the Old Regime* (Cambridge: Harvard University Press, 1982), 167. Darnton also notes that "eighteenth-century journalism frequently reflected the interests of journalists rather than those of their readers" (176).

11. For a more complete treatment of familial history, see Philippe Ariès, *L'Enfant et la vie familiale sous l'Ancien Régime* (Paris: Plon, 1960); Jacques Donzelot, *The Policing of Families* (New York: Pantheon Books, 1979); Jean-Louis Flandrin, *Familles: parenté, maison, sexualité, dans l'ancienne société* (Paris: Seuil, 1984); René Pillorget, *La Tige et le rameau. Familles anglaise et française, XVIe–XVIIIe siècles* (Paris: Calmann-Levy, 1979); Edward Shorter, *The Making of the Modern Family* (New York: Basic Books, 1975); Lawrence Stone, *The Family, Sex and Marriage* (New York: Harper and Row, 1979); J. F. Traër, *Marriage and the Family in Eighteenth-Century France* (Ithaca: Cornell University Press, 1980); and Eli Zaretsky, *Capitalism, the Family, and Personal Life* (New York: Harper and Row, 1986).

12. Donzelot, *Policing of Families*, xx.

13. Flandrin, *Familles*, 152; Stone, *Family, Sex and Marriage*, 88.

14. The high birth and mortality rates were certainly another factor in the lack of strong parent–child bonding: before the turn of the century in France only half the babies born ever reached their twenty-first birthdays (Shorter, *Making of the Modern Family*, 203).

15. Louis Althusser, "Ideology and Ideological State Apparatuses," in *Lenin and Philosophy* (New York: Monthly Review Press, 1971).

16. Of course, both ISAs and RSAs were simultaneously at play in both the traditional authoritarian state and in early forms of the modern state. As Althusser points out, it is a question of degree (*Lenin and Philosophy*, 145). The repressive public rules of the traditional authoritarian state had always depended on and been naturalized by what Althusser terms ISAs (including literature, for example). But in the eighteenth century the relationship between RSAs and ISAs changed. Althusser tells us: "No class can hold State power over a long period without at the same time exercising its hegemony over and in the State Ideological Apparatuses" (146).

17. Flandrin, *Familles*, 14.

18. Ibid., 10.

19. For some graphic descriptions of intrafamilial conflict during this period, see *Le Désordre dans les familles: Lettres de cachet des archives de la Bastille* (1728–1758), eds. Arlette Farge and Michel Foucault (Paris: Gallimard, 1982).

20. Stone, *The Family, Sex and Marriage*, 426.

21. Erica Harth, *Cartesian Women: Versions and Subversions of Rational Discourse in the Old Regime* (Ithaca, New York: Cornell University Press, 1992), 6.

22. Again, it is important to recognize just how careful one must be in defining the moment when the representational (courtly) sphere shifts and becomes the basis of an oppositional public sphere. The monarchy of Louis XIV and Colbert was hugely invested in the very processes of change that would eventually make dissent possible. As Harth points out with regard to the *Académie des sciences*: "The new philosophy that was institutionalized by the state in 1663 was closely allied with the

emerging sociopolitical regime. Technological innovations were essential to Colbert's mercantilism and to France's nascent capitalism; the academicians' pragmatic values were those of an embryonic bourgeoisie" (*Cartesian Women*, 143).

23. Joan Landes, *Women and the Public Sphere in the Age of the French Revolution* (Ithaca: Cornell University Press, 1988), 53. Habermas addressed this phenomenon in his 1992 (German) edition of *The Structural Transformation of the Public Sphere* reprinted in English in *Habermas and the Public Sphere*, ed. Craig Calhoun (Cambridge: Massachusetts Institute of Technology Press, 1992), 425:

> Apart from introducing a greater internal differentiation of the bourgeois public, which by means of a more detail-oriented focus could also be accommodated within my model, a different picture emerges if from the very beginning one admits the coexistence of competing public spheres and takes account of the dynamics of those processes of communication that are excluded from the dominant public sphere.

24. While Habermas privileges the novel, it, and literature more generally, are but one of the many cultural institutions that inform his model. Habermas also discusses coffee houses, clubs, reading and language societies, lending libraries, concert halls, opera houses, theaters, publishing companies, lecture halls, salons, and of course the press. Habermas was not trying to account for the novel in the ways that I am exploring here. My intention is not to attack Habermas's model, but rather to consider some of its implications and, while using it as a starting point, to go beyond his interests in an effort to better understand my subject, that is, the relation between women-authored novels and the shifts in society on which he focuses.

25. Françoise de Graffigny, *Lettres portugaises, Lettres d'une Péruvienne et d'autres romans d'amour par lettres*, eds. Bernard Bray and Isabelle Landy-Houillon (Paris: Flammarion, 1983), 267. All subsequent quotations from *Lettres d'une Péruvienne* will be taken from this edition and cited parenthetically in the text.

26. See Isabelle Brouard-Arends, *Vies et images maternelles dans la littérature française du dix-huitième siècle* (Oxford: Voltaire Foundation, 1991).

27. In his biography of Graffigny, Noël suggests the historical preface was not Graffigny's own work—rather that of one of her "adorateurs," Antoine Bret ("*Une Primitive oubliée*," 178). No other documentation currently available supports this view. This does not, however, mean that Noël is necessarily mistaken. Noël had access to letters from Brett to Graffigny, which have since been lost. It is probably these that led him to believe that Brett had written the historical preface. It is clear from the novel as a whole (even in its first version, which did not include the historical preface) that Graffigny had read Garcilaso as well as other ethnographic sources. The preface to her second edition might well be an example of salon writing in which both Brett and Graffigny had a hand.

28. For another view, see Janet Altman, "Making Room for Peru," in *Writing the Female Voice*, ed. Elizabeth C. Goldsmith (Boston: Northeastern University Press, 1989), 172–202. Altman cites this passage to support her argument that Graffigny exploits descriptions of Inca and Peruvian culture from Garcilaso's *Histoire des Incas* to present a culture characterized by a more egalitarian social structure than that of France.

29. James Higgins, *A History of Peruvian Literature* (Wolfeboro, N.H.: Francis Cairns Publications Ltd.), 1987.

30. Garcilaso de la Vega, *Histoire des Incas, rois du Pérou*, ed. trans. Thomas François Dalibard (Paris: Prault fils, 1744). Julia Douthwaite charts the use of Peruvian imagery and themes in the work of other seventeenth- and eighteenth-century writers (*Exotic Women:* Literary Heroines and Cultural Strategies [Philadelphia: University of Pennsylvania Press, 1992], 102–110).

31. See Katharine Ann Jensen, *Writing Love: Letters, Women, and the Novel in France, 1605–1776* (Carbondale and Edwardsville: Southern Illinois University Press, 1995), 103.

32. Zilia's condemnation of this "usage barbare établi parmi les grands seigneurs du pays" is seemingly at odds with her praise for the Inca marriage tradition, which, according to Zilia, cloisters women like herself to assure the success of the rigidly hierarchical marriage system that favors the lucky few.

33. Zilia's notion that warmth and tenderness are the "natural" attributes of motherliness is not to be found in Garcilaso's rendition of Peruvian culture. In *Histoire des Incas*, we read: "Les mères ne prenoient jamais leurs enfans dans leur bras, disant que les enfans n'en vouloient point sortir quand on les avoit accoutumés. Ils élevoient leurs enfans avec très peu de délicatesse" (72). Garcilaso admires coldness on the part of mothers. Zilia's allegiance to new notions of good and natural motherhood betrays once again her eighteenth-century (rather than sixteenth-century) origins.

34. I emphasize this passage because the parallel made by Zilia between her relationship with Aza and Déterville's with his sister Céline is key to my reading Aza and Zilia as siblings rather than simply as close relations.

35. Marie Fleming's comments, in her discussion of Habermas, are useful here:

> Whereas the publicity of representation typical of the court had been located in the person of the sovereign, the site of the new publicity was the "people." Early bourgeois writers soon identified this new publicity with openness and the "rule of the law," the very opposite of the secrecy and arbitrariness typical of courtly practices. ("Women and the Public Use of Reason," 124)

Graffigny presents "les hommes de la loi" and "les juges" against "les seigneurs du pays" in the establishment of justice for the Déterville siblings against the tyranny of parents, here represented by Madame Déterville, "la mère dénaturée." Graffigny's novel provides a remarkable *mise-en-abyme* of the phenomenon described by Fleming and points to Zilia's participation as a novelist in the early forms of public discourse in the Habermassian sense.

36. In her reading, which focuses on the writing topos, Nancy Miller underscores the symbolic import of this passage: "The ambitious project to create a *text* for posterity is cut off when the movement that was to mark the climax is also cut off by the violent invasion of the virginal feminine space.... Zilia must stop memorializing their happiness as text in order to retrieve her own identity in the epistolary novel over which she has suddenly lost narrative control. Though fatal to the story she inhabits, this double swerve from genre is utterly generative of the story whose heroine she is to become" (*Subject to Change* [New York: Columbia University Press, 1988], 140).

37. Lynn Hunt, *The Family Romance of the French Revolution* (Berkeley: University of California Press, 1992), 34–35.

38. Pierre Fauchery, *La Destinée féminine dans le roman européen du dix-huitième siècle 1713–1807, Essai de gynécomythie romanesque*, (Paris: Armand Colin, 1972), 150.

39. Habermas, *Structural Transformation*, 55. Despite the change in the way that marriage and family began to be imagined, "the contractual form of marriage, imputing the autonomous declaration of will on the part of both partners, was largely a fiction especially since a marriage, to the extent that the family owned capital, could not remain unaffected by considerations regarding the latter's preservation and augmentation" (Habermas, *Structural Transformation*, 47). See too Lévi-Strauss, *Les Structures élémentaires de la parenté*, (Paris: Mouton, 1967), xx. Lévi-Strauss makes the same point as Habermas with regard to the relationship between marriages of convenience and love matches: "Reconnaissons que les notions de mariage préscriptif et de mariage préférentiel son relatives. . . ."

40. Foucault, *History of Sexuality*, trans. Robert Hurley, vol. 1 (New York: Random House), 108–9.

41. The status of the relationship between Aza and Zilia is somewhat contested. As I have already argued, the parallel between the Déterville–Céline bond and the Aza–Zilia bond underscores the brother-sister nature of their relationship.

42. We might read this as an indication that the development of the father figure as marker of the Oedipus complex charted by Pelckmans is not firmly embedded in the collective unconscious until well after the French Revolution. This confusion between father–daughter incest and sister–brother incest points to the lack of definite form of the Oedipal structure before the revolution. See Lynn Hunt's *Family Romance of the French Revolution* for a view of eighteenth-century fathers that differs from that presented by Pelckmans.

43. Garcilaso de la Vega, *Histoire des Incas*, ix. Garcilaso's work was published with the express approval of the Inquisition. We should not underestimate the role that the power of the Inquisition and its censors may have played in Garcilaso's decision to preface his work with these passages.

44. Showalter, "*Les Lettres d'une Péruvienne*," 27.

45. Graffigny, of course, simplifies the very complicated issue of Peruvian incest: "La question n'est donc pas de savoir s'il existe des groupes permettant des mariages que d'autres excluent, mais plutôt s'il y a des groupes chez lesquels aucun type de mariage n'est prohibé. La réponse doit être, alors, absolument négative, et à un double titre: d'abord, parce que le mariage n'est jamais autorisé entre tous les proches parents, mais seulement entre certaines catégories (demi-soeur à l'exclusion de soeur, soeur à l'exclusion de mère, etc.); ensuite, parce que ces unions consanguines ont, soit un caractère officiel et permanent, mais restent, dans ce dernier cas, le privilège d'une catégorie sociale très restreinte" (Lévi-Strauss, *Structures élémentaires de la parenté*, 11). Important in our reading is not the degree to which Peruvian marriage was or was not based on what we think of as incest, but rather the *symbolic* role that Zilia's attachment to an incestuous relationship plays within Graffigny's novel set in eighteenth-century France.

46. Miller, *Subject to Change*, 141.

47. Douthwaite, *Exotic Women*, 114.

48. We might see here too an analogous situation for the woman writer. She could participate in the new genre on the terms described by Turgot and Fréron, that is, by writing a marriage plot. She thereby participated in the new literary market, but symbolically excluded herself from the public sphere at the same time by

presenting a model that would ultimately keep women out of all social circulation (except the continuing marriage market). For Graffigny this paradox is less glaring. In *Lettres* she presents a model in which it makes sense for a woman to participate as an agent in the exchange of words and money by removing her protagonist from the domestic family narrative.

49. Douthwaite points out that despite some aristocratic pretensions, Zilia's "emphasis on personal *industrie* reveals a rather bourgeois concern with productivity and individual accountability, with using time to worthwhile purpose" (*Exotic Women*, 124–25).

50. Jensen, *Writing Love*, 102.

51. Paul Hoffman, "*Les Lettres d'une Péruvienne*: Projet d'autarcie sentimentale," in *Vierge du soleil/Fille des Lumières: La Péruvienne de Mme de Graffigny et ses suites*, ed. Groupe d'étude du dix-huitième (Strasbourg: Université de Strasbourg II, 1989), 66.

52. DeJean, *Tender Geographies*, 122.

53. Harth rightly notes: "The opposition of public/private, which is freighted with the ideology of industrial capitalism, is not strictly applicable to the seventeenth century" (*Cartesian Women*, 17).

54. Fleming, "Women and the Public Use of Reason," 120.

55. Richard Terdiman, *Discourse/Counter-Discourse: The Theory and Practice of Symbolic Resistance in Nineteenth-Century France* (Ithaca: Cornell University Press, 1980), 75. See Fleming too: "Habermas views the culture of the 'town' and the salons as a bridge between the collapsing courtly form of publicity connected with the emerging bourgeois public sphere" ("Women and the Public Use of Reason," 121).

56. Harth, *Cartesian Women*, 54.

57. "Les précieuses savent que pour l'heure, les femmes n'ont pas, en majorité, fait des mariages d'amour et que beaucoup d'entre elles ne sont pas heureuses en ménage. Pour celles-ci, elles osent envisager une certaine forme d'amour en dehors du mariage. Non pas un grossier adultère . . . mais 'l'amitié tendre' d'un chevalier servant ou d'un amant de coeur. . . . Il régnera surtout entre eux une étroite communion de sentiments et de goûts. Un amour d'ordre néo-platonicien, dégagé de tout ce qui peut être intéressé, bas, charnel" (Pillorget, *La Tige et le rameau*, 67).

58. Landes, *Women and the Public Sphere*, 49.

59. Joan DeJean, "Teaching Frenchness," *French Review* 61.3 (1988): 398–413.

60. Gutwirth, *Twilight of the Goddesses*, 1–22.

61. Pierre Fauchery, *La Destinée féminine dans le roman européen du dix-huitième siècle 1713–1807, Essai de gynécomythie romanesque* (Paris: Armand Colin, 1972), 93.

62. For a treatment of Graffigny's own disastrous marriage, see DeJean's *Tender Geographies*, 153–155. I agree with DeJean, who feels that while Graffigny's experience is usually subordinated to a general "defense of women," there are certain passages of *Lettres*, particularly those dealing with the injustice of marriage laws, in which "the hard edge of the personal still resists [such] generalization" (154).

63. Fauchery, *La Destinée féminine*, 102.

Chapter 2: The Mother–Daughter Plot in Isabelle de Charrière's *Lettres écrites de Lausanne*

1. Henri Coulet, *Le Roman jusqu'à la Révolution* (Paris: Armand Colin, 1967), 149.

2. Georges May, *Le Dilemme du roman au dix-huitième siècle: etude sur les rapports du roman et de la critique (1715–1761)* (Paris: Presses universitaires de France, 1963), 248.

3. Robert Darnton, *The Great Cat Massacre and Other Episodes in French Cultural History* (New York: Basic Books, 1984), 249. See too Claude Labrosse, *Lire au dix-huitième siècle: La Nouvelle Héloïse et ses lecteurs* (Lyon: Presses universitaires de Lyon; Paris, Editions du CNRS, 1985); and Anna Attridge, "The Reception of *La Nouvelle Héloïse*," *Studies on Voltaire and the Eighteenth Century* 120 (1974): 227–67.

4. Cited in Labrosse, *Lire au dix-huitième siècle*, 70.

5. Jean-Marie Goulemot, "Tensions et contradictions de l'intime dans la pratique des Lumières", *Littérales* 17 (1995): 19.

6. Cited in Labrosse, *Lire au dix-huitième siècle*, 67–68.

7. Cited in Labrosse, *Lire au dix-huitième siècle*, 58.

8. Cited in Carol Blum, *Rousseau and the Republic of Virtue: The Language of Politics in the French Revolution* (Ithaca: Cornell University Press, 1986), 146.

9. Cited in Labrosse, *Lire au dix-huitième siècle*, 100.

10. *Structural Transformation*, 48.

11. Goulemot, "Tensions et Contradictions," 19.

12. Cited in Labrosse, *Lire au dix-huitième siècle*, 36.

13. Cited in Labrosse, *Lire au dix-huitième siècle*, 108.

14. Joan DeJean, *Literary Fortifications: Rousseau, Laclos, Sade*, (Princeton: Princeton University Press, 1984), 189.

15. Attridge, "The Reception of *La Nouvelle Héloïse*," 259.

16. William Ray, "Reading Women: Cultural Authority, Gender, and the Novel. The Case of Rousseau," *Eighteenth-Century Studies* (1988): 438.

17. Tony Tanner, *Adultery in the Novel* (Baltimore: The Johns Hopkins University Press), 178.

18. Ibid., 386.

19. Cited in Darnton, *Great Cat Massacre*, 236.

20. Rousseau repeatedly waxes nostalgic over the nuclear family, which he presents as the natural (and preexisting) unit from which the French had strayed:

> Il n'y a plus d'éducation privée dans les grandes villes. La société y est si générale et si mêlée qu'il ne reste plus d'azile pour la retraite et qu'on est en public jusques chez soi. A force de vivre avec tout le monde on n'a plus de famille, à peine connoit-on ses parens; on les voit en étrangers, et la simplicité des moeurs domestiques s'éteint avec la douce familiarité qui en faisoit le charme. C'est ainsi qu'on suce avec le lait le gout des plaisirs du siécle et des maximes qu'on y voit régner. (Rousseau, *Emile*, in *Oeuvres complètes*, eds. Bernard Gagnebin and Marcel Raymond, vol. 4 [Paris: Gallimard, 1969], 739)

21. Rousseau, *Emile*, 738.

22.. Patrick Coleman, *Rousseau's Political Imagination* (Geneva: Droz, 1984), 109.

23. Ray, "Reading Women," 428.

24. Rousseau, *Emile*, 258–60.

25. Medical treatises were filled with prescriptions to women that they nurse and with observations of the wonders that occurred when they did. In 1786, a certain Doctor Chambaud noted the new trend toward maternal nursing that had commenced in Paris, and he attributed this change to Rousseau:

> The wise teachings of Locke about infancy presented through the eloquent pen of Rousseau, have started to gather fruit in this city. Among the upper orders for several years now an ever greater number of mothers have discovered that the tiresomeness of nursing is compensated by many pleasures and advantages. People are now giving more liberty to children.... Pap has been banned from their regime and they are given more exercise. (cited in Shorter, *Making of the Modern Family*, 38)

By the time of the French Revolution, in certain regions of France, over 90 percent of mothers breastfed their children (Shorter, *Making of the Modern Family*, 67).

26. Mary Trouille, *Sexual Politics in the Enlightenment: Women Writers Read Rousseau* (Albany: State University of New York Press, 1997), 55.

27. Thomas Laqueur points to the complicated ways that both personal issues and politics motivated Rousseau's doctrines: "Rousseau was enraged by the cultural influence of women not only for idiosyncratic reasons or because relations with women represented the prototypical case of man's slavish dependency: his obsessions on the matter developed in the great age of the salon where women had in fact created a genuine new public space within the old regime" (*Making Sex: Body and Gender from the Greeks to Freud* [Cambridge: Harvard University Press, 1990], 197–98). For a good discussion of the role of women, literary salons, and shifting definitions of aristocracy in the early part of the eighteenth century, see Thomas DiPiero, *Dangerous Truths and Criminal Passions: The Evolution of the French Novel, 1569–1791* (Stanford: Stanford University Press, 1992), 244–46.

28. Rousseau, *Emile*, 768.

29. This passage follows another in which Rousseau suggests that any work published by a woman was actually written by a man: "On sait toujours quel est l'artiste ou l'ami qui tient la plume ou le pinceau quand elles travaillent. On sait quel est le discret homme de lettres qui leur dicte en secret leurs oracles. Toute cette charlatanerie est indigne d'une honnête femme" (*Emile*, 768).

30. Ray, "Reading Women," 421–47.

31. At the age of 19, Germaine Necker wrote the following words in her journal: "Que les femmes sont peu faites pour courir la même carrière que les hommes, lutter contre eux, exciter en eux une jalousie si différente que celle que l'amour leur inspire. Une femme ne doit avoir rien à elle et trouver toutes ses jouissances dans ce qu'elle aime! Non, notre bonheur est d'aimer, notre gloire est d'admirer celui que le sort où notre choix nous a destiné; malheur à nous quand nous renversons l'ordre de la nature!" Cited in Georges Solovieff, *Madame de Staël: Choix de textes, Thématique et Actualité* (Paris: Klincksieck, 1974), 37. Later Staël would come to have a more critical view of Rousseau's views.

32. See Jean-Claude Bonnet, "Naissance du Panthéon," *Poétique* 33 (1978): 46–65. Bonnet considers the implications of the Academy's shift in its essay competitions from philosophical themes to the praises of great men.

33. This is with the exception of *Le Noble*, published in 1758 when Charrière was just eighteen years old.

34. Raymond Trousson, "Isabelle de Charrière et Jean-Jacques Rousseau," *Bulletin de l'Académie royale de langue et de littérature françaises* 43.1 (1985): 6.

35. In her biography of Charrière, C. J. Courtney refers to her subject as "Belle" throughout the early part of her work, which is devoted to life before marriage, and as "Isabelle de Charrière" thereafter (*Isabelle de Charrière [Belle de Zuylen]* [Oxford: Voltaire Foundation, 1993]). See too Jenene Allison, *Revealing Differences: The Fiction*

of *Isabelle de Charrière* (Newark: University of Delaware Press, 1995), especially the insightful chapter "Belle/Agnès/Zélide/Madame de Charrière" (107–26).

36. Isabelle de Charrière, *Oeuvres complètes*, eds. Jean-Daniel Candaux et al. (Amsterdam: G. A. van Oorschot, 1979–1984), vol. 1, 204–5.

37. The next time she identified with a character in Rousseau's life, it was with a real rather than a fictional one. This identification too suggests a certain distance from Rousseau, or at least from the role he accorded women. Many years after Rousseau's death, the question of whether Thérèse Levasseur should receive a part of the proceeds of Rousseau's posthumously published *Confessions* was discussed. In the meantime, Levasseur had remarried with a man who had been in Rousseau's employ. A flood of antipathy for Rousseau's widow sprang forth from many different sources, including Germaine de Staël and Charrière's friend DuPeyrou. Barruel-Beauvert, a particularly indignant and brutal critic, had this to say on the subject: "Est-ce qu'on est obligé de fournir de la pâture aux coulèvres? Non, mais les laisser vivre est une cruauté" (cited in Trousson, "Isabelle de Charrière et Jean-Jacques Rousseau," 18). In her "Plainte et Défense de Thérèse Levasseur," Charrière counters Staël's implication that Levasseur was not good enough for Rousseau, with a biting critique of issues of both class and gender implied in what was meant by being "good enough":

> Quoi, parce que M. Rousseau a fait à une pauvre fille qui ne savoit ni lire, ni écrire, ni voir l'heure qu'il étoit sur un cadran, l'honneur de lui donner son linge à blanchir et son potage à cuire; parce qu'il lui a fait partager parfois son lit, et longtemps après son nom; il faudroit que cette pauvre fille devînt une héroïne, un grand esprit, une belle dame à la manière de celles qu'on fabrique dans les livres! . . . Oui, madame la baronne, vous manquez de bonté; car vous dites du mal d'une pauvre femme qui ne vous en a point fait, et qui est dans des circonstances moins brillantes que les vôtres. Mon célèbre ami est mort, votre célèbre et respectable pere est, Dieu merci, plein de vie; vous êtes riche, vous êtes baronne et ambassadrice, et bel esprit; et moi, que suis-je? Vous manquez de justice; car vous avancez des faits qu'il vous est impossible de prouver, comme à moi de les réfuter pleinement; de sorte que je reste chargée à jamais d'une accusation grave et d'un soupçon odieux. (*Oeuvres complètes*, vol. 10, 173–74)

38. Charrière, *Oeuvres complètes*, vol. 1, 224–25. Charrière's sentiments call to mind those of Graffigny's heroine Zilia. Charrière "*pour un throne . . . ne renoncerai*[t] *pas* [à] [*ses*] *leçons, lectures et écritures*" (my emphasis). Zilia's early wish to live alone "afin de [se] livrer sans relâche" (*Lettres d'une Péruvienne*, 296) to her writing skills, is fulfilled through the transformation of her (and Aza's) throne into a home complete with library. In the cases of both Charrière and Zilia, the vocation of reading and writing is symbolically opposed to aristocratic privilege bestowed by the throne. Both associate writing with change and consciously position themselves as writers within a framework that opposes itself to the monarchical tradition. They thereby demand a voice in a society shifting away from the structures of the ancien régime.

39. Rousseau, *Emile*, 768.

40. Charrière, *Oeuvres complètes*, vol. 1, 224.

41. In a letter dated 5 December 1764, Boswell wrote to Rousseau: "Si vous voulez vous amuser de lire quelques pièces de cette Demoiselle, vous les trouverez dans un petit paquet à part. Je voudrais bien avoir vos sentiments sur son caractère" (*Correspondance complète de Jean-Jacques Rousseau*, ed. R. A. Leigh, vol. 22, (Geneva

and Banbury: The Voltaire Foundation, 1974), 171. There is no record of any response from Rousseau.

It should be noted here that Boswell himself contemplated marriage to his "Zélide," as is testified to in the following letter addressed to a close friend: "And must I then marry a Dutchwoman? Where shall he find a more amiable wife? Is he not a man of a most singular character? and would not an ordinary woman be insupportable to him? Should he not thank the Powers Above for having shown him Zélide, a young lady free from all the faults of her sex, with genius, with good humour, with elegant accomplishments?" Apparently he thought better of it, for a few days later he wrote to the same friend using precisely the term Rousseau used in his condemnation of women writers: "I shall correspond with her as a *bel esprit,* but I think it would be madness to marry her." Cited in Courtney, *Isabelle de Charrière,* 202, 207.

42. Charrière, *Oeuvres complètes,* vol. 10, 345.

43. Rousseau, *Emile,* 768.

44. Much of the work done on Charrière has focused on her life rather than her work. Five book-length biographies have appeared over the past century: Philippe Godet's *Madame de Charrière et ses amis* (1906; Reprint, Geneva: Slatkine, 1973; Geoffrey Scott's *The Portrait of Zélide* (London: Constable and Co., 1925); Simone Dubois's *Leven op afstand* (Zaltbomme: Europese Bibliotheek, 1969); C. P. Courtney's *Isabelle de Charrière (Belle de Zuylen)* (Oxford: Voltaire Foundation, 1993); and Paul Pelckmans's *Isabelle de Charrière: une correspondance au seuil du monde moderne* (Amsterdam: Rodopi, 1995). In all of these works, Charrière's novels are read for the most part as biographical footnotes to a life. In the case of Godet and Scott, the attention paid to Charrière, while highly respectful, is largely in homosocial terms. Her body is a connector of more prestigious (male) (writing) bodies, namely those of Boswell, Diderot, Rousseau, and the two Constants, Hermenches and Benjamin.

With the appearance of recent work on women writers, a literary web including the work of both male and female writers allows us to trace the relationships between women writers even as they pass through male writers. The recent work of Trousson and Showalter, for example, lets us to read Rousseau as an intermediary between Graffigny and Charrière. Both women had interactions with the famous writer, and both expressed profound ambivalence about his work, particularly his exacerbation of the conflict for women writers between domesticity and writing, or to use Marianne Hirsch's terms, between "reproductivity and productivity" (*The Mother/Daughter Plot* [Bloomington: Indiana University Press], 44). Jenene Allison's *Revealing Differences: The Fiction of Isabelle de Charrière,* the first book-length study to focus on the author's work rather than her biography, points to promising new directions for a truly literary history that includes women writers.

45. This passage is quoted in Alan Sheridan, *Michel Foucault: The Will to Truth* (New York: Tavistock Publications, 1980), 217.

46. The narrator, like Charrière herself, who published *Lettres* anonymously, is fastidious about keeping her name out of her correspondence: "Je ne me signe pas et je ne nomme personne; les accidents qui peuvent arriver aux lettres me font toujours peur" (48). Interestingly, the excluded name, in the case of the married woman, is the name of the husband and the husband's father, which is hereby also excluded. In other words, one of the privileges of anonymity is the disassociation of the female writer from the ubiquitous name of the father.

47. Isabelle de Charrière, *Lettres écrites de Lausanne,* ed. Claudine Hermann

(Paris: Editions des femmes, 1979), 23. All subsequent references to *Lettres écrites de Lausanne* will be taken from this edition and cited parenthetically in the body of the text.

48. Nadine Bérenguier, "From Clarens to Hollow Park: Isabelle de Charrière's Quiet Revolution," *Studies in Eighteenth-Century Culture* 21 (1991): 230.

49. The novel itself has an ambiguous status, as it is both a marriage plot (with regard to Cécile) and a post-marriage plot (with regard to the narrator herself). Nadine Bérenguier provides an excellent reading of another of Charrière's novels, *Les Lettres de Mistriss Henley*, which she describes as "a fictional treatment of Rousseau's marriage narrative and of its consequences for women" ("From Clarens to Hollow Park," 223). We might read *Les Lettres écrites de Lausanne* as another version of a post-marriage response to Rousseau, or perhaps, as the narrator is widowed, a *post* post-marriage plot.

50. I should say rather that nobility is being redefined as and/or replaced by what Charrière, in an ironic note she added to the second edition of her *Lettres*, calls "les gens les plus distingués de Lausanne" (59). In Switzerland, as in France, "a new noble ideology arose premised less on hereditary or institutionalized virtue, and more on moral attitudes and the rendering of service" within bourgeois systems of exchange (DiPiero, *Dangerous Truths and Criminal Passions*, 250).

51. Habermas makes a similar point in *The Structural Transformation of the Public Sphere*:

> The conjugal family's self-image of its intimate sphere collided even within the consciousness of the bourgeoisie itself with the real functions of the bourgeois family. . . . [The family] played its precisely defined role in the process of the reproduction of capital. As a genealogical link it guaranteed a continuity of personnel that consisted materially in the accumulation of capital and was anchored in the absence of legal restrictions concerning the inheritance of property. As an agency of society it served especially the task of that difficult mediation through which, in spite of the illusion of freedom, strict conformity with societally necessary requirements was brought about. (46)

52. Sandra Lee Bartky, "Foucault, Femininity, and the Modernization of Patriarchal Power," in *Feminism and Foucault: Reflections of Resistance*, eds. Irene Diamond and Lee Quinby (Boston: Northeastern University Press, 1988), 61.

53. See Laurence Mall, "Perdues dans les détails: *Les Lettres de Mistriss Henley* de Charrière et l'écriture de la désintégration," *Orbis Litterarum* 52 (1997): 178–93.

54. Biddy Martin, "Feminism, Criticism, and Foucault," in *Feminism and Foucault: Reflections on Resistance*, eds. Irene Diamond and Lee Quinby (Boston: Northeastern University Press, 1988), 9.

55. It is worth citing the passage from which this is taken: "We should be aware . . . of the extent to which the period was one of linguistic transition. Raymond Williams argues that the eighteenth century saw the beginning of a major new emphasis on language as activity, in close relation to the demystified understanding of society as a set of structures and inventions 'made' by human beings. 'Language' and 'reality' were no longer systematically perceived, as they had been in all previously dominant traditions, as decisively separated. . . . Scrutiny of the works of female novelists suggests evidence of just such a move toward language as operative. . . . One discerns in a number of women writers an inchoate realization of the opacity of the signifier and the degree to which everyday speech may sustain patriarchal

arrangements—social, political and sexual" (Joan Hinde Stewart, "The Novelists and Their Fictions," in *French Women and the Age of Enlightenment*, ed. Samia I. Spencer [Bloomington: Indiana University Press, 1984], 203).

56. There are some exceptions to Foucault's general focus on male bodies. His words about women in the nineteenth century are apt here: "It is worth remembering that the first figure to be invested by the deployment of sexuality, one of the first to be 'sexualized,' was the 'idle' woman. She inhabited the outer edge of the 'world,' in which she always had to appear as a value, and of the family, where she was assigned a new destiny charged with conjugal and parental obligations" (*History of Sexuality*, vol. 1, 121).

57. May, *Le Dilemme du roman*, 249. I am not arguing that Charrière does not participate in the art of illusion so dear to her contemporaries. She does, and all the more so, because of her technique of calling her readers' attention to the constructed nature of plots and realities. These techniques, like Diderot's self-conscious authorial interventions, create the illusion of including the audience in her work, thereby "plac[ing] a final veil over the difference between reality and illusion" (Habermas, *Structural Transformation*, 50). Charrière does not reject a certain identification on the part of readers with fictional characters; she simply creates a different illusion, one that opposes itself to those she shows "torment" women.

58. Béatrice Didier points out that the disarticulation of women's body is typical in literature of this period: "Le corps féminin—beaucoup plus que le corps masculin—était, dans la littérature, un corps morcelé. . . Les stéréotypes romanesques limitaient le corps de la femme à peu de choses: yeux, cheveux, front, bras, cheville, etc., et le roman féminin acceptait ces limites, les renforçait peut-être encore, par souci de bienséance" (*L'Ecriture-femme* [Paris: Presses universitaires de France, 1981], 36).

59. Charrière was criticized from many quarters for including what was considered the rather repugnant detail of Cécile's goiter. Fifty years later the anatomical detail was still being commented on by journalists like Paul de Molènes, who in the *Journal des débats* of July 8, 1845 refers to Cécile's thickish neck as "le plus inutile et le plus malencontreux de tous les traits." Cited in Godet, *Madame de Charrière et ses amis*, 304. Cécile is a far cry from delicate Sophie, who, Rousseau tells us again and again, did not need to wear high heels to create the illusion of small feet. The inclusion of unseemly details in Charrière's novel works to de-idealize the fictional marriage plot.

60. Shorter, *Making of the Modern Family*, 64.

61. Lévi-Strauss presents a sentimentalized description of the interplay between woman as object of exchange and woman as a value *en soi*: "Dans le dialogue matrimonial des hommes, la femme n'est jamais, purement, ce dont on parle; car si les femmes, en général, représentent une certaine catégories de signes, destinés à un certain type de communication, chaque femme conserve une valeur particulière, qui provient de son talent, avant et après le mariage, à tenir sa partie dans un duo. A l'inverse du mot, devenu intégralement signe, la femme est donc restée, en même temps que signe, valeur" (*Structures elémentaires de la parenté*, 569). With the emergence of the modern plot, the value side of the equation came to play a much larger role.

62. Rousseau, *Emile*, 697–98.

63. Coleman, *Rousseau's Political Imagination*, 117. See too DiPiero, *Dangerous Truths and Criminal Passions*, 252. DiPiero underlines the inseparable link between the bourgeois family, female sexual restraint, and new socioeconomic codes: "Sexual restraint, particularly as it concerned women, formed the keystone of bourgeois order, since promiscuous feminine sexuality threatened the stability of the family name and, consequently, its fortune. The cohesive bourgeois family thus correlated the interwoven systems of reason, exchange, and social integrity."

64. Luce Irigaray, *Ce Sexe qui n'en est pas un* (Paris: Editions de minuit, 1977).

65. DeJean, *Tender Geographies*, 8.

66. The narrator refers to female virtue as one of God's laws (63).

67. *Emile*, 741.

68. The narrator follows this passage with a set of supposedly bad examples: accounts of women who transgressed the codes of behavior she has been teaching Cécile. The examples of Adrienne le Couvreur and Agnès Sorel seem to suggest not that they are dangerous, but rather, that they are endangered! Both women took lovers, and both were eventually poisoned. But the way in which the narrator presents the examples does not mention their deaths. On the contrary, from the snippets the narrator includes, it seems as though the women's successes were the direct *result* of their transgression: "La Le Couvreur n'aurait pu envoyer au maréchal de Saxe le prix de ses diamants si on ne les lui avait donnés, et elle n'aurait eu aucune relation avec lui si elle n'avait été sa maîtresse. Agnès Sorel n'aurait pas sauvé la France, si elle n'avait été celle de Charles VII" (69).

69. Shorter, *Making of the Modern Family*, 184.

70. Raymond Williams describes ideology as "a conscious system of ideas and beliefs, but [in addition] the whole lived social process as practically organized by specific and dominant meanings and values. . . . [It is] a saturation of the whole process of living. . . , of the whole substance of lived identities and relationships. . . , a whole body of practices and expectations. . . , our senses and assignments of energy, our shaping perceptions of ourselves and our world. It is a living system of meanings and values—constitutive of and constituting—which . . . appear as reciprocally confirming . . . a sense of absolute reality beyond which it is very difficult . . . to move." Cited in Richard Terdiman, *Discourse/Counter-Discourse: The Theory and Practice of Symbolic Resistance in Nineteenth-Century France* (Ithaca: Cornell University Press, 1985), 42.

71. Joan Kelly, *Women, History, and Theory* (Chicago: University of Chicago Press, 1984), 2.

72. Mary Jacobus, "Incorruptible Milk: Breast-Feeding and the French Revolution," in *Rebel Daughters: Women and the French Revolution*, eds. Sara E. Melzer and Leslie W. Rabine (Oxford: Oxford University Press, 1992), 55. The many *fontaines de la regénération* represented in prints throughout the revolutionary period are a particularly striking example of the relationship between maternal roles for women and universal (male) citizenship. These prints portray a large, seated woman whose breasts spurt milk into crowds of men holding forth in public squares. Jacobus, who calls breast milk "the nectar of the Age of Reason," suggests that it is the anxiety associated with the threat to old-regime blood-ties "that gives advocacy of maternal breast-feeding its special urgency" during the revolutionary period (66).

73. During a parlor game, the question "A qui doit-on sa première éducation?" generates the (anonymous) response: "A sa nourrice" (56). The term "nourrice"

may or may not indicate the mother. In another of Charrière's novels, the issue of breastfeeding is discussed explicitly. The protagonist has long internal debates on whether to breastfeed her child, turning around the issues tenderness, health, and duty (*Lettres de Mistriss Henley publiées par son amie* [New York: Modern Language Association, 1993], 36–38).

74. See Carol Duncan, *The Aesthetics of Power: Essays in Critical Art History* (Cambridge: Cambridge University Press, 1993), 208.

75. Rousseau, *Emile*, 757.

76. Ibid., 697.

77. Ibid., 246.

78. "Lettres écrites de Lausanne," *Journal Encyclopédique* 52 (1786; Geneva: Slatkine Reprints, 1967), 266.

79. Rousseau, *Emile*, 718.

80. "The new mother was faced with the choice of nursing her child or fulfilling her conjugal duty; she could not do both, for sexual intercourse, opinion held, would spoil or dry up her milk. This situation put the woman in a double bind. A mother nursing her child would safeguard the baby's physical health, but risk the moral well-being of her husband, who might be tempted to adultery or, even worse, onanism. If she fulfilled her conjugal duty, she did so by putting the nursling's safety in jeopardy" (Mary Sheriff, "Fragonard's Erotic Mothers and the Politics of Reproduction," in *Eroticism and the Body Politic*, ed. Lynn Hunt [Baltimore: The Johns Hopkins University Press, 1991], 21).

81. Rousseau, *Emile*, 702.

82. "Adèle et sa mère" refers to the Comtesse Stéphanie de Genlis's widely read *Adèle et Théodore ou Lettres sur l'éducation* (1782). Genlis, who served as the governess to many members of the royal family, integrated Rousseauian precepts in a Christian context. The main character of Genlis's work has much in common with Charrière's narrator's correspondent. She is a baroness who moves to Languedoc, far from the distractions of the social life of Paris. Moreover, her lessons are Rousseauian in their emphasis on the rewards for women to be found in the private sphere: "Home education—although she was not unaware of its limitations—was highly recommended by Mme de Genlis, for the benefit of both children and mothers. While it provided a solid foundation for the child, it gave the mother a strong sense of identity and made her life happier, more meaningful, and more fulfilled—a sharp contrast with the salon life of Paris" (Samia I. Spencer, "Women and Education," in *French Women and the Age of Enlightenment*, ed. Samia I. Spencer [Bloomington: Indiana University Press, 1984], 92).

83. We find here a *mise-en-abîme* of the situation of Charrière the novelist. She, like the narrator, must react to and simultaneously rewrite novelistic convention. Charrière's dissenting voice manifests itself in the tone of ambivalence that pervades the narrator's presentation of her daughter's marriage plot.

84. We might also see an element of desire in the narrator's description of the process of "showing" her daughter to potential suitors. Throughout her presentation she places herself in the position of the male suitor, seeing her daughter through his eyes, that is, she looks at her daughter as a lover does.

85. Reactions to the novel suggest that such transgressions of French customs were hardly typical of the Swiss or at least of those Swiss who controlled the general representation of Swiss customs and who greeted Charrière's work with strong dis-

approval. One pamphlet condemned the narrator for her *distance* from proper Swiss norms: "On dira: la mère de Cécile n'est point un modèle; les leçons qu'elle donne à sa fille, à cet enfant de dix-huit ans, ne produisent d'autre effet que celui de scandaliser le lecteur; elles ont au moins le mérite d'être extraordinaires." Cited in Godet, *Madame de Charrière et ses amis*, 314.

86. Lévi-Strauss, *Les Structures elémentaires*, 569.

87. Ibid., 570.

88. Didier, *L'Ecriture-femme* (Paris: Presses universitaires de France, 1981), 101. More recently Gutwirth too has underscored the importance of the mother–daughter bond in the novel (*Twilight of the Goddesses*, 187): "Charrière locates maternal dignity in the mother–daughter bond: it is in educating a daughter to cope with her bewilderingly rigged lot, that a mother can demonstrate her effectiveness to society, while finding in the sweetness of that bond some reparation for the disillusionment of marriage, which offers her nothing of the kind." I would go on to suggest that this bond between mother and daughter represents more broadly the valorization of bonding between women. Recall the narrator's brief reference to the cousin who taught her how to speak English. She writes: "Ne vous souvient-il pas que nous avions, vous et moi, une tante qui s'était retirée en Angleterre pour cause de religion? Sa fille, ma tante à la mode de Bretagne, a passé trois ans chez mon père dans ma jeunesse, peu après mon voyage en Languedoc. C'était une personne d'esprit et de mérite. Je lui dois presque tout ce que je sais, et l'habitude de penser et de lire" (52).

89. Didier, *L'Ecriture-femme*, 101.

90. Sigyn Minier, "*Les Lettres écrites de Lausanne* de Madame de Charrière: Rapports familiaux et exigences sociales au dix-huitième siècle," *Selecta: Journal of the Pacific Northwest Council on Foreign Languages* 4 (1983): 25. Jean Starobinski too notes "un climat d'absurdité et de désolation qui envahit le roman" ("*Les Lettres écrites de Lausanne* de Mme. de Charrière," *Romans et lumières au dix-huitième siècle* [Paris: Editions sociales, 1970], 130–51).

91. Susan Jackson reads the ending in a very different way: "No longer, in Charrière's hands, is female life possessed of but a single shape. Rather it is rendered shapeless, open-ended, subject to change for better or for worse, perhaps tedious, even trivial, but at least not necessarily or uniformly tragic" ("The Novels of Isabelle de Charrière, or, A Woman's Work Is Never Done," *Studies in Eighteenth-Century Culture* 14 (1985): 303).

92. Elsewhere, Minier rightfully points out that "beaucoup trop d'importance a été attribuée à Cécile au détriment de [sa mère] qui précisément, [fait] la narration de leur histoire et dont il apparaît injuste de négliger les sentiments personnels," and goes on to stress that "c'est en effet la mère de Cécile, et avec elle un aspect bien précis de la destinée féminine, la maternité, qui . . . occupe le centre du roman" (*Trois Femmes*, 50). Despite these apt observations, Minier ultimately sees the mother as a passive player in the events recounted: "Bien sûr, la mère disparaît devant sa fille, dans le roman comme dans la vie: c'est son rôle, son destin de mère, et Madame de Charrière l'a bien vu" (50). On the contrary, I believe that, through the maternal narrator, Charrière quite actively explores the boundaries of power and authority allotted the mother in the bourgeois family.

93. Elizabeth Fox-Genovese, "Women and Work" in *French Women and the Age of Enlightenment*, ed. Samia I. Spencer (Bloomington: Indiana University Press, 1984), 123.

94. Cited in Godet, *Madame de Charrière et ses amis*, 134.

95. Cited in Godet, *Madame de Charrière et ses amis*, 134.

96. Cited in Godet, *Madame de Charrière et ses amis*, 134.

97. Gutwirth calls her "the original of the great-souled, inadequately-loved courtesans of nineteenth-century literature" (*Twilight of the Goddesses*, 185).

98. See Paul Pelckmans, "La Fausse Emphase de la mort de toi," *Neophilologus* 72.4 (1988): 499–515. Pelckmans explores the ways in which *Caliste* subverts certain conventions of the marriage plot.

99. Susan Lanser considers the ways in which Caliste joins a male literary tradition focused on male subjectivity: "[In *Caliste*] questions of gender were subordinated to a more general distress. One can see this muting of sexual politics not only in Charrière's complete abandonment of Cécile's story, but also in the choice of a suffering, romantic male narrator who emphasizes those aspects of Caliste's story that denote a shared and bisexual plight. What Charrière actually helped to inaugurate in this gesture was a tradition of romantic narratives in which subjectivity, and hence narrative voice, becomes almost exclusively male" ("Courting Death: Romans, Romanticism, and *Mistriss Henley*'s Narrative Practice," *Eighteenth-Century Life* 13 [1989]: 57). Allison disagrees and argues instead that the continuation along with three other very short fragments of sequels included in the *Oeuvres complètes* turn the novel from a monophonic into a much richer polyphonic novel (*Revealing Differences*, 64–65).

100. Elizabeth MacArthur, "Devious Narratives: Refusal of Closure in Two Eighteenth-Century Epistolary Novels," *Eighteenth-Century Studies* 21 (1987): 17.

101. Sainte-Beuve, "Portrait de femmes" in *Oeuvres complètes de Sainte-Beuve*, ed. Maxime Leroy (Paris: Librarie Gallimard, 1951), 757.

102. Cited in Godet, *Madame de Charrière et ses amis*, 407.

103. Cited in Godet, *Madame de Charrière et ses amis*, 326.

104. Cited in Godet, *Madame de Charrière et ses amis*, 319.

105. Starobinski, "*Les Lettres écrites de Lausanne* de Mme. de Charrière," 132–33.

106. Susan Lanser, "Courting Death," 58.

107. MacArthur, "Devious Narratives," 17.

108. One of these "activities" is caring for a dying African who had worked for an English family that had left the area. The experience provides Cécile with the opportunity for metaphysical ponderings on death and power that go far beyond the confines of domestic concerns: "Mourir dans son pays ou ailleurs, avoir vécu longtemps ou peu de temps, avoir eu un peu plus ou un peu moins de peine ou de plaisir, il vient un moment où cela est bien égal: le roi de France sera un jour comme ce nègre" (107).

109. Julia Douthwaite, "Female Voices and Critical Strategies," in *Feminism*, eds. A. Maynor Hardee and G. Henry Freeman (Columbia: University of South Carolina Press, 1989), 73.

110. MacArthur, "Devious Narratives," 13. I would point out too that the lessons on the dangers of novels presented in the original novel inevitably condition our reading of William's "histoire tout romanesque." Indeed, his story might be read as a case study on the dangers of these "novelistic conventions and their imposition on life." Caliste provides a well-worthwhile lesson when we remember the romantic ambiguity between the original narrator and the ubiquitous guest in her parlor. . . . Whatever ambiguity may have been in the earlier letters with regard to the relationship between the two is crushed by the Caliste story.

111. Cited in Godet, *Madame de Charrière et ses amis*, 313.

Chapter 3: After the Revolutions(s): George Sand's *Indiana*

1. Antoine Caritat marquis de Condorcet, "Lettres d'un bourgeois de New Haven," in *Recherches historiques et politiques sur les Etats-Unis de l'Amérique séptrionale, par un citoyen de Virginie*, ed. Filippo Mazzei (Paris: Froullé, 1788), vol. 1, 284.

2. Siméon-Prosper Hardy. Cited in Women in Revolutionary Paris: Selected Documents Translated, eds. Darline Gay Levy, Harriet Branson Applewhite, and Mary Durham Johnson (Urbana: University of Illinois Press, 1980), 35.

3. Among the most (in)famous cross-dressers of the revolutionary period was Théroigne de Méricourt, a former courtesan and active participant in revolutionary societies, including *Les Amis de la loi* and *La Société fraternelle*. She often appeared in trousers on horseback with a pistol at each hip, or so the legend goes (Landes, *Women and the Public Sphere*, 110). In the following decades, women retrospectively were given "credit" for the worst excesses of the Revolution. In other words, while their power was hardly overpowering during the Reign of Terror, the fact that they did play a role at all was used later as a lesson on the dangers of public activity for women. Consider, for example, Baudelaire's quatrain devoted to Méricourt in *Les Fleurs du mal* (1857):

> Avez-vous vu Théroigne, amante de carnage,
> Excitant à l'assaut un peuple sans souliers,
> La joue et l'oeil en feu, jouant son personnage,
> Et montant, sabre au poing, les royaux escaliers.

4. Olympe de Gouges, "Les Droits de la femme," in *Ecrits politiques (1788–1791)*, ed. Olivier Blanc (Paris: Côté-Femmes, 1993), 205–6.

5. Cited in *Women in Revolutionary Paris*, 219–20.

6. These laws are again in keeping with Rousseau's views concerning the different degree of seriousness of the crime of adultery for men and for women: "Tout mari infidelle . . . est un homme injuste et barbare: mais la femme infidelle fait plus, elle dissout la famille et brise tous les liens de la nature" (Rousseau, *Emile*, 698).

7. Michelle Perrot, *A History of Private Life: From the Fires of Revolution to the Great War*, vol. 4. ed. trans. Arthur Goldhammer (Cambridge: Harvard University Press, 1990), 47.

8. To some degree this tendency was already present before the Revolution. Marie-Antoinette went to great lengths to convince the French she was a good mother. We need only think of the portrait she commissioned by Elisabeth Vigée-Lebrun in which she is portrayed with a happy infant in her lap and her other children gathered around. See Gutwirth, *Twilight of the Goddesses*, 180.

9. Cited in Marguerite Iknayan, *The Idea of the Novel in France: The Critical Reaction 1815–1848* (Geneva: Droz, 1961), 60.

10. Leyla Ezdinli, *George Sand's Literary Transvestism: Pre-texts and Contexts*, Ph.D. dissertation, Princeton University, 1987, 201.

11. There was an attempt on the part of women to break this masculine control of journals. In 1832, the year Sand published *Indiana*, appeared *La Femme Libre*, a

journal devoted exclusively to the words of women. This journal and a series of sister publications were, sadly, short-lived enterprises, subject to much ridicule.

12. This was true as well in the popular *contes fantastiques* and the gothic novel, replete with persecuted maidens "whose innocence was equaled only by their helplessness" (Priscilla Clark, *Battle of the Bourgeois: The Novel in France, 1789–1848* [Paris: Librairie Marcel Didier, 1973], 63).

13. D. Madelénat, "Romantisme," in *Dictionnaire de la littérature française et francophone* (Paris: Larousse, 1987).

14. A similar evolution occurred in England, under very different social and political circumstances. The great Victorian women novelists also wrote under male or ungendered pen names. This similarity really reinforces the case made by Habermas, that a fundamental change in mentality was underway, having to do with the basic economic and ideological structures of European society, not with local conditions.

15. To my knowledge, Sand never makes mention of revolutionary women and the role they played in the events of 1789–1793. If she did know about them, it is highly unlikely she would have made any effort to associate herself with them. The cross-dressers and women involved in any way in the Revolution, had, by the nineteenth century, become symbols of the dangers associated with the disruption of the "natural" order. Cross-dressing was so threatening that it had already been reason for arrest before the Revolution under the terms of fraud. For an examination of cross-dressing in the eighteenth century, see Lynn Friedli, " 'Passing Women': A Study of Gender Boundaries in the Eighteenth Century," in *Sexual Underworlds of the Enlightenment*, eds. G. S. Rousseau and Roy Porter (Chapel Hill: University of North Carolina Press, 1988), 234–60.

16. George Sand, *Histoire de ma vie* (Paris: Stock, 1945), 281.

17. That Sand was aware of this hostility to women is manifest in a letter written to her friend Charles Duvernet. She stresses the fact that, without the cover of a male name, she would have little hope of publishing in *La Revue*, given the editor's misogyny: "Il est bon que je vous dise que M. Véron, le rédacteur en chef de *La Revue* [*de Paris*] déteste les femmes et n'en veut pas entendre parler" (*Correspondance*, ed. Georges Lubin [Paris: Garnier frères, 1964], vol. 1, 784).

18. In fact, the spines of many late-nineteenth-century editions of Sand's works bear the name Dudevant rather than Sand. The fact that even the editors (and presumably admirers) of Sand's work felt impelled to associate this woman writer with her "real" name, that is, the name of her father or husband, rather than the name that she chose to identify herself by, bears witness to the tenacity of the need to categorize women according to "the name of the father" from which Sand was trying to escape. For a discussion of women writers and the complicated question of names, see Marie Maclean, *Name of the Mother* (London, New York: Routledge), 7–9; and DeJean *Tender Geographies*, 1–16.

19. Cited in Annarosa Poli, "George Sand devant la critique, 1831–1833," in *George Sand*, ed. Simone Vierne (Paris: Editions SEDES, 1983), 95, 96.

20. Ezdinli, *George Sand's Literary Transvestism*, iii.

21. George Sand, *Indiana* (Paris: Gallimard, 1984), 40. All subsequent references to *Indiana* and its prefaces will be to this edition, and page numbers will be cited parenthetically in the text.

22. The scene is then quite unlike the novels Georges May and Henri Coulet

point to as typical of the genre at the end of the eighteenth century, novels that openly support bourgeois family values of which Marmontel's *Contes moraux* (1761, 1789–1792) are a striking example. In Sand's first preface she comments: "Si vous voulez absolument qu'un roman finisse comme un conte de Marmontel, vous me reprocherez peut-être les dernières pages" (39). She claims to write self-consciously against these late-eighteenth-century plots.

23. Delmare, entirely a creation of his position within the greater world, talks to Indiana "sur un ton moitié père, moitié mari." In the Freudian paradigm a woman falls in love with a man reminiscent of her father. This is an organizing principle of bourgeois plots on which Freud based his theory of the Oedipus complex. In a sense Indiana fits into this world (as did Julie in *La Nouvelle Héloïse*). She does marry someone reminiscent of her father. But in Sand's novel this father is hardly a revered figure. He is described as "un père bizarre et violent" (88) who neglected his daughter. We are told that when Indiana married she simply changed masters and prisons: "En épousant Delmare elle ne fit que changer de maître, en venant habiter Lagny que changer de prison et de solitude."

24. Clark, *Battle of the Bourgeois*, 170–71.

25. Poli, "George Sand devant la critique," 96.

26. This decision to use a male-gendered narrating voice has been seen by many recent critics as profoundly antifeminist in its impulse. One calls Sand's choice to use a male authorial voice "anathema to the feminist spirit" (Nancy Rogers, "George Sand and Germaine de Staël: The Novel as Subversion," in *West Virginia George Sand Conference Papers*, eds. Armand E. Singer et al. [Morgantown: West Virginia University, Dept. of Foreign Languages, 1981], 94). Another writes, "The mask that the novelist is compelled to wear denies her sexual identity, and, from this false stand, she writes about women in a distorted, unfaithful, and sometimes disloyal, fashion" (Pierrette Daly, "The Problem of Language in George Sand's *Indiana*," in *West Virginia George Sand Conference Papers*, eds. Armand E. Singer et al. [Morgantown: West Virginia University, Dept. of Foreign Languages, 1981], 26). And another: "To the most deeply rooted part of her self, Sand was as ruthless as any male model of exterior domination she had encountered" (Erdmute Wenzel-White, "George Sand: She Who Is Man and Woman Together," in *West Virginia George Sand Conference Papers*, eds. Armand E. Singer et al. [Morgantown: West Virginia University, Depart. of Foreign Languages], 1981, 103). I would argue that the readings of these critics do not sufficiently account for the limitations placed on women writers during the early nineteenth century, nor the ways in which women like Sand were actually able to exploit the *form* of the constraints (male authorial voice, distance from female point of view, disclaimers, and so forth) to undermine the male domination of the profession and to present feminist alternatives.

27. In his *Dictionnaire* (1863–1872), Littré writes: "Private life should be lived behind walls. No one is allowed to peer into a private home or to reveal what goes on inside." Cited in Perrot, *Histoire de la vie privée*, vol. 4, 341.

28. This is true even though the money that fronted Delmare's manufacturing business came from Indiana's aunt, Mme de Carjaval.

29. Of these hysterical symptoms, René Doumic writes in 1909: "La femme incompromise . . . elle est pâle, elle est frêle, elle est sujette à s'évanouir. A la page 99, j'ai compté le troisième évanouissement; je n'ai pas compté plus loin. Ne croyez pas que ce soit l'effet d'une mauvaise santé! Mais c'est la mode" (*George Sand: Dix Conferences sur sa vie et son oeuvre*, [Paris: Perrin, 1909], 93).

30. In Charrière's *Lettres* we saw an exploration of the discipline of the marriageable female body, implicit in the bourgeois marriage plot. In Sand's novel we find an exploration of the constraints imposed on the female body in the bourgeois *post-*marriage plot.

31. Fauchery, *La Destinée féminine dans le roman européen du dix-huitième siècle,* 799.

32. Raymon at one point actually makes this explicit when he cries: "Elle s'est tuée, afin de me laisser l'avenir. Elle a sacrifié sa vie à mon repos" (184). But because Raymon's reaction is so blatantly self-interested, the event loses its poignancy.

33. A link between Noun's death in a plot concerning what the narrator calls "de bourgeois amours" and a larger economic system is suggested by the fact that she dies in the river whose water makes Delmare's manufacturing firm function; she is surrounded, moreover, by workers of the factory.

34. We find in this scene another instance of the narrator using cross-voicing. Interspersed with his critique of Raymon's view of women, he actually takes Raymon's point of view of Indiana and borrows his voice: "Le principal charme des créoles, selon moi, c'est que l'excessive délicatesse de leurs traits et de leurs proportions leur laisse longtemps la gentillesse de l'enfance" (153). The male narrator adopts Raymon's perspective in this passage. He does so after systematically showing his reader that Raymon is, in fact, a despicable character. His words echo Raymon's hackneyed ideas about Créole women, but they do so with an ironic distance not present when Raymon's thoughts are transcribed directly. Again, the words in the narrator's mouth seem to almost parody Raymon's (and romantic literature's) obsession with virginal girl-children.

35. Though he always rationalizes his political views with a social justification—"Raymon soutenait sa doctrine de monarchie héréditaire, aimant mieux, disait-il, supporter les abus, les préjugés, toutes les injustices, que de voir relever les échafauds et couler le sang innocent" (167)—he supports the monarchy out of self-interest rather than abstract conviction.

36. We have seen that Sand's narrator moves in and out of omniscience. Sometimes, as is the case here, he knows everything. Other times he is more tentative: "Le gonflement de ses narines trahit je ne sais quel sentiment de terreur ou de plaisir" (161). This shifting allows Sand a certain ironic distance vis-à-vis her narrator.

37. "Comment eût-on pu persuader à ces jeunes appuis de la monarchie constitutionnelle que la constitution était déjà vieille, qu'elle pesait sur le corps social et le fatiguait, lorsqu'ils la trouvaient légère pour eux-mêmes et n'en recueillaient que les avantages? Qui croit à la misère qu'il ne connaît pas?" (130). Raymon's relationship with Indiana suggests the injustice of the constitution vis-à-vis "le corps social," as well as the injustice of relationships between men and women within such a system. Raymon is a grand exploiter of both the social body in his work, and of specific women's bodies in his private life. The love story doubled by a political allegory plays out dramatically the relationship between injustice at the level of public and private spheres.

38. Gérard Genette, *Figures II* (Paris: Seuil, 1969), 73–75.

39. Rousseau's *Emile* was condemned for its similarly iconoclastic views of God, particularly in the "Profession de foi" portion. For women, however, Rousseau felt that religion, regardless of whether it were true, was necessary to keep women firmly entrenched in their "natural" roles: "Quand cette religion seroit fausse, la

docilité qui soumet la mère et la fille à l'ordre de la nature efface auprès de Dieu le pêché de l'erreur. Hors d'état d'être juges elles mêmes, elles doivent recevoir la décision des pères et des maris comme celle de l'Eglise" (*Emile*, 721).

40. "En 1832, la France subit les transformations de la révolution industrielle, connaît la misère urbaine, on est en plein saint-simonisme" (Frank Bowman, "La Nouvelle en 1832: la société, la misère, la mort et les mots," *Cahiers de l'association internationale des études françaises* 27 [1975]: 198).

41. "During this time, the Saint-Simonians were particularly active in Paris and Lyons, where they presented lectures several times a week to audiences that commonly numbered in the hundreds" (Claire Goldberg Moses, *French Feminism in the Nineteenth Century* [Albany: State University of New York, 1984], 45).

42. "De vives sympathies me lient de coeur et d'intention aux saint-simoniens; mais je n'ai pas encore trouvé une solution aux doutes de tout genre qui remplissent mon esprit et je ne pourrais en accepter aucune que je n'eusse bien examinée. . . . Comme je ne puis me défendre de l'intérêt et de la sympathie, je ne crains pas de déclarer que j'aime le saint-simonisme parce que l'avenir qu'il offre aux hommes est admirable de vigueur et de charité." Cited in Jehan d'Ivray, *L'Aventure saint-simonienne et les femmes* (Paris: Félix Alcan, 1930), 11.

43. Moses, *French Feminism in the Nineteenth Century*, 47.

44. Sailors brutally attack the dog as she swims after Indiana, who is clandestinely being rowed to the boat that will carry her to Raymon in France.

45. Cited in Ivray, *L'Aventure saint-simonienne*, 1.

46. Bernardin de Saint-Pierre was known as Bernardin during his lifetime.

47. Hunt, *Family Romance of the French Revolution*, 31.

48. Bernardin de Saint-Pierre, *Paul et Virginie* (Paris: Editions Gallimard, 1979), 1.

49. Ibid., 16.

50. Ibid., 58.

51. Rousseau instituted the modern father figure in *La Nouvelle Héloïse*. That the father figure in *Paul et Virginie* is left out in no way changes the novel's complicity with a bourgeois social structure. Lynn Hunt suggests that the absence of the father figure in novels published during the revolutionary period played an important role in mitigating anxieties related to the removal of the king father-figure from his sacred place of power in the old regime. We might also note that, while no actual fathers are present, there is, much as in Rousseau's *Emile*, a tutor figure. This "vieillard" dispenses Rousseauian words of wisdom to his charge at intervals throughout the novel.

52. Goulemot, "Tensions et contradictions de l'intime dans la pratique des Lumières", 19.

53. Bernardin de Saint-Pierre, *Paul et Virginie*, 66.

54. Ibid., 102.

55. Jean-Marie Goulemot, "L'Histoire littéraire en question: l'exemple de Paul et Virginie," in *Etudes sur Paul et Virginie et l'oeuvre de Saint-Pierre*, ed. Jean-Michel Racault (Paris: Didier-Erudition, 1986), 203.

56. Before Ralph's story and after the exchange of letters between Indiana and Raymon, Sand's novel loops back into the Raymon–Indiana plot. Raymon, moved by Indiana's words, writes her a letter asking her to return to him. At great peril she does. Her trip takes months, and by the time she arrives in France, Raymon has

forgotten all about his letter to her. In fact, confronted with "une société prête à se dissoudre," he is taken with a sudden urge for bourgeois comforts: "Raymon en tira cette conclusion, qu'il fallait à l'homme, en état de société, deux sortes de bonheur, celui de la vie publique et celui de la vie privée, les triomphes du monde et les douceurs de la famille" (262). He marries the daughter of the rich bourgeois who bought Lagny from M. Delmare, and the newlyweds are living there by the time Indiana arrives. Indiana enters her old bedroom and falls at the knees of Raymon, who had been reading. He is stupefied. Then, sensing an opportunity to ravish Indiana at last, moves to shut the door. Not quickly enough, however, for his wife enters and bids him to arrange Indiana's immediate departure. The coach leaves her at the pension where Ralph finds her.

57. This reference to Rousseau is interesting. Sand doubles Rousseau's "promeneur solitaire" to include a woman in this foray into a natural paradise. As we will see, however, this nominal inclusion of woman does not change the entirely Rousseauian presentation of the Ralph–Indiana marriage plot. Indiana's earlier solitary vagaries through the wilderness during her "promenades solitaires" (254) are far more suggestive of a truly new social vision.

58. In case we are not sufficiently moved by Ralph's story, or convinced this is the true marriage plot as opposed to the "simulacrum légal" of the Delmare marriage, the narrator, addressing us directly, prods us into appreciation:

> Si le récit de la vie intérieure de Ralph n'a produit aucun effet sur vous, si vous n'en êtes pas venu à aimer cet homme vertueux, c'est que j'ai été l'inhabile interprète de ses souvenirs, c'est que je n'ai pas pu exercer non plus sur vous la puissance d'un homme profondément vrai dans sa passion. (329)

59. The couple's new life bears resemblance to the characters of another Bernardin novel, *La Chaumière indienne*, the title of which actually makes up the final words of Sand's novel: "Souvenez-vous de notre chaumière indienne" (344). Sand has already waxed nostalgic about the privatized family earlier:

> Raymon apporta dans leur solitude toutes les subtilités de langage, toutes les petitesses de la civilisation. . . . C'est une grande imprudence d'introduire la politique comme passe-temps dans l'intérieur des familles. Si il en existe encore aujourd'hui de paisibles et d'heureuses, je leur conseille de ne s'abonner à aucun journal, de ne pas lire le plus petit article de budget, de se retrancher au fond de leurs terres comme dans un oasis, et de tracer une ligne infranchissable entre elles et le reste de la société; car, si elles laissent le bruit de nos contestations arriver jusqu'à elles, c'en est fait de leur union et de leur repos. (170–71)

The irony here is that, by the time we read this passage, we have already seen what a disaster the Delmare family was before Raymon's arrival. The narrator seems to blame the disintegration on the "subtilités de langage" that Raymon introduces into the household, but we know there were serious problems in the Delmare family from the moment the novel opens.

60. Carol Richards argues just this: "Indiana's dependence on Ralph to supply her [vindication against conjugal tyranny], as well as to save her from the consequences of her own folly, mark the limits to which Sand's feminist thought was developed in this, her first novel" ("Structural Motifs and Limits of Feminism in

Indiana," in *George Sand Papers*, ed. Natalie Datlof [New York: AMS Press, 1978], 19).

61. For another reading of Sand's ending and her use of the exotic landscape, see Nancy K. Miller, "Arachnologies: The Woman, the Text, and the Critic," in *Poetics of Gender*, ed. Nancy K. Miller (New York: Columbia University Press, 1986).

Works Cited

Allison, Jenene J. *Revealing Differences: The Fiction of Isabelle de Charrière*. Newark: University of Delaware Press, 1995.

Althusser, Louis. *Lenin and Philosophy*. New York: Monthly Review Press, 1971.

Altman, Janet Gurkin. "Graffigny's Epistemology and the Emergence of Third World Ideology." In *Writing the Female Voice*. Ed. Elizabeth C. Goldsmith. Boston: Northeastern University Press, 1989, 172–202.

———. "Making Room for 'Peru': Graffigny's Novel Reconsidered." In *Dilemmes du roman: Essays in Honor of Georges May*. Ed. Catherine Lafarge. Stanford: Anma Libri (Stanford French and Italian Studies), 1990, 33–46.

Ariès, Philippe. *L'Enfant et la vie familiale sous l'Ancien Régime*. Paris: Plon, 1960.

Attridge, Anne. "The Reception of La Nouvelle Héloïse." *Studies on Voltaire and Eighteenth-Century France* 120 (1974): 227–67.

Bartky, Sandra Lee. "Foucault, Femininity, and the Modernization of Patriarchal Power." In *Feminism and Foucault: Reflections on Resistance*. Eds. Irene Diamond and Lee Quinby. Boston: Northeastern University Press, 1988, 61–86.

Bérenguier, Nadine. "From Clarens to Hollow Park: Isabelle de Charrière's Quiet Revolution." *Studies in Eighteenth-Century Culture* 21 (1991): 219–42.

Blum, Carol. *Rousseau and the Republic of Virtue: The Language of Politics in the French Revolution*. Ithaca: Cornell University Press, 1986.

Bonnet, Jean-Claude. "Naissance du Panthéon." *Poétique* 33 (1978): 46–65.

———. "La Malédiction paternelle." *Dix-huitième siècle* 12 (1980): 195–208.

Bowman, Frank Paul. "La Nouvelle en 1832: la société, la misère, la mort et les mots." *Cahiers de l'association internationale des études françaises* 27 (1975): 189–208.

Brouard-Arends, Isabelle. *Vies et images maternelles dans la littérature française du dix-huitième siècle*. Oxford: Voltaire Foundation, 1991.

Charrière, Isabelle de. *Caliste, ou Les Lettres écrites de Lausanne*. Ed. Claudine Hermann. Paris: Editions des femmes, 1979.

———. *Lettres de Mistriss Henley publiées par son amie*. New York: Modern Language Association, 1993.

———. *Oeuvres complètes*. Eds. Jean-Daniel Candaux et al. Amsterdam: G. A. van Oorschot, 1979–1984.

Chartier, Roger. *Les Origines culturelles de la révolution française*. Paris: Seuil, 1990.

Cherpack, Clifton. *Mythos and Logos: Ideas and Early French Narratives*. Lexington, Ky.: French Forum, 1983.

Cixous, Hélène, and Catherine Clément. *La Jeune Née*. Paris: Unions générale d'éditions, 1975.

Clark, Priscilla. *Battle of the Bourgeois: The Novel in France, 1789–1848*. Paris: Librairie Marcel Didier, 1973.

Coleman, Patrick. *Rousseau's Political Imagination: Rule and Representation in the Lettre à d'Alembert.* Geneva: Droz, 1984.

Condorcet, Antoine Caritat marquis de. "Lettres d'un bourgeois de New Haven." In *Recherches historiques et politiques sur les Etats-Unis de l'Amérique séptrionale, par un citoyen de Virginie.* Ed. Filippo Mazzei. Paris: Froullé, 1788.

Coulet, Henri. *Le Roman jusqu'à la Révolution.* Paris: Armand Colin, 1967.

Courtney, C. P. *Isabelle de Charrière (Belle de Zuylen).* Oxford: Voltaire Foundation, 1993.

Daly, Pierrette. "The Problem of Language in George Sand's Indiana." In *West Virginia George Sand Conference Papers.* Eds. Armand E. Singer et al. Morgantown: West Virginia University, Dept. of Foreign Languages, 1981, 22–27.

Darnton, Robert. *Forbidden Best-Sellers of Pre-Revolutionary France.* New York and London: Norton, 1995.

———. *The Great Cat Massacre and Other Episodes in French Cultural History.* New York: Basic Books, 1984.

———. *The Literary Underground of the Old Regime.* Cambridge: Harvard University Press, 1982.

DeJean, Joan. *Literary Fortifications: Rousseau, Laclos, Sade.* Princeton: Princeton University Press, 1984.

———. "Teaching Frenchness." *French Review* 61.3 (1988): 398–413.

———. *Tender Geographies: Women and the Origins of the Novel in France.* New York: Columbia University Press, 1991.

Didier, Béatrice. *L'Écriture-femme.* Paris: Presses universitaires de France, 1981.

DiPiero, Thomas. *Dangerous Truths and Criminal Passions: The Evolution of the French Novel, 1569–1791.* Stanford: Stanford University Press, 1992.

Donzelot, Jacques. *The Policing of Families.* New York: Pantheon Books, 1979.

Doumic, René. *George Sand: Dix Conferences sur sa vie et son oeuvre.* Paris: Perrin, 1909.

Douthwaite, Julia. *Exotic Women: Literary Heroines and Cultural Strategies in Ancien Régime France.* Philadelphia: University of Pennsylvania Press, 1992.

———. "Female Voices and Critical Strategies: Montesquieu, Mme de Graffigny, and Mme de Charrière." In *Feminism.* Eds. A. Maynor Hardee and G. Henry Freeman. French Literature Series. Columbia: University of South Carolina Press, 1989.

Dubois, Simone. *Leven op afstand.* Zaltbommel: Europese Bibliotheek, 1969.

Duncan, Carol. *The Aesthetics of Power: Essays in Critical Art History.* Cambridge: Cambridge University Press, 1993.

Etienne, Louis. "Une socialiste d'autrefois." *Revue des deux mondes* 94 (1871): 454–64.

Ezdinli, Leyla. *George Sand's Literary Transvestism: Pre-texts and Contexts.* Ph.D. dissertation. Princeton University, 1987.

Farge, Arlette, and Michel Foucault. *Le Désordre des familles: lettres de cachet des archives de la Bastille.* Paris: Editions Gallimard, 1982.

Fauchery, Pierre. *La Destinée féminine dans le roman européen du dix-huitième siècle 1713–1807, Essai de gynécomythie romanesque.* Paris: Armand Colin, 1972.

Flandrin, Jean-Louis. *Familles: parenté, maison, sexualité, dans l'ancienne société.* Paris: Seuil, 1984.

Fleming, Marie. "Women and the Public Use of Reason." In *Feminists Read Habermas.* Ed. Johanna Meehan. New York: Routledge, 1995, 117–37.

Foucault, Michel. *History of Sexuality.* Trans. Robert Hurley. Vol. 1. New York: Random House, 1980.

———. *Power/Knowledge: Selected Interviews and Other Writings, 1972–1977.* Ed. Colin Gordon. New York: Random House, 1972.

Fox-Genovese, Elizabeth. "Women and Work." In *French Women and the Age of Enlightenment.* Ed. Samia I. Spencer. Bloomington: Indiana University Press, 1984, 111–27.

Fraser, Nancy. "What's Critical About Critical Theory? The Case of Habermas and Gender." *New German Critique* 35 (1985): 97–121.

Freud, Sigmund. "Family Romances." In *The Standard Edition of the Complete Works.* Vol. 9. Trans. James Strachey. London: Hogarth Press, 1964, 235–41.

Friedli, Lynne. " 'Passing Women': A Study of Gender Boundaries in the Eighteenth Century." In *Sexual Underworlds of the Enlightenment.* Eds. G. S. Rousseau and Roy Porter. Chapel Hill: University of North Carolina Press, 1988, 234–60.

Genette, Gérard. *Figures II.* Paris: Seuil, 1969.

Godet, Philippe. *Madame de Charrière et ses amis.* 1906. Reprint, Geneva: Slatkine Reprints, 1973.

Goldsmith, Elizabeth C. "Authority, Authenticity, and the Publication of Letters by Women." In *Writing the Female Voice: Essays on Epistolary Literature.* Ed. Elizabeth C. Goldsmith. Boston: Northeastern University Press, 1989.

Goodman, Dena. "Public Sphere and Private Life: Toward a Synthesis of Current Historiographical Approaches to the Old Regime." *History and Theory* 31 (1992): 1–20.

———. "Seriousness of Purpose: Salonnières, Philosophes, and the Shaping of the Eighteenth-Century Salon." In *Proceedings of the Annual Meeting for the Western Society for French History* 15 (1988): 111–21.

Gouges, Olympe de. "Les Droits de la femme." *Ecrits politiques (1788–1791).* Ed. Olivier Blanc Paris: Côté-Femmes, 1993.

Goulemot, Jean-Marie. "L'Histoire littéraire en question: l'exemple de Paul et Virginie." *Etudes sur Paul et Virginie et l'oeuvre de Saint-Pierre.* Ed. Jean-Michel Racault. Paris: Didier-Erudition, 1986, 201–214.

———. "Tensions et contradictions de l'intime dans la pratique des Lumières", *Littérales* 17 (1995): 13–21.

Graffigny, Françoise de. *Lettres d'une Péruvienne et autres romans d'amour par lettres.* Eds. Bernard Bray and Isabelle Landy-Houillon. Paris: Flammarion, 1983.

———. *Lettres d'une Péruvienne.* Introd. Joan DeJean and Nancy K. Miller. New York: Modern Languages Association, 1993.

Gutwirth, Madelyn. *Twilight of the Goddesses: Women and Representation in the French Revolutionary Era.* New Brunswick, N.J.: Rutgers University Press, 1992.

Habermas, Jürgen. "Further Reflections on the Public Sphere." In *Habermas and the Public Sphere.* Ed. Craig Calhoun. Cambridge: Massachusetts Institute of Technology Press, 1992.

———. *Structural Transformation of the Public Sphere: An Inquiry into a Category of Bourgeois Society.* Trans. Thomas Burger. Boston: Massachusetts Institute of Technology Press, 1989 (orig. *Strukturwandel der Öffentlichkeit: Untersuchungen zu einer Kategorie de bürgerlichen Gesellschaft.* Neuwied and Berlin: Hermann Luchterhand, 1962. Fr. trans. *L'Espace public: archéologie de la publicité comme dimension constitutive de la société bourgeoise.* Trans. Marc B. de Launay. Paris: Payot, 1978).

Harth, Erica. *Cartesian Women: Versions and Subversions of Rational Discourse in the Old Regime.* Ithaca: Cornell University Press, 1992.

Hartmann, Pierre. "Turgot lecteur de Mme de Grafigny." In *Vierge du Soleil/Fille des Lumières: La Péruvienne de Mme de Grafigny et ses Suites.* Ed. Groupe d'étude du dix-huitième siècle. Strasbourg: University of Strasbourg, 1989, 113–20.

Higgins, James. *A History of Peruvian Literature.* Wolfeboro, N.H.: Francis Cairns Publications Ltd., 1987.

Hirsch, Marianne. *The Mother/Daughter Plot.* Bloomington: Indiana University Press, 1989.

Hoffmann, Paul. *La Femme dans la pensée des Lumières.* Paris: Ophrys, 1977.

———. "*Les Lettres d'une Péruvienne:* un projet d'autarcie sentimentale." *Vierge du soleil/Fille des Lumières: la Péruvienne de Mme de Grafigny et ses suites.* Ed. Groupe d'étude du dix-huitième siècle. Strasbourg: Université de Strasbourg II, 1989, 49–76.

Hunt, Lynn. *The Family Romance of the French Revolution.* Berkeley: University of California Press, 1992.

Iknayan, Marguerite. *The Idea of the Novel in France: The Critical Reaction 1815–1848.* Geneva: Librairie E. Droz, 1961.

Irigaray, Luce. *Ce Sexe qui n'en est pas un.* Paris: Editions de Minuit, 1977.

Ivray, Jehan de. *L'Aventure saint-simonienne et les femmes.* Paris: Librairie Félix Alcan, 1930.

Jackson, Susan. "The Novels of Isabelle de Charrière, or, A Woman's Work Is Never Done." *Studies in Eighteenth-Century Culture* 14 (1985): 299–306.

———. "In Search of a Female Voice: Les Liaisons dangereuses." In *Writing the Female Voice: Essays on Epistolary Literature.* Ed. Elizabeth C. Goldsmith. Boston: Northeastern University Press, 1989, 154–71.

Jacobus, Mary. "Incorruptible Milk: Breast-Feeding and the French Revolution." In *Rebel Daughters: Women and the French Revolution.* Eds. Sara E. Melzer and Leslie W. Rabine. Oxford: Oxford University Press, 1992.

Jacquin, Armand-Pierre. *Entretiens sur les romans.* 1755. Reprint, Geneva: Slatkine Reprints, 1970.

Jensen, Katharine Ann. *Writing Love: Letters, Women, and the Novel in France, 1605–1776.* Carbondale and Edwardsville: Southern Illinois University Press, 1995.

Kelly, Joan. *Women, History, and Theory.* Chicago: University of Chicago Press, 1984.

Labrosse, Claude. *Lire au dix-huitième siècle: La Nouvelle Héloïse et ses lecteurs.* Lyon: Presses universitaires de Lyon; Paris: Editions du CNRS, 1985.

Landes, Joan. *Women and the Public Sphere in the Age of the French Revolution.* Ithaca: Cornell University Press, 1988.

Lanser, Susan. "Courting Death: Romans, Romanticism, and *Mistriss Henley*'s Narrative Practices." *Eighteenth-Century Life* 13 (1989): 49–59.

Laqueur, Thomas. *Making Sex: Body and Gender from the Greeks to Freud.* Cambridge: Harvard University Press, 1990.

Lenglet-Dufresnoy, N.-A. *De L'Usage des romans.* 1734. Reprint, Geneva: Slatkine Reprints, 1970.

"Lettres écrites de Lausanne." Review. *Journal Encyclopédique* 52 (1786). Geneva: Slatkine Reprints, 1967.

Lévi-Strauss, Claude. *Les Structures élémentaires de la parenté.* Paris: Mouton, 1967.

Levy, Darline Gay, Harriet Branson Applewhite, and Mary Durham Johnson, eds. *Women in Revolutionary Paris: Selected Documents Translated.* Urbana: University of Illinois Press, 1980.

MacArthur, Elizabeth. "Devious Narratives: Refusal of Closure in Two Eighteenth-Century Epistolary Novels." *Eighteenth-Century Studies* 21 (1987): 1–20.

Maclean, Marie. *The Name of the Mother.* London and New York: Routledge, 1994.

Madelénat, D. "Romantisme." *Dictionnaire de la littérature française et francophone.* Paris: Larousse, 1987.

Mall, Laurence. "Perdues dans les détails: *Les Lettres de Mistriss Henley* de Charrière et l'écriture de la désintégration." *Orbis Litterarum* 52 (1997): 178–93.

Martin, Biddy. "Feminism, Criticism, and Foucault." *Feminism and Foucault: Reflections on Resistance.* Eds. Irene Diamond and Lee Quinby. Boston: Northeastern University Press, 1988, 3–19.

May, Georges. *Le Dilemme du roman au dix-huitième siècle: Etude sur les rapports du roman et de la critique (1715–1761).* Paris: Presses universitaires de France, 1963.

Maza, Sara. "Only Connect: Family Values in the Age of Sentiment." *Eighteenth-Century Studies* 30.3 (1997): 207–12.

Meyer, Martine Darmon. *Relationships Between Mothers and Daughters in Laclos, Rousseau, and Mme de Charrière.* Selected Proceedings of the Pennsylvania Foreign Language Conference. Ed. Martin L. Gregario. Pittsburgh: Duquesne University, Department of Modern Languages, 1988, 117–25.

Miller, Nancy K. "Arachnologies: The Woman, the Text, and the Critic." In *Poetics of Gender.* Ed. Nancy K. Miller. New York: Columbia University Press, 1986, 270–95.

———. *The Heroine's Text: Readings in the French and English Novel, 1722–1782.* New York: Columbia University Press, 1980.

———. *Subject to Change.* New York: Columbia University Press, 1988.

Minier, Sigyn. *Madame de Charrière: Les premiers romans.* Paris and Geneva: Editions Champion-Slatkine, 1987.

———. "*Les Lettres écrites de Lausanne de Madame de Charrière.* Rapports familiaux et exigences sociales au dix-huitième siècle." *Selecta: Journal of the Pacific Northwest Council on Foreign Languages* 4 (1983): 23–27.

Mitchell, Juliet. *Psychoanalysis and Feminism.* New York: Vintage Books, 1974.

Moses, Claire Goldberg. *French Feminism in the Nineteenth Century.* Albany: State University of New York Press, 1984.

Noël, Georges. *Madame de Graffigny: Une "Primitive" oubliée de l'école des "coeurs sensibles."* Paris: Librairie Plon, 1913.

Pelckmans, Paul. "La Fausse emphase de la 'mort de toi.' " *Neophilologus* 72.4 (1988): 499–515.

———. *Isabelle de Charrière: Une Correspondance au seuil du monde moderne.* Amsterdam: Rodopi, 1995.

———. *Le Sacre du père: fictions des Lumières et historicité d'Oedipe, 1699–1775.* Amsterdam: Rodopi, 1983.

Perrot, Michelle. *A History of Private Life: From the Fires of Revolution to the Great War.* Ed. Trans. Arthur Goldhammer. Vol. 4. Cambridge: Harvard University Press, 1990.

Pillorget, René. *La Tige et le rameau. Familles anglaise et française, XVIe–XVIIIe siècle.* Paris: Calmann-Levy, 1979.

Poli, Annarosa. "George Sand devant la critique, 1831–1833." In *George Sand.* Ed. Simone Vierne. Paris: Editions SEDES, 1983, 95–100.

Ray, William. "Reading Women: Cultural Authority, Gender, and the Novel. The Case of Rousseau." *Eighteenth-Century Studies* 27.3 (1994): 421–47.

Reid, Roddey. *Families in Jeopardy: Regulating the Social Body in France, 1750–1910.* Stanford: Stanford University Press, 1993.

Richards, Carol V. "Structural Motifs and Limits of Feminism in *Indiana.*" In *George Sand Papers.* Eds. Natalie Datlof et al. New York: AMS Press, 1978, 12–20.

Rogers, Nancy. "George Sand and Germaine de Staël: The Novel as Subversion." In *West Virginia George Sand Conference Papers.* Eds. Armand E. Singer et al. Morgantown: West Virginia University, Department of Foreign Languages, 1981, 61–73.

Rossum-Guyon, Van. "A propos d'*Indiana*: La préface de 1832." *George Sand.* Ed. Simone Vierne. Paris: Editions SEDES, 1983, 71–83.

Rousseau, Jean-Jacques. *Les Confessions.* Paris: Gallimard, 1973.

———. *Correspondance complète de Jean-Jacques Rousseau.* Ed. R. A. Leigh. Vol. 22. Geneva and Banbury: Voltaire Foundation, 1974.

———. *Emile. Oeuvres complètes.* Eds. Bernard Gagnebin and Marcel Raymond. Vol. 4. Paris: Gallimard, 1969.

Rubin, Gayle. "The Traffic in Women." In *Toward an Anthropology of Women.* Ed. Rayna R. Reiter. New York: Monthly Review Press, 1975, 157–210.

Rustin, Jacques. "Sur les suites des *Lettres d'une Péruvienne.*" *Vierge du soleil/Fille des Lumières: La Péruvienne de Mme de Graffigny et ses suites.* Ed. Travaux du groupe d'étude du dix-huitième siècle. Strasbourg: Université de Strasbourg II, 1989.

Sainte-Beuve. "Portrait de femmes." *Oeuvres complètes de Sainte-Beuve.* Ed. Maxime Leroy. Paris: Gallimard, 1951, 985–1422.

Saint-Pierre, Bernardin de. *Paul et Virginie.* Paris: Gallimard, 1979.

Salomon, Pierre. "Introduction." *Indiana.* Ed. Pierre Salomon. Paris: Garnier frères, 1962, i–lii.

Sand, George. *Histoire de ma vie.* Paris: Editions Stock, 1945.

———. *Correspondance.* Ed. Georges Lubin. Vol. 1. Paris: Garnier frères, 1964.

———. *Indiana.* Paris: Gallimard, 1984.

Schor, Naomi. "Le Féminisme et George Sand: Lettres à Marcie." *Revue des sciences humaines* 226 (1992): 21–35.

Scott, Geoffrey. *The Portrait of Zélide.* London: Constable and Co., 1925.

Sheriff, Mary. "Fragonard's Erotic Mothers and the Politics of Reproduction." In *Eroticism and the Body Politic.* Ed. Lynn Hunt. Baltimore: The Johns Hopkins University Press, 1991, 14–40.

Shorter, Edward. *The Making of the Modern Family.* New York: Basic Books, 1975.

Showalter, English. "*Les Lettres d'une Péruvienne:* composition, publication, suites." *Archives et Bibliothèques de Belgique* 54.1–4 (1983): 14–28.

Smith, David W. "The Popularity of Madame de Graffigny's *Lettres d'une Péruvienne:* The Bibliographical Evidence." *Eighteenth-Century Studies* 3 (1990): 1–20.

Solovieff, Georges (Ed.). *Madame de Staël: Choix de textes, Thématique et Actualité.* Paris: Klincksieck, 1974.

Spencer, Samia I. "Women and Education." In *French Women and the Age of Enlightenment.* Ed. Samia I Spencer. Bloomington: Indiana University Press, 1984, 83–96.

Stackelberg, Jürgen von. "Die Kritik an de Zivilisationsgesellschaft aus der Sich einer 'guten Wilden': Mme de Grafigny und ihre *Lettres d'une Péruvienne.*" *Die Französische Autorin, vom Mittelalter bis sur Gegenwart.* Eds. Renate Baader and Dietmar Fricke. Wiesbaden: Athenaion, 1979, 131–45.

Staël, Germaine de. *Delphine.* Geneva: J. J. Paschoud, year 11 (1802).

Starobinski, Jean. "*Les Lettres écrites de Lausanne* de Mme de Charrière." In *Romans et lumières au dix-huitième siècle.* Paris: Editions sociales, 1970, 130–51.

Stewart, Joan Hinde. "The Novelists and Their Fictions." *French Women and the Age of Enlightenment.* Ed. Samia I Spencer. Bloomington: University of Indiana Press, 1984, 197–211.

Stone, Lawrence. *The Family, Sex and Marriage.* New York: Harper and Row, 1979.

Tanner, Tony. *Adultery in the Novel.* Baltimore: The Johns Hopkins University Press, 1979.

Terdiman, Richard. *Discourse/Counter-Discourse: The Theory and Practice of Symbolic Resistance in Nineteenth-Century France.* Ithaca: Cornell University Press, 1985.

Traer, J. F. *Marriage and the Family in Eighteenth-Century France.* Ithaca: Cornell University Press, 1980.

Trouille, Mary S. *Sexual Politics in the Enlightenment: Women Writers Read Rousseau.* Albany: State University of New York Press, 1997.

Trousson, Raymond. "Isabelle de Charrière et Jean-Jacques Rousseau." *Bulletin de l'Académie royale de langue et de littérature françaises* 43.1 (1985): 5–57.

Undank, Jack. "Graffigny's Room of Her Own." *French Forum* 13.3 (1988): 297–318.

Vega, Garcilaso de la. *Histoire des Incas, rois du Pérou.* Ed. Trans. Thomas François Dalibard. Paris: Prault fils, 1744.

Wenzel-White, Erdmute. "George Sand: She Who Is Man and Woman Together."

In *West Virginia George Sand Conference Papers*. Eds. Armand E. Singer et al. Morgantown: West Virginia University, Department of Foreign Languages, 1981, 85–95.

Zaretsky, Eli. *Capitalism, the Family, and Personal Life*. New York: Harper and Row, 1986.

Acknowledgments

It is a great pleasure to reflect back on all of those who contributed to the completion of this book. First and foremost, I wish to thank Joan DeJean for inspiring this project, and for her guidance. I am indebted too to Katharine Conley, Lucienne Frappier-Mazur, Kathleen Hart, Lynn Hunt, and Gwendolyn Wells, all of whom helped me considerably with reading, talking, and advice in the early stages.

My warm thanks goes as well to those who read and commented on parts or all of the manuscript at various stages of revision: Faith Beasley, Brigitte Cazelles, Leo Damrosch, Julia Douthwaite, and Catherine Spencer. I offer special thanks to Julie Candler Hayes and to Michael Ryan for insightful and generously detailed readings of the manuscript in its final stages. The friendship and collegiality of many others sustained me throughout the project: Mireille Baurens, Celeste Goodridge, Nancy Halloran, Frances Hurwitz, Michael Iarocci, Laurence Mall, David Patton, Julie Rivkin, Jaymes Anne Rohrer, and Marjorie Salvodon. To Mary Donaldson-Evans, my thanks for her wonderful teaching and for her encouragement to pursue graduate studies in French literature. To my family, I wish to express my heartfelt thanks for their enthusiastic and unwavering support.

I am grateful to the University of Pennsylvania and the Mellon Foundation for the financial support that gave me the time I needed to begin to research and write this project. In the form of a Fairchild Grant, Connecticut College provided the resources and time necessary to work full-time on the research, writing, and revision of the manuscript.

At Bucknell University Press, I wish to thank the editor, Greg Clingham, for his belief in the project, and my reviewers, for their very helpful suggestions. At Associated University Presses, I want to express my appreciation to Julien Yoseloff, Christine Retz, Brian Haskell, and Ellen Kazar, who together so ably saw the manuscript through production. Finally, I wish to thank Susan Finkelstein for her thoughtful copyediting.

A part of Chapter 1 originally appeared in *Romance Languages Annual 1994*, vol. 6. I wish to thank the journal for granting me permission to use that material in this book.

Index

Adorno, Theodor, 10
adultery: Rousseau's views on, 165n.6; treated in the Napoleonic Code, 106, 109
Allison, Jenene, 156–57n.35, 158n.44, 164n.99
Althusser, Louis, 27, 72; "Ideological State Apparatuses," 24, 150n.16
Altman, Janet, 20, 151n.28
Ancien Moniteur, L', 105
architecture, as indicator of familial change, 22
Ariès, Philippe, 23
Attridge, Anne, 61
authorial voice: Sand's use of male-gendered narrator, 107–11; undermined, 114–15, 167n.26; used to critique characters, 113; Zilia's claim to, 47–48

Balzac, Honoré de, 106
Bartky, Sandra Lee, 72
Batteux, l'Abbé: *Les Beaux Arts réduits à un seul principe*, 54; *Cours de belles-lettres*, 54
Battle of the Bourgeois, The (Clark), 114
Baudelaire, Charles, 165n.3
Beaux Arts réduits à un seul principe, Les (Batteux), 54
Bérenguier, Nadine, 159n.49
Bernardin de Saint-Pierre, Jacques Henri: *Paul et Virginie*, 134–40, 169n.51; *La Chaumière indienne*, 170n.59
Blanchard, Antoine, 24
Blum, Carol, 147n.9
bloodlines: and incest, 44; and the fidelity of wives, 77
body: the narrator's, 142; in the marriage plot, 31, 69, 72–76, 158n.44, 160n.58, 168nn.30 and 37; language of the body, 109, 118–19, 167n.29; the male, 160n.56; exploitation of the social 168n.37
Bonnet, Jean-Claude, 12–13
Boswell, James: relations with Charrière, 67, 157–58n.41, 158n.44
bourgeois, the: emergence of a distinct sense of identity, 10–11; as the culprit in Romantic literature, 113–14
bourgeois public sphere, the, 9–10, 147n.9
bourgeoisie, the: and courtly-noble society, 52–53, 150–51n.22, 159n.51; of Lausanne, 95
Bowman, Frank Paul, 169n.40
breast-feeding: discussed in the *Convention*, 105; in iconography of the revolutionary period, 84, 161n.72 as key part of Rousseau's vision, 64; and republican notions of good motherhood, 83–85, 155n.25; and the sexual unavailability of wives to husbands, 87, 162n.80
business: and gender, 63, 94–95

Caliste, ou Suite des Lettres écrites de Lausanne (Charrière), 96–100
capitalism, 150–51n.22, 154n.53; and the creation of the modern subject, 10, 135
Catholicism: and the work of Garcilaso de la Vega, 45–46
Charrière, Isabelle de: *Caliste, ou Suite des Lettres écrites de Lausanne*, 96–100; *Lettres de Mistress Henley*, 159n.49; *Lettres écrites de Lausanne*, 14–15, 58, 66–102, 140, 144; *Le Noble*, 156n.33;

181

INDEX

"Plainte et Défense de Thérèse Levasseur"; as reader of Rousseau, 66–69, 103, 145
Chartier, Roger, 7
Chaumette, Pierre, 104–5, 112
chastity: and the "law" of female virtue, 78–83, 87; of Romantic heroines, 106–7
childbearing: critique of, 28, 53
childhood: modern conception of, 27–29; in Garcilaso, 30; Graffigny's use of Peru as metaphor for, 32; and incest, 42; and new family paradigm, 23–25, 27–29, 35–37, 143; Noun and Indiana's, 130; as presented in *Paul et Virginie*, and motherhood, 63–64, 77–78, 86–89
citizenship: and gender, 11, 84, 103, 106; and horizontal power relations, 37; and the public sphere, 37; and *pudeur*, 77; and reading, 7
Cixous, Hélène, and Catherine Clément, *La Jeune Née*, 118
class, 95–96, 102, 106, 116, 133; and gender, 13, 53, 77, 104, 119–20, 157n.37; and Saint-Simonianism, 129
Clément, Pierre, 20
Coleman, Patrick, 63, 77
Condorcet, Antoine Caritat de: *Lettre d'un bourgeois de New Haven*, 103
confessional manuals, 22–24
Courtney, C. J., 156–57n.35, 158n.44
cultural contradictions: and the role of heroine's death, 102; underscored, 75
Consolations, Les (Sainte-Beuve), 107
Correspondance littéraire (Grimm), 59
Coulet, Henri: *Le Roman jusqu'à la Révolution*, 57–58, 101–2
Courrier français, Le, 106
Cours de belles-lettres (Batteux), 54
counter-discourse, 52
cross-dressing: and revolutionary heroines, 165n.3, 166n.15; Sand's, 108, 112, 115
cross-voicing: and "bi-textuality," 111; and cross-dressing, 141–42; leading to questions about author's gender, 109; as means to publish in journals hostile to women writers, 108; used to critique male characters, 113–14; used parodically, 114–15, 168n.34
culte du moi, le: and masculinization of authorship, 107

Darnton, Robert, 58, 62, 150n.10
death of the heroine: in *Caliste*, 96–97; deromanticized in *Indiana*, 119–20; the economics of, 168n.33; in *Paul et Virginie*, 137; as means of resolving social contradictions, 119
DeJean, Joan, 51–52, 61, 78; *Tender Geographies*, 149n.24, 154n.62
Déstinée féminine dans le roman européen du dix-huitième siècle, La (Fauchery), 55, 79
details, and the workings of power, 73
Didier, Béatrice, 91, 160n.58
DiPiero, Thomas, 156n.27, 159n.50, 161n.63
domesticity, 73–74, 116; and the market economy, 72, 139–40, 145; in Rousseau's vision, 63
Doumic, René, 167n.29
Douthwaite, Julia, 20, 48, 99, 152n.30, 154n.49
Droits de la femme, Les (Gouges), 103–4
Dubois, Simone, 158n.44

economy, the: and the gendered public/private divide, 11, 26, 28–29, 60, 139; and publishing, 25–26; and marriage, 72; libidinal, 118; of association and the Saint-Simonians, 130; new sexual economy imagined, 131; and *Paul and Virginie*, 135–36, and modern models of subjectivity, 143
education of women, the, 27–28, 87–89
Emile (Rousseau), 58, 155n.20, 169n.51; and adultery, 165n.6; condemnation of, 101; on gender and religion, 168–69n.39; and interpellation of gendered subjectivities, 62–63, 65–66; and mother-daughter intimacy, 85; and the woman writer, 65, 68, 156n.29
Enfantin, "le Père," 129

Enlightenment, the: Frankfurt school critique of, 10; and happiness, 32; and selfish individualism, 83
epistolary novel: conventions of, 34, 74; and the creation of inner life, 8–9; and epistolary communication, 57–61; first female-authored, 19; and identity, 152n.36; monophonic, 70
eroticism: of brother-sister bond, 38; of family bonds, 42; and the male gaze, 75–76; non-conjugal, 51, 53, 132; egalitarian, 122
exoticism, 20, 29–30, 120, 171n.61
Ezdinli, Leyla, 106

family: bourgeois, 89, 117, 143–44, 159n.51, 161n.63; critique of, 139; first modern definition, 24; and incest, 41–43; and Rousseau, 14, 62–66; 155n.20; as shared unit of stability in unstable political times, 106; and the Saint-Simonians 129–30; in transition, 22–25, 41
"family romance" : defined, 12, Freud's use of the term, 148n.16
fan mail: Rousseau and modern phenomenon of, 58–63; and Bernardin de Sainte-Pierre, 134–35
father figures, 12–13, 44, 97, 153n.42, 169n.51; absence of, 69, 102, 169n.51
fathers, 24, 30, 32, 63; absence of, 71–72, 91; in Freud, 148n.16, 167n.23; name of the father, 158n.46, 166n.18; and Rousseau, 77
Fauchery, Pierre, 41, 119; *La Destinée féminine dans le roman européen du dix-huitième siècle*, 55–56, 79
female sexuality, 79–80; and social vision, 131–32
Femme libre, La, 165–66n.11
Feuilles d'automne (Hugo), 107
Figaro, Le, 108
Flandrin, Jean, 24
Fleming, Marie, 14, 152n.35, 154n.55
Foucault, Michel, 47; and the "indispensable pivot" of incest, 42–43; and the mechanics of power, 70–73, 160n.56

Fox-Genovese, Elizabeth, 95
France littéraire, La, 109
Fraser, Nancy, 11
free enterprise, 143
French Revolution, the: "family romance" of, 97, 153n.42; and gender, 11, 13, 77, 83, 97, 103, 143, 161n.72; and new definitions of nobility, 95; nostalgia for, 133; and reading, 7; and women's activism, 103–4, 165n.3
Fréron, Elie: *Lettres sur quelques écrits*, 20–22
Freud, Sigmund: and the eighteenth-century novel, 12–13; and the "family romance," 12, 148n.16; on hysterical symptoms as hieroglyphs, 118

gaze: cross-gendered, 113; Garcilaso's Peru subjected to female, 32; and implied reader in Rousseau's *Emile*, 65; male gaze in the marriage plot, 75–76; mother's upon her daughter, 162n.84
gender: ambiguity of the novel genre, 15; and class, 13, 53, 77, 104, 116, 119–20, 157n.37; versus nationality, 32–33; and nature, 103–4; and public sphere/private sphere divide, 11–15, 26, 53, 106, 115, 139, 141, 143–45; and the professions, 84; and Rousseauian family values, 63–64; transgression of gender roles, 71, 102, 141
Genette, Gérard, 127–28
Genlis, Stéphanie de, *Adèle et Théodore ou Lettres sur l'éducation*, 62n.82
Godet, Philippe, 98, 158n.44
Goodman, Dena, 147n.10, 149n.23
Gouges, Olympe, *Les Droits de la femme*, 103–104; death of, 106
Goulemot, Jean-Marie, 58, 60, 136
Graffigny, Françoise de: *Lettres d'une Péruvienne*, 13–15, 19–56, 58, 99, 140; marriage of, 154n.62
Gramsci, Antonio, 24, 72, 82–83
Grimm, Melchior de, *Correspondance littéraire*, 59
Gutwirth, Madelyn, 11, 54, 163n.88

Habermas, Jürgen, 22, 54, 74, 152n.35, 154n.55; and dual role of modern family, 42, 153n.39; and the intimate sphere of the nuclear family, 26–28; and the novel, 39, 57, 113, 151n.24; and the oppositional public sphere, 81, 94, 102; on Rousseau, 59–60; and salon culture, 54–55, 151n.23; *Structural Transformation of the Public Sphere*, 9–14, 26, 146n.5

Harth, Erica, 26–27, 52, 150n.22, 154n.53

Hermenches, Constant d', 66–77

heroine, the: in the epistolary tradition, 34; hysterical, 118; sexualized versus virginal in *Indiana*, 120–24, 127; tragic, 41; suitable endings for, 20, 93, 97–102, 119–20

Heroine's Text, The (Miller), 20

Higgins, James, 32

Hirsch, Marianne, 158n.44

Histoire des Incas, rois du Pérou (Garcilaso de la Vega): and Catholicism, 45; Graffigny's transformation of, 31–35; and the Inquisition, 153n.43; and motherhood, 152n.33

Histoire de ma vie (Sand), 108

Hoffman, Paul, 50

Horkheimer, Max, 10

Hugo, Victor: *Feuilles d'automne*, 107

Hunt, Lynn, 41, 97, 153n.42

hieroglyphs: in descriptions of île Bourbon, 142; hysterical symptoms as, 118; as signs of the repressed in the nineteenth-century novel, 145

ideology: and culture, 82–83; defined, 161n.70; and plausibility, 127; and ideological state apparatuses 24, 27

incest, and the incest taboo: as force in the eighteenth-century imagination, 29; in *Lettres d'une Péruvienne*, 14, 38–39, 41–51, 144, 153nn.42 and 43

Indiana (Sand), 15, 107–42, 145

inner life: paradoxical link to public life, 8–9; Rousseau and the creation of, 60. *See* private life

Irigaray, Luce: *Ce sexe qui n'en est pas un*, 78–79

Jackson, Susan, 13, 98, 163n.91

Jacobus, Mary, 84, 161n.72

Jacquin, Armand-Pierre, 20

Janin, Jules, 106

Jaucourt, Louis de, 24

Jensen, Katharine, 20, 49

Jeune Née, La (Cixous and Clément), 118

Kelly, Joan, 83

kinship systems, 13, 15, 23–24, 48, 116

Labrosse, Claude, 59–60

Laclos, Pierre Choderlos de, *Les Liaisons dangereuses*, 117

Lafayette, Marie Madeleine de, *La Princesse de Clèves*, 51

Lamarche-Courmont, Hugary de: *Les Lettres d'Aza*, 21–22

Landes, Joan, 11, 27, 74

Lanser, Susan, 164n.99

Laqueur, Thomas, 156n.27

Launay, Marc de, 146n.5

laws: on adultery, 106; favoring the bourgeois family, 15, 143; favoring younger siblings, 37–38, 137n.35; against incest, 50; and Rousseauian gender roles, 105, 116–17, violence condoned by, 130

Lettre à d'Alembert (Rousseau), 63

Lettre d'un bourgeois de New Haven (Condorcet), 103

Lettres à Marcie (Sand), 141

Lettres d'Aza (Lamarche-Courmont), 21–22

lettres de cachet de famille, 23

Lettres de Mistress Henley, Les (Charrière), 159n.49; and breastfeeding, 161–62n.73

Lettres d'une Péruvienne (Graffigny), 13–15, 19–56, 58, 99, 140

Lettres écrites de Lausanne (Charrière), 14–15, 58, 66–102, 140, 144

Levasseur, Thérèse, 157n.37

Lévi-Strauss, Claude, 48, 76; *Les Structures élémentaires de la parenté*, 90, 153n.39, 160n.61

Liaisons dangereuses, Les (Laclos), 117

MacArthur, Elizabeth, 20, 97–98

marriage: changing conception of, 22–25; critiqued by courtly *salonnières*,

52–54; modern model in *Lettres d'une Péruvienne*, 36–39; negative examples of, 80, 92; Peruvian model in *Lettres d'une Péruvienne*, 34–35; in post-revolutionary setting, 113
marriage plot: critiqued in *Indiana*, 120; in *Lettres d'une Péruvienne*, 34–41; in *Lettres écrites de Lausanne*, 69, 70–78, 80, 93, 101; reaffirmed in *Indiana*, 138–40, 170n.58
Marianne: replaced by Hercules during the Reign of Terror, 104
Marmontel, *Contes moraux*, 166–67n.22
masculinization, of the writing profession, 106
May, Georges, 56–58, 81, 100–102
Miller, Nancy, 47; *The Heroine's Text*, 20; 171n.61
Minier, Sigyn, 93–94
monarchy, 8, 10, 30, 136; constitutional, 124; and literary salons, 53–54, 57, 147n.9, 150n.22
Moses, Claire Goldberg, 169n.41
mother-daughter relationship: in conflict with conjugal duties, 87; intimacy and confession in, 85–86; in the marriage plot, 71; privileged in *Lettres écrites de Lausanne*, 69; in traditional family, 36; as replacement for marriage, 90–92, 144, 145, 163n.88; as means to escape domestic confinement, 94; and resistance to "suitable" closure of marriage or death, 99–100
motherhood, 25; critique of limitations imposed by, 27–28; and the French Revolution, 11; model of bad, 36–39; and modern social organization, 83–87, 152n.33; Rousseau and, 63–64
Mythos and Logos (Cherpack), 19

name of the father, and women writers, 156–57n.35; 158nn.44 and 66, 166n.18
Napoleonic Code, the: and the exclusion of women from public life, 105; and husbands' increased power, 113–14, 116; Indiana's exagerrated submission to, 117

narrator, male-gendered: and ironic distance, 168n.36; used to critique characters, 113–14; used parodically, 114–15, 168n.34; in voice and body, 141–42
Nicoletti, Gianni, 19
Noble, Le (Charrière), 156n.33
Noël, Georges, 151n.27
Nouvelliste, La (Rabou), 114
Nouvelle Héloïse, La (Rousseau), 28, 113, 116, 134, 159n.61; Charrière's identification with Rousseau's Julie, 66; reader response to, 58–61; rewritten versions of, 61–62; and valorization of *la vie intérieure*, 64; Switzerland in, 101–2
novel, the: and ambiguous relationship to gender, 15; as bastard genre, 8, 146n.3; conventions of, 96; and the creation of inner life, 8–9, 57, 73; debates on the social role of, 146n.2; eighteenth-century developments of, 9–10, 22–29, 57–58, 61, 143–45, 149n.1; as crucible of modern identity, 12; as "family romance," 12–13; Graffigny's gendering of the ethnographic novel, 33, 47; as marriage plot, 20; masculinization of the genre, 78, 106–7; and the modern nuclear family, 10, 22–29; and negotiation of new female subjectivities, 144; and new social rules, 15, 26–27; and the public/private divide, 10–12, 14–15, 26–27, 73, 81, 144, 146nn.2 and 3; and seventeenth-century *salonnières*, 53–54; undoing conventions of, 13; as paradox for women writers, 153–54n.48

Oedipus complex: in *Indiana*, 167n.23; as marker of the modern subject, 28–29, and the novel, 12–13; Oedipal symbolism in *Caliste*, 97; origins of, 12, 28
old regime: association with public women, 14, 52–53, 137; and origins of the public sphere, 149n.23; strictly defined hierarchy of, 23, 37; values critiqued in *Paul et Virginie*, 136–37

Olivier, Madame Juste, 98
Ormoy, Charlotte Chaumet d', 66

Paul et Virginie (Bernardin de Saint-Pierre), 123, 134–40
Pelckmans, Paul, 12–13, 22, 29, 42, 148n.21, 158n.44; *Le Sacre du père*, 28
Pillorget, René, 154n.57
political views: of Charrière's narrator, 78; of Sand's characters, 133–34, 168nn.35 and 37
précieuses. See *salonnières*
primogeniture, the law of: function in traditional family paradigm, 23–24, in *Lettres d'une Péruvienne*, 36–37
Princesse de Clèves, La (Lafayette): and tradition of *refus*, 51
printing system: and the creation of the public sphere, 14; in the Restoration period, 137
private life: as counterbalance to economic man, 63; and the court, 147n.9; defined in *Littré*, 167n.27; establishment among all classes, 196; and novels, 8–9; Rousseau and the creation of, 60; Sand's emphasis of link with public life, 112–14
psychoanalytic approaches, to the early French novel, 12–13, 28–29, and *Caliste*, 97
public space, 52
public sphere: defined, 10; and gender, 10–12; 11, 14, : multifaceted nature of, 26–27, 74, 151n.23; Zilia and, 112–14, 133, 135, 141–42, 144–45, 147nn.9 and 10, 149n.23, 150n.22; bourgeois, 9, 10
pudeur, 77, 82

Ray, William, 61, 63–65
readers: and creation of the bourgeois public sphere, 9; and Rousseau, 58–61
reading: and social change, 7; privatization of the experience, 8
reading beyond the ending: in *Indiana*, 138–43; in *Lettres d'une Péruvienne*, in *Lettres écrites de Lausanne*, 98–102
Reign of Terror, 104, 165n.3

Repressive State Apparatuses (RSAs), 24, 150n.16
Rêveries d'un promeneur solitaire (Rousseau), 144, 170n.57
Richards, Carol, 170–71n.60
Roland, Marie-Jeanne: guillotined, 105
Romanticism, and domesticity, 107
Rousseau, Jean-Jacques, 14, 27, 73–74, 158n.44, 159n.49; and Bernardin de Saint-Pierre, 137; and Charrière, 66–70; *Emile*, 58, 62, 64–66, 68, 85, 101, 168–69n.39; and infidelity, 77, 165n.6; influence on readers, 58–61; as inspiration to women writers, 66; *Lettre à d'Alembert*, 63; on motherhood, 83, 86; *La Nouvelle Héloïse*, 28, 58–59, 61–64, 66, 101, 102, 113, 116, 134; and the "natural" moral qualities of women; on nature and the family, 104, 135, 144; *Rêveries d'un promeneur solitaire*, 144, 170n.57; on the social role of women, 63–63; on social stability, 69; and Thérèse Levasseur, 157n.37; views on women and religion, 168–69n.39; on women writers, 65, 106, 156n.29

Sacre du père, Le (Pelckmans), 28
Saint-Simonians, 108, 128–32, 133, 140, 169nn.40, 41 and 42
salons and *salonnières*, 14, 26, 48, 52–53, 147n.10, 149n.23
Sainte-Beuve, 97; *Les Consolations*, 107
Sand, George: as cross-dresser, 108; *Histoire de ma vie*, 108; *Indiana*, 15, 103–42; *Lettres à Marcie*, 141; and the post-revolutionary position of women, 106–7; and Rousseau, 66; use of conventional characters, 112; viewed as anti-feminist writer, 167n.26; 170–71nn.59 and 60
Sandeau, Jules, 108
Schor, Naomi, 111
Scott, Geoffrey, 158n.44
Scudéry, Madeleine de, 52
sex/gender system, 26; and the novel genre, 52
Sexe qui n'en est pas un, Ce (Irigaray), 78–79

sexual politics, 164n.99
Sexual Politics in the Enlightenment (Trouille), 64
Sheriff, Mary, 162n.80
Shorter Edward, 25, 76
Showalter, English, 19–20
"siblification," of Aza-Zilia bond, 38
Stackelberg, Jürgen von, 19
Staël, Anne-Louise-Germaine Necker de: journal entries of, 156n.31; and Rousseau, 66
Starobinski, Jean, 98
Stendahl, 106
Stewart, Joan Hinde, 73, 159n.55
Stone, Lawrence, 25
Structural Transformation of the Public Sphere, The (Habermas): dual role of modern family, 153n.39; feminist critiques of, 11–12; and Freud, 12; on the novel, 26; on oppositional public sphere, 9–14, 147n.9; reception of 146n.5
Structures élémentaires de la parenté (Lévi-Strauss), 48, 76, 90, 153n.39, 160n.61
style indirect libre, 125
subjectivity, 60; female, 48, 117; male, 148n.21, 164n.99
Switzerland, 102, 159n.50

Tanner, Tony, 62
tendre amitié, 48, 51–56, 154n.57
Terdiman, Richard, 52
transgression, 161n.68; incest as symbol of, 43; and the novel, 62; of public/private divide, 87–92
Trouille, Mary: *Sexual Politics in the Enlightenment*, 64
Turgot, Anne-Robert-Jacques, 20–22

Undank, Jack, 20

Vega, Garcilaso de la, 32; *Histoire des Incas, rois du Pérou*, 31–32, 34–35, 45, 151n.27, 151n.28, 152n.33, 153n.43
virginity: fetishized in Romantic heroines, 107; of Sand's heroine, 117, 122, 152n.36; woman's responsibility for, 80
virtue: republican, 83, 147n.9; the "law" of female, 79–80

wedding whites, 139
Williams, Raymond, 159–60n.55, 161n.70
women writers: and homosociality, 158n.44; and negotiation of the terms of the eighteenth-century family romance, 13, 143–44; and the name of the father, 156–57n.35, 158nn.44 and 46, 166n.18; nineteenth-century denigration of, 106–7; and the opacity of the signifier, 159n.55; and the paradox of the marriage plot, 153nn.48; Rousseau on, 65–66
work, 95, 168n.33

Zuylen, Belle de. *See* Charrière, Isabelle de